CH

SUPER-MINI GRAMMAR

edited by
David Edmonds

CHAMBERS

CHAMBERS

An imprint of Chambers Harrap Publishers Ltd
7 Hopetoun Crescent
Edinburgh EH7 4AY

Copyright © Chambers Harrap Publishers Ltd 1998

We have made every effort to mark as such all words which we believe to be trademarks. We should also like to make it clear that the presence of a word in the dictionary, whether marked or unmarked, in no way affects its legal status as a trademark.

All rights reserved. No part of this publication may be reproduced, stored in a retrieval system or transmitted by any means, electronic, mechanical, photocopying or otherwise, without the prior permission of the publisher.

A CIP catalogue record for this book is available from the British Library.

ISBN 0-550-14030-1

Typeset by Chambers Harrap Publishers Ltd, Edinburgh
Printed in Great Britain by Clays Ltd, St Ives plc

Preface

This book is designed to help people whose native language is English and who wish to be able to speak and write the standard form of British English correctly and effectively. Even though (like me) you learnt the language at your mother's knee and have used it ever since, there have probably always been things you (like me) have never been quite clear about: dictionaries never seem to explain them, and grammar books are so full of technical jargon that even if they contain the answer, it is impossible to find. These problems don't worry us when we are chatting with our friends, but they suddenly become urgent when your English is "on trial" — when there is an essay or an important letter to write, or when you have to go for an interview or speak at a meeting. This book is designed to give you the answers you will need, quickly and clearly.

The book is arranged like a dictionary: the articles are short and self-contained, so that one stop will give you all you need to know. Areas covered include:

Spellings — How many *t*s and *l*s in *battalion*? Is *bellyfull* right, or is it *bellyful*?

Pronunciations — Where is the stress in *banal*? Does *blessed* have one syllable or two? How is *bass* pronounced? Is it the same for the singer and the fish?

Confusables — Is a tumour *benign* or *benignant*? Is a fool *barmy* or *balmy*?

Usage — Do we say *the media is* or *the media are*? Does it make any difference whether we say *because of* or *due to*?

Grammar — Do *I shall go* and *I will go* mean different things? What is a *count noun*?

Inflections — Do we say *brother-in-laws* or *brothers-in-law*? What is the past tense of *bid* — or does it have two, each with a different meaning?

This snapshot approach is enriched by a series of **topic entries** (see the list on p. v) which give a comprehensive overview of certain major topics (such as punctuation, political correctness and American English) that are best understood when seen as a whole. In compiling this book I owe thanks for help and encouragement to Robert Allen, George Davidson and Megan Thomson.

David Edmonds
June 1996

Introduction

All the articles in this book are arranged in a single alphabetical sequence, and cross-references have been kept to an absolute minimum; as a result, almost all articles (except for feeders into the topic entries) are complete in themselves, and any cross-references point to information elsewhere which may enrich (often by contrast, such as **common noun** ... *see also* **proper noun**), but is not essential to an adequate understanding of the topic discussed. One result of this policy is that articles discussing confusables (eg **balmy / barmy**) will appear again at the alphabetic position of the second (or later) alternative, unless this second appearance would be within easy sight (usually computed as a distance of five articles or less) of the first; where necessary the text of the second article will have been adjusted or amplified to reflect the fact that it will be consulted by readers whose principal interest is in the second of the headword alternatives (here **barmy**) rather than the first.

Apart from the self-evident *eg*, *ie* and *etc*, scarcely any abbreviations have been used. *AmE* and *BrE* mean American and British English respectively, while the signs ✓ and ✗ are used to indicate examples of correct and incorrect usage. In the topic entries (but not elsewhere in the book) notes are used to draw attention to important exceptions or amplifications of the rules given in the main text without interrupting the flow of its presentation.

Where alternative inflections are given without comment (eg *in general use*, *in scientific use* etc), the first alternative is (sometimes only marginally) to be preferred, though both are correct in all contexts.

Pronunciation

The following symbols are used:

Consonants:

>   ch as in church
>   dh as in then
>   kh as in loch
>   zh as in pleasure

>   ng as in sing
>   sh as in ship
>   th as in thing

All other consonants are pronounced as in normal everyday English

Vowels:

>   a as in cat
>   ar as in car
>   a^{ng} as in French vin
>   aw as in caught
>   ay as in hay
>   e as in egg and air
>   ee as in deep
>   i as in hit
>   iy as in fight
>   o as in pot

>   oh as in coat
>   oh^{ng} as in French bon
>   oo as in book
>   o^{ng} as in French dans
>   oy as in boil
>   ow as in cow
>   u as in cup
>   uh as in French chauffeur
>   uh^{ng} as in French un
>   uu as in boot

Stressed syllables are shown by ***bold italic type***, the others in *light italic*.

Any vowel or group of vowels which is pronounced as a neutral "uh" (or *schwa*) sound is represented by u.

List of Topic Entries

- abbreviations
- adjectives
- adverbs
- agreement
- American spellings, vocabulary and usage
- apostrophes
- articles
- capitalization
- clauses and phrases
- conditionals
- dates
- hyphens
- negatives
- nouns
- political correctness
- pronouns
- punctuation
- register
- standard / non-standard English
- verbs

Contributors

Editor
David Edmonds

Editorial staff
Sandra Anderson, Penny Hands, Megan Thomson

Prepress department
Louise McGinnity

a / an

▷ use **a** before words that begin (or sound as if they begin) with a consonant (eg *a book*, *a cat*, *a one-way street*, *a UNESCO grant*) and **an** before words that begin (or sound as if they begin) with a vowel (eg *an egg*, *an hour*, *an FT report*).

-a / -ums

▷ most words ending in *-um* form plurals by adding an *s* in the usual way (eg *referendums*, although *referenda* is not incorrect), but a few (eg *addendum*, *desideratum*) still reflect their Latin origin by replacing the *-um* by *-a*, and are listed at their alphabetical place in this book.

abandon

▷ has a present participle ***abandoning*** and a past tense ***abandoned***.

abbreviate, abbreviation

▷ are spelt *-bb-*.

---

abbreviations

Abbreviations are shortened forms of well-known words and phrases that are used to save space in writing and time in speaking. They are formed in various ways:

○ By using only the first part of the word (eg *Tues.*, *approx.*) followed by a full stop. These are called ***abbreviations***, and are written in the short forms but read or spoken in full.

abbreviations ...

- By taking (some or all of) the middle out of the word or phrase but leaving (at least) its first and last letters, eg *St* (meaning *Street*), *sthg* (meaning *something*), *he'll* (meaning *he shall* or *he will*), *it's* (meaning *it is*). These are called **contractions** and are not followed by a full stop. Contractions of the *St* and *sthg* kind are read or spoken in full, but those of the *he'll*, *it's* type are spoken and read as written.

- By using only the first letters of each of a group of words (eg *BBC*, *PhD*, *RSPCA*, *pm*, *eg*). These are called **initialisms** if (as in the above examples) the letters in the resultant string are pronounced separately (eg *bee-bee-see* for *BBC*), but **acronyms** if the whole string can be (and is) pronounced as a single word (eg *NATO*, *Benelux*). Acronyms tend to be treated as 'proper' words (see separate entry at **acronym**). Initialisms are nowadays written without full stops between the letters. If more than the first letter of any capitalized word is used to make an initialism (as in *PhD*), the second and subsequent letters taken from that word are not capitalized; but they are still pronounced as separate letters (eg *pee-aych-dee*) unless (as in *BMus*) they themselves make a pronounceable word (*bee-muz*).
  ➤ For the use of *a* and *an* before initialisms see **a / an**.

• plurals

There are three simple rules:

- Add a lower-case s to initialisms (eg *MPs*, *bcgs*); use *'s* only when there is a danger of s being taken as part of a lower-case initialism (eg *how many of those duties are pm's?*).

abbreviations ...

- Not many abbreviations that end in a full stop have a plural form; those that do put the *s* before the full stop (eg *vols. 5 and 6*).

- A few initialisms make a plural by doubling their singular form, or a part of it (eg *p/pp* for *page* or *pages*, *MS/MSS* for *manuscript* or *manuscripts*, *qv/qqv* for *quod vide* meaning *for which see*).

• weights and measures

Whether they are abbreviations, contractions or initialisms, and whether they refer to metric or imperial units, the following general rules apply:

- Use no full stop (eg *cwt*, *°C*).

- Do not add *s* to make a plural (eg *3kg, 4lb*).

• 'Unimportant' words in initialisms and acronyms

'Unimportant' words are those that would not be given a capital first letter if the term were written out in full, as *of the* in *Department of the Environment*. They are treated in one of the following ways:

- Sometimes their initials are omitted from the abbreviated form, as in *RSPCA* (which is in full *Royal Society for the Prevention of Cruelty to Animals*).

- Sometimes they are kept in the abbreviated form, but given a lower-case letter, as in *DoE* (*Department of the Environment*).

- Sometimes they are kept in the abbreviated form and given a capital letter, as in *FOE* (*Friends of the Earth*).

Follow the style used by the organization concerned, who will probably have devoted some time to the selection of an eye- (or ear-)catching string of letters or sounds.

➤ See also **acronym, clipped form, symbol**.

abetter

abetter or abettor
▷ the spelling *-er* is in general use; *-or* is found only in legal writing.

abhorrence, abhorrent
▷ are spelt *-ence*, *-ent*.

abide
▷ has a past tense and past participle *abode* (*abided* is also found).

ability or capability or capacity
▷ *ability* means 'being able' or 'competence' (eg *showed above average ability in the practical exam*); *capability* refers to an aptitude or potential, mental or physical, to cope with a situation (eg *still amazed at my mother's organizational capabilities*); *capacity* has both meanings (eg *the new job was beyond her capacities*).

-able / -ible
▷ although the first of these suffixes is the more common, there are no simple rules for remembering which a particular word will take. All the commonest *-able* and *-ible* words are listed at their alphabetical place in this book.

Aboriginal / Aborigine
▷ the preferred forms for referring to the original inhabitants of Australia are now
  ○ singular noun ***Aborigine***.
  ○ plural noun ***Aboriginals***.
  ○ adjective ***Aboriginal***.

abscissa
▷ has plurals *abscissas* and *abscissae*.

absolute
▷ denotes

○ a clause that is not grammatically connected with the rest of the sentence in which it stands (eg *Time permitting, we will visit the museum tomorrow*).

○ a transitive verb that has an object that is understood but not stated (eg *Soldiers are trained to kill* — where 'people' is understood).

abstinence, abstinent
▷ are spelt *-ence, -ent*.

abstract noun
▷ denotes a noun which names something that has no physical form or existence, eg *anger, courage, dancing*.
➤ See also **concrete noun, nouns**.

abundance, abundant
▷ are spelt *-ance, -ant*.

abuse or misuse
▷ ***abuse*** tends to refer to the use of things for the wrong purposes (eg *the President's abuse of his powers in giving Government posts to all his friends*), ***misuse*** to the use of things in the wrong way (eg *years of misuse finally made the handle drop off*).

accelerate, acceleration
▷ are spelt with two *c*s and one *l*.

accelerator
▷ is spelt with two *c*s and one *l*, and ends with *-or*.

accent
▷ denotes
○ one of the marks `` ` ``, ´, ˆ written or printed above a vowel in a foreign word to show how it is pronounced or which syllable is stressed (eg *blasé, raison d'être*).
➤ Also called **diacritic**.

acceptance

- ○ the emphasis (also called the *stress*) placed upon a syllable in a word or a word in a sentence in speech; where pronunciations are given in this book the stressed syllable is printed in ***bold italic*** type; the word *accept* is, for example, stressed on the second syllable, giving a pronunciation
  - ✓ ak-***sept***

  rather than
  - ✗ ***ak***-sept
- ○ the set of ways in which a person pronounces English, which is usually an indicator of his or her geographical or social origins (eg *a Yorkshire/posh accent*).

acceptance
▷ is spelt *-ance*.

accessible
▷ is spelt *-ible*.

accessary or accessory
▷ ***accessory*** is now acceptable in all senses, but ***accessary*** is sometimes used in legal writing (eg *accessary after the fact*).

accommodate
▷ is spelt with two *c*s and two *m*s.

accursed
▷ is pronounced with three syllables.

accusative case
▷ is another name for the ***objective case of the direct object***, which denotes the form taken by pronouns which are the direct object of a verb, as *him* in *she hit him*.

acknowledge
▷ is spelt *ack-* and *-dge*.

acoustics
▷ denotes
  ○ the scientific study of sound, and is singular (eg *acoustics is still a new science*).
  ○ the sound characteristics of a concert hall, etc; it is plural (eg *the Albert Hall's acoustics have been improved*).

acquaintance
▷ is spelt *acqu-* and *-ance*.

acquiesce
▷ is spelt *acqu-* and *-esce*.

acquiescence, acquiescent
▷ are spelt *acqu-*, and have *-e-* in their final syllable.

acquire
▷ is spelt *acqu-*.

acreage
▷ is spelt *-eage*.

acronym
▷ denotes an abbreviation that is pronounced as a word and is made from the initial letters or syllables of the words for which it stands, eg *NATO* or *Nato* from <u>N</u>orth <u>A</u>tlantic <u>T</u>reaty <u>O</u>rganization, and *Benelux* from <u>Be</u>lgium, <u>Ne</u>therlands, <u>Lux</u>embourg. Heavily used acronyms tend in time to lose their capitalization, and eventually (as with *radar*, *sonar* and *laser*) come to be regarded as words in their own right, their origin as a bunch of initials being forgotten by most of their users.
➤ See also **abbreviations**.

active voice
▷ denotes those forms of the verb that are used when its subject performs (instead of suffering or experiencing) the action it describes (eg *Fred kicked the donkey* instead

of *Fred was kicked by the donkey*); for the forms taken by English verbs to denote this voice see **verbs**. Compare **passive voice**.

actor
▷ is spelt *-or*.

acute accent
▷ denotes the mark or diacritic ´ written or printed above a letter in certain foreign languages (eg French), or in English words (eg *fiancée*) borrowed from them, to indicate its pronunciation or stress.

-acy / -asy
▷ only four nouns have the *-asy* ending: ***apostasy***, ***ecstasy***, ***fantasy***, ***idiosyncrasy***. All the others of this type end in *-acy*.

adaptor
▷ is still the standard spelling, although ***adapter*** is increasingly found.

addendum
▷ has a plural ***addenda***.

adherence, adherent
▷ are spelt *-ence*, *-ent*.

adherence or adhesion
▷ both words mean 'sticking'; generally, ***adherence*** is used for the metaphorical senses (eg *adherence to middle-class values*) and ***adhesion*** for the literal ones (eg *this glue gives a good adhesion to wet surfaces*).

adieu
▷ has plurals ***adieus*** or ***adieux***.

adjacent / adjoining / contiguous
▷ ***adjacent*** things may have space between them, but ***adjoining*** or ***contiguous*** things do not.

adjectives

adjectival clause
▷ denotes a group of words in a sentence that do the work of an adjective (eg *the reason why she did it is still unclear*).

adjectival noun
▷ is an adjective used as a noun, as in *Help the Aged*.

adjectival phrase
▷ denotes a phrase consisting of an adjective with one or more adverbs that qualify it, as in *a very big lorry*.

adjectives

An adjective is a word that provides more information about a noun or pronoun. There are two basic types:

○ ***Descriptive adjectives*** answer the question 'what kind?': examples of descriptive adjectives are *big, green, stupid*.

○ ***Limiting adjectives*** (also called ***determiners***) answer the question 'which one?': examples of limiting adjectives are *this, my, some, every*.

• Descriptive adjectives

Most (but not all) descriptive adjectives can do all the following:

○ Precede the noun or pronoun they qualify eg
      ✓   *this is the big one*
but not
      ✗   *this is the asleep one*

when they are called ***attributive adjectives***.

○ Follow a linking verb eg
      ✓   *the pudding looked good*
but not
      ✗   *this fool is utter*

when they are called ***predicative adjectives***.

adjectives ...

- Be preceded by adverbs of degree eg
  - ✓ *a <u>very</u> fat man*
  - *she is <u>quite</u> beautiful*

  but not
  - ✗ *a <u>very</u> infinite number*

- Form comparatives and superlatives (eg *fatter*, *fattest*, but not *asleeper*, *asleepest*).

A few descriptive adjectives (eg *professor <u>emeritus</u>, president <u>elect</u>*) must follow the noun they qualify; they are called ***post-positive adjectives***.

• Comparison of descriptive adjectives

These adjectives have three degrees of comparison:

- ***Positive*** (eg *small, resourceful, good*).
- ***Comparative*** (eg *smaller, more resourceful, better*).
- ***Superlative*** (eg *smallest, most resourceful, best*).

As the preceding examples show, there are three basic ways of forming the comparative and superlative:

- By adding *-er* and *-est* to the positive form.
- By placing *more* and *most* before the positive form.
- By changing the positive form completely: all the adjectives that do this are explained at their alphabetical place.

To find how an adjective that is not explained at its alphabetical place forms its comparative and superlative, follow the general rules given below:

- ***One-syllable adjectives*** add *-er* and *-est* (eg *faster, fastest*) except for past participles (eg *more bored, most worn*).

  NOTE Many adjectives whose stem is modified when taking *-er* and *-est* (eg *bi<u>gg</u>er, fa<u>tt</u>est*) are explained at their alphabetical place.

- **Longer adjectives** add *more* and *most* (eg *more resourceful, most hard-bitten*); however, **two-syllable adjectives** in *-er, -le, -ow* and *-ure* may also add *-er* and *-est* (eg *cleverer / more clever, shallowest / most shallow*), and **two-syllable adjectives** in *-ey* and *-y* may also add *-ier* and *-iest* (eg ✓*friendliest* / ✓*most friendly*).

• **Limiting adjectives**

There are seven types of limiting adjective, all of which precede the noun or pronoun they qualify:

- ○ **Demonstrative adjectives** (eg <u>this</u> book, <u>those</u> flowers).
- ○ **Interrogative adjectives** (eg <u>which</u> books?, <u>what</u> flowers?).
- ○ **Possessive adjectives** (eg <u>my</u> books, <u>his</u> flowers).
- ○ **Indefinite adjectives** (eg <u>any</u> books, <u>some</u> flowers).
- ○ **Distributive adjectives** (eg <u>each</u> book, <u>every</u> flower).
- ○ **Relative adjectives** (eg *the woman* <u>who</u> *gave me the book*).
- ○ **Definite and indefinite articles** (ie *the, a / an*).
- ○ **Cardinal and ordinal numbers** (eg *seven, seventh*).

adjudicator
▷ is spelt *-or*.

admissible
▷ is spelt *-ss-* and *-ible*.

admission / admittance
▷ both mean 'the act of entering' or 'permission/right to enter', but **admission** is generally used of a public place such as a theatre (eg *we have paid admission*) and **admittance** of private ones (eg *could not gain admittance to the party*).

admittance
▷ is spelt -ance.

adolescence, adolescent
▷ are spelt -en-.

adopted / adoptive
▷ generally, **adopted** is used of the child and **adoptive** of its new parents.

adverbial clause
▷ denotes a group of words in a sentence that do the work of an adverb (eg *I'll come when I'm ready*).

adverbial phrase
▷ denotes a phrase consisting of an adverb with one or more adverbs that qualify it (eg *she ran very quickly*).

adverbs

An adverb is a word that answers questions like 'how?' or 'how much?'. It can be used with:

- Verbs (eg *she ran quickly* modifies *ran*).
- Adjectives, (eg *a very big house* modifies *big*).
- Other adverbs (eg *she ran very quickly* modifies *quickly*).
- Prepositions (eg *fell right under the wheels of the bus* modifies *under*).
- Conjunctions (eg *I'll show you exactly how she did it* modifies *how*).

• Types of adverb
There are seven types of adverb:

- **Adverbs of place** (eg *she sat there for a while and then went out*).
- **Adverbs of manner** (eg *they ran quickly*).

advice

advice / advise
▷ the noun is spelt -ice and the verb -ise.

advisedly
▷ is pronounced with four syllables, ie ad-**viyz**-id-li.

-ae / -as
▷ certain words of Latin origin whose singular ends in -a have a plural in -ae; the commonest ones are listed at their alphabetical place in this book. Other words in -a make their plural in the usual English way by adding s.

-ae- / -e-
▷ except for **medieval** and **encyclopedia**, British English (unlike American) prefers the -ae- spelling.

aegis
▷ is pronounced **ee**-jis.

aeon
▷ is spelt ae- and pronounced **ee**-on.

aerate
▷ is spelt aer- and pronounced **ay**-er-ayt.

aerobics
▷ is spelt aer- and is singular (eg aerobics has become very fashionable) except when referring to a series of exercises considered as separate units (eg that gym's aerobics are exhausting).

aerodynamics
▷ is singular.

aeroplane / airplane / aircraft
▷ use **aeroplane** in British English, and **airplane** in American; **aircraft** (plural same) is used in both languages, but has a wider meaning covering any flying machine (eg balloons, gliders, helicopters) and is mostly found in technical writing.

- ○ **Adverbs of time** (eg *do it <u>now</u>*).
- ○ **Adverbs of degree** (eg *this is <u>completely</u> unacceptable*).
- ○ **Adverbs of negation** (eg *she's <u>not</u> coming*).
- ○ **Interrogative adverbs** (eg *<u>how</u> did you do that?*).
- ○ **Conjunctive adverbs** (eg *I don't know <u>how</u> he did it*).

• **Comparison of adverbs**

Like descriptive adjectives (see under adjectives), adverbs have three degrees of comparison:

- ○ **Positive** (eg *fast, resourcefully, well*).
- ○ **Comparative** (eg *faster, more resourcefully, better*).
- ○ **Superlative** (eg *fastest, most resourcefully, best*).

As the preceding examples show, there are three basic ways of forming the comparative and superlative:

- ○ Adverbs whose positive form is exactly the same as that of their related adjective (eg *fast*) add *-er* and *-est* or *-ier* and *-iest* to it, just as the adjective does.
- ○ Adverbs whose positive form is made by adding *-ly* to the positive of their related adjective (eg *resourcefully*) place *more* and *most* before the positive form.
- ○ Some adverbs (eg *well, badly*) change their positive form completely: all these are explained at their alphabetical place.

adverse / averse

▷ **adverse** means 'unfavourable, hostile, harmful' (eg *train delayed due to adverse weather conditions*); **averse** means 'disliking, disinclined' and is usually found in a negative sentence (eg *not averse to the occasional drink*).

advertise

▷ is spelt *-ise*.

affect / effect
▷ **affect** is a verb meaning 'to cause a change in, have influence upon' (eg *the accident has affected his eyesight*); **effect** is a noun meaning 'result, impression' (eg *repeated warnings have had no effect upon him*), and a verb meaning 'bring about' (eg *tried to effect a reconciliation between her parents*).

affirmative
▷ denotes a phrase or sentence that states something to be the case: its opposite is **negative**.

affix
▷ denotes a word-forming element that is added to the beginning or end of a word or word-root to form another word (eg *un-* + *known* = *unknown*, *drink* + *-able* = *drinkable*).

affluent, affluence, effluent
▷ **affluent** is an adjective meaning 'rich'; **affluence** is a noun meaning 'riches'; **effluent** is a noun meaning 'outflow'. All three words are spelt *-en-*.

aficionado
▷ is spelt with one *f* and one *c*, and pronounced *a-fish-ee-on-ah-doh*. It has a plural **aficionados**.

aged
▷ is pronounced **ay**-*jid* when meaning 'elderly' (eg *an aged gentleman, Help the Aged*) and *ayjd* when meaning 'being of the specified age' (eg *a boy aged two*).

ageing / aging
▷ **ageing** is the standard spelling, although *aging*, which is awkward to read, is also found.

ageism, ageist
▷ are spelt with an *-e-*.

agent

agent
▷ denotes the noun or pronoun that performs the action of the verb (eg *Fred* in the active sentence *Fred kicked the ball* and *a bomb* in the passive sentence *she was killed by a bomb*).
➤ See also **active voice**, **passive voice**.

aggravate
▷ means 'to make worse' and 'to annoy'; although the second sense is thought by many people to be incorrect, it has been in use for some 300 years.

aggressor
▷ is spelt *-gg-*, *-ss-* and *-or*.

aghast
▷ is spelt *-gh-*.

agitator
▷ is spelt *-or*.

agreement

In Grammar, a word is said to *agree* with some other word when it takes a particular form because of the other word's influence on it. In English:

○ **Verbs** must agree with their subject in person and number:
✓ *I am*
is correct because the *am* is the form for the first person singular of the verb *to be* and *I* is the first person singular of the personal pronoun.

○ **Demonstrative adjectives** must agree in number with the nouns they qualify:
✓ *this cat*
is correct because both adjective and noun are singular in form, and

> ✗ *this cats*

is wrong because the adjective is in the singular form, and the noun in the plural.

- The **relative pronouns** *who* and *which* must agree in gender with the noun or nouns to which they refer. Basically, persons are referred to by 'who' and things by 'which' (eg *the girl who came in, the books which were on the shelf*). Pet animals tend to be treated grammatically as if they were persons (eg *my cat, who was not very well*), other animals as if they were things (eg *ran into a cow which had strayed onto the road*).

- **Personal and reflexive pronouns, and possessive adjectives** must agree with the noun to which they refer in person, number and (with a third-person-singular verb) sex (eg *she found Richard and said to him, 'I have hurt myself: can you fetch Mother her shawl?'*).

Agreement is also known as **concord**.

➤ There can be exceptions to these rules when a noun that is singular in form is thought to be plural in meaning, and so takes a plural verb, pronouns, etc: see the entries at **choir**, **committee**, **majority**, **number of**, **rest of**; see also **what**.

ague
▷ is pronounced ***ay**-gyuu*.

aircraft / airplane / aeroplane
▷ use ***aeroplane*** in British English, and ***airplane*** in American; ***aircraft*** (plural same) is used in both languages, but has a wider meaning covering any flying machine (eg balloons, gliders, helicopters) and is mostly found in technical writing.

alga
▷ has a plural ***algae***.

alias

alias / alibi
▷ an **alias** (pronounced **ay**-lee-us) is a false name; an **alibi** (pronounced **al**-ih-biy) is an accused person's proof that he or she was elsewhere at the time the crime was committed. The use of **alibi** in informal English to mean 'excuse' is considered incorrect by many people.

alight
▷ has a past tense **alighted**.

all / all of
▷ use **all of** when a personal pronoun follows (eg *and so say all of us* / *all of us want to go*); in all other cases either can be used (eg *he ate all of my cheese* / *he ate all my cheese, all the girls laughed at him* / *all of the girls laughed at him*).

allege
▷ is spelt without a *-d-*.

allegedly
▷ is pronounced with four syllables, ie *u-**lej**-id-li*.

alleluia / alleluya / hallelujah
▷ the third spelling is more common.

alliance
▷ is spelt *-ance*.

allowance
▷ is spelt *-ance*.

all right / alright
▷ although increasingly common, **alright** is still considered incorrect by many people and should be avoided in formal writing.

all together / altogether
▷ **all together** means 'all at the same time or place' (eg *went

ambiance

off all together to the pub); ***altogether*** means 'in total' (eg *it's altogether too much*).

almighty
▷ is spelt with one *-l-*.

almost
▷ is spelt with one *-l-*.

alms
▷ is pronounced *ahms*; it is plural and has no singular form.

alternate / alternative
▷ ***alternate*** is pronounced *awl-ter-nayt* as a verb and *awl-ter-nit* as an adjective. The verb ***alternate*** means 'to switch back and forward between two things' (eg *each week he alternates between cycling and swimming*); the adjective ***alternate*** refers to things or events that come after each other by turns (eg *alternate bursts of rain and sunshine*) or which happen on every other occasion (eg *visited her on alternate Mondays*). The adjective ***alternative*** is pronounced *awl-**ter**-na-tiv* and refers to something offering a choice between two possibilities (eg *an alternative menu is available on payment of a supplement*).

aluminium
▷ is spelt with two *i*s (AmE ***aluminum***).

alumna
▷ has a plural ***alumnae***.

alumnus
▷ has a plural ***alumni***.

ambiance / ambience
▷ ***ambience*** is the usual spelling for the word's general senses ('surroundings, environment'); ***ambiance*** is less often found in these senses, and some speakers use it

ambidextrous

only in the visual-art sense ('arrangement of the background objects in a picture etc').

ambidextrous
▷ is spelt *-tr-*.

ambiguous / ambivalent
▷ ***ambiguous*** means 'having more than one possible meaning' (eg *the sentence 'she does not enjoy good health' is ambiguous*); ***ambivalent*** means 'uncertain, having mixed feelings about' (eg *I'm pretty ambivalent about the new road: it will make travel quicker, but you can't get away from the noise*).

amend / emend
▷ ***amend*** means 'change (the style or content of a document) in order to improve'; ***emend*** means 'correct the mistakes (eg spellings, miscopyings) in'.

American spellings, vocabulary and usage

This entry highlights the main differences between American English and British English, rather than being a comprehensive guide to American English. American variants which might be confused with their British counterparts are listed at their alphabetical place.

• Spellings
These are a few key areas to watch out for:

○ Word endings: ***-er*** instead of ***-re*** (eg *center, fiber*); ***-l*** instead of ***-ll*** (eg *appal, enrol*); ***-or*** instead of ***-our*** (eg *labor, color*); ***-yze*** instead of ***-yse*** (eg *analyze, paralyze*); ***-ize*** instead of ***-ise*** (eg *organize, personalize*), although the ***-ize*** version is also used in British English.

○ Word middles: ***l, p, t*** instead of ***ll, pp, tt*** (eg *panelist, woolen, kidnaped, clarinetist*).

American vocabulary ...

○ Anywhere: *e* instead of *ae* or *oe* (eg *esthetic*, *esophagus*).

Note also the following: *ax*, *catalog*, *check* (for BrE *cheque* and *check*), *cigaret* (*cigarette* also used), *cozy*, *defense*, *draft* (for BrE *draft* and *draught*), *gray*, *jewelry*, *license* (noun and verb), *maneuver*, *mustache*, *offense*, *pajamas*, *practise* (noun and verb), *pretense*, *program* (all senses), *skeptic*, *sulfur*, *story* (of a building), *tire* (on a wheel).

• **Vocabulary**

There are many differences in vocabulary between British and American English. Some of the most common terms are listed below.

BrE	AmE
aubergine	eggplant
autumn	fall
biscuit	cookie
bonnet (car)	hood
boot (car)	trunk
camp bed	cot
candy floss	cotton candy
caravan	trailer
car park	parking lot
chips	French fries
condom	rubber
cot	crib
courgette	zucchini
crisps	potato chips
cupboard	closet
drawing-pin	thumb tack
first floor	second floor
garden	yard
ground floor	first floor
handbag	purse, pocketbook
holiday	vacation

American usage ...

BrE	AmE
lift	elevator
paraffin	kerosene
pavement	sidewalk
petrol	gasoline (gas)
suppose	guess
sweets	candy
tap	faucet
tights	pantihose
trousers	pants
vest	undershirt
waistcoat	vest

- **Usage**

Some key differences are:

- A collective noun is usually followed by a singular verb (eg *the committee <u>was</u> dumbfounded by her resignation*) regardless of sense; for the British use see the entry at **committee**.

- American English uses **gotten** as well as **got** as past participles of *get*, and they are not interchangeable. **Has gotten** is used to mean 'has obtained' (eg *she's inherited her aunt's fortune but still hasn't gotten herself a decent car*), and **has got** to mean 'possesses'; **has got to** means 'must', and **has gotten to** 'has obtained permission or has the opportunity, etc' (eg *I see he's gotten to go on the free trip next week*).

- American English often uses a simple past tense where British English would use a perfect (eg *did she leave yet?* as opposed to *has she left yet?*).

- American English is more prone than British to use the subjunctive after verbs, nouns and adjectives that denote ordering, urging, requiring, etc (eg *it is essential that she <u>leave</u> tomorrow*).

among

- American English uses **will** rather than **shall** with the first person of the simple future tense (eg *I will be back in a week or so*); for the British use see **will, shall**.
- In American English a comma is generally inserted before the *and* that introduces the last item in a list (eg *bread, jam, and pickles*).
- In all-figure dates of the type '1/11/96' American usage takes the first figure to refer to the *month* and the second to refer to the *day*, so that the figures written above would denote 11 January 1996, not 1 November 1996, and is written by Americans as January 11, 1996.

amiable / amicable
▷ *amiable* means 'friendly, pleasant, good-natured' and is usually applied to persons or their appearance, mood, etc; *amicable* means 'done in a friendly way, showing goodwill' and is usually applied to actions.

amniocentesis
▷ is spelt with a -c- and pronounced *am-ni-oh-sen-**tee**-sis*.

amoeba
▷ is pronounced *am-**ee**-ba* and has plurals **amoebae** and **amoebas**.

amok / amuck
▷ the first spelling is more common.

among / between
▷ in sentences of dividing or sharing use **between** when only two persons or groups are involved and **among** when larger numbers are involved (eg *share the clothes out between Fred and Bert / between the boys and the girls / among all the children*). In other senses use **among** when the subject participates in what is described and **between** when it does not (eg *the village is situated between two*

amoral

mountains — where the implication is that it stands apart on lower ground from the mountains — and *the village is situated among the mountains* — where the implication is that it is itself on the high ground).

amoral / immoral
▷ an *amoral* person believes that there are no moral rules; an *immoral* person accepts that there are such rules, but disobeys them.

ampere
▷ refers to an electrical unit and is spelt with a lower-case initial and without an accent.

amphora
▷ has plurals *amphoras* and *amphorae*.

an / a
▷ use *a* before words that begin (or sound as if they begin) with a consonant (eg *a book*, *a cat*, *a one-way street*, *a UNESCO grant*) and *an* before words that begin (or sound as if they begin) with a vowel (eg *an egg*, *an hour*, *an FT report*).

anaesthetic
▷ is spelt *-ae-*.

analogous / similar
▷ *analogous* (which is pronounced with a hard *g*) means 'similar in certain respects only'.

analogy
▷ denotes a process by which a word or grammatical structure is altered over the years to bring it into line with what is thought to be the norm (eg the replacement of *eyen* — the former plural of *eye* — with the 'regular' *eyes*).

analysis
▷ has a plural *analyses*.

-ance / -ence
▷ there are no easy rules to find which ending is used by a given word; all the commonest *-ance* and *-ence* words are listed at their alphabetical place in this book.

ancillary
▷ is spelt with a *c*, two *l*s and ends in *-ary*.

and
▷ the use of **and** after words such as **try** and **sure** (eg *try and finish it before bedtime*) is acceptable only in informal English; in formal contexts use **to** (eg *be sure to lock the door before opening the safe*).

annex / annexe
▷ **annex** is the verb and **annexe** the noun.

annual / perennial
▷ when used of plants **annual** means 'lasting for one year only' and **perennial** means 'lasting for more than two years'. Otherwise **annual** means 'happening once every year' (eg *the annual dinner will be held on 23 March*) or 'of one year' (eg *what is his annual income?*), and **perennial** means 'lasting a whole year' or 'continual' (eg *can't stand his perennial whingeing*).

annul, annulment
▷ are spelt with one *l*.

-ant / -ent
▷ there are no easy rules to find which ending is used for a given word; all the commonest *-ant* and *-ent* words are listed at their alphabetical place in this book.

Antarctic
▷ is pronounced *ant-**ark**-tik* and spelt with a *-c-*.

ante- / anti-
▷ **ante-** means 'before, in front of', and **anti-** means 'against'.

antecedent
▷ denotes the word, phrase or clause to which a following relative pronoun refers, such as 'he drank a lot' in *he drank a lot, which didn't please his new wife*. Some grammarians also use this term for the word, phrase or clause to which a following personal pronoun refers, such as 'Fred' in *when Fred arrives give him the note*.

antelope
▷ has two plurals
- ○ *antelope*, when the group is thought of as a whole (eg *saw a large herd of antelope charging across his path*).
- ○ *antelopes*, when the group is thought of as a set of individuals (eg *a few antelopes came past, some limping badly*).

antenna
▷ has a different plural for each of its meanings
- ○ *antennae*, meaning 'insect's feelers'.
- ○ *antennas*, meaning 'aerials'.

Antigua
▷ is pronounced *an-**tee**-gu*.

antipasto
▷ has plurals *antipasti* and *antipastos*.

antiquary
▷ is pronounced with stress on ***an-***.

antithesis
▷ has a plural *antitheses*.

antonym
▷ denotes a word that is the opposite of another; so *buy* is an antonym of *sell*, and *big* is an antonym of *little*.
➤ Compare **synonym**.

any one / anyone
▷ **anyone** has the same meaning as *anybody* (eg *he dropped it on the station platform — anyone could have picked it up*); **any one** always refers back to a list of persons or things previously mentioned, as in *Fred, Bert and Mary were all there that night: any one of them could have done it*.

any time
▷ is two words.

any way / anyway
▷ **any way** means 'in any manner, by any means' (eg *do it any way you can*); **anyway** means 'at all events' (eg *anyway, once the drawbridge is up we won't be troubled by chance callers*).

apartheid
▷ is spelt *-heid* and pronounced *a-**part**-hayt*.

apex
▷ has a plural **apices**.

apologize
▷ is spelt with one *p*.

apophthegm
▷ is spelt *-phth-* and *-gm*, and pronounced ***ap**-oh-them*.

apostasy
▷ is spelt *-asy*.

apostrophes

An **apostrophe** is a punctuation mark (') which is used for three main purposes:

○ To indicate the point or points at which letters have been omitted in contractions of two or more words.

○ To create the possessive form of a noun.

○ To create the plural form of certain nouns.

apostrophes ...

• The apostrophe in contractions

These are found with combinations of:

○ Personal pronouns and verbs (eg *I've* is a contraction of *I have* and *she'd've* is a contraction of *she would have*).

○ A verb with *not* (eg *didn't* is a contraction of *did not* and *wouldn't've* is a contraction of *would not have*).

○ Two nouns linked by *and* that express a single idea (eg *fish'n'chips / worse'n'worse*).

Occasionally they are also used to contract long place-names on signposts, etc (eg *SO'TON* for Southampton, *B'HAM* for Birmingham).

Be sure to:

○ Use enough apostrophes eg
        ✓   *wouldn't've*
not
        ✗   *wouldnt've*

— one for each set of letters omitted.

○ Put the apostrophes in the right place eg
        ✓   *wouldn't've*
not
        ✗   *would'nt've*

— put them where the letters are omitted, *not* where the words end.

• The apostrophe with possessives

There are two basic rules for nouns:

○ The possessive form of a noun is shown in writing by adding *'s* (eg *the child's dog / the children's dog / Fred's dog*).

○ But if the noun is plural and already ends in *-s*, add the apostrophe only (eg *the boys' dog / in two months' time*).

apotheosis

For proper nouns ending in -s the rules are:

- Single-syllable names take 's (eg *James's bike*).
- Longer names can also take 's; but if this makes the name a 'mouthful' to pronounce, add the apostrophe only (eg *Fostiropoulos'* instead of the (also correct, but awkward to say) *Fostiropoulos's*).

For the possessive form of pronouns the apostrophe is not used (eg *the cat licked its paws / the book is hers / whose book is that?*).

NOTE
1. As an exception, the possessive form of the indefinite pronoun **one** is **one's** (eg *the Olympics is about doing one's best*).
2. *It's* and *who's* are not possessive forms, but contractions of *it is* and *who is* (eg *it's no use complaining / who's making that row?*).

• The apostrophe with plural nouns

This should not be used except in a few cases where misunderstanding or mispronunciation would otherwise be possible:

- With very short words (eg *do's and don'ts*).
- To make the plural of a word or letter that is quoted from somewhere else (eg *there are too many that's in that sentence / take more care with writing your t's*).

As an alternative to using the apostrophe, in printing or word-processing such words or letters can be made clearer by using a reverse fount (eg *too many thats / writing your ts*), whilst in handwriting an underline may be used (eg *thats*).

➤ See also **abbreviations**.

apotheosis
▷ has a plural *apotheoses*.

apparatus

apparatus
▷ has plurals **apparatuses** and **apparatus**; the first is in general use.

appearance
▷ is spelt *-ance*.

appendix
▷ has plurals **appendixes** and **appendices**; the first is in more general use.

appliqué
▷ the verb has a present participle **appliquéing** and a past tense **appliquéd**.

apposition
▷ denotes two or more words or phrases that have the same grammatical role in the sentence they are in: for example, *my secretary* and *Mr Strobes* are both subjects of the verb in the sentence *My secretary Mr Strobes will deal with you*. They are therefore 'in apposition' to each other. The apposed elements may be some distance apart in the sentence and the second may be introduced by a word or phrase such as *namely* or *that is to say*.

appraise / apprize
▷ to **appraise** is to assess the value of; to **apprize** is to inform.

approve / approve of
▷ to **approve** is to accept or authorize (eg *council has approved the expenditure plans for 1997*); to **approve of** is to think well of or consider to be good (eg *his rowdy behaviour was not approved of by many*).

apt / liable / likely / prone
▷ **apt** means 'tending to, in the habit of' (eg *grandma is apt to nod off after supper*); **prone** is similar in meaning, but should only be used of persons or of things composed

of persons (eg *the motor industry is prone to wildcat strikes*), and usually refers to what is considered to be bad actions. ***Likely*** means 'will probably' (eg *since he's a keen music-lover you're likely to see him at the concert*). ***Liable*** means 'runs the risk of, will probably', and usually refers to an unpleasant consequence of the subject of the sentence's previous action (eg *children who play in the road are liable to end up in hospital*).

aquarium
▷ is spelt without a *c* and has plurals ***aquariums*** and (less usually) ***aquaria***.

-ar / -er / -or
▷ these suffixes denote 'doers' (eg *beggar, runner, actor*); the *-er* form is by far the most common and is used on all new coinings. All words ending in *-ar* and *-or* are listed at their alphabetical place in this book.

Arab / Arabian / Arabic
▷ use ***Arab*** of the people and the horses they breed (eg *an Arab stallion*), ***Arabian*** of the region (eg *Arabian oil*) and ***Arabic*** of the language (eg *she speaks fluent Arabic*).

arbiter / arbitrator
▷ an ***arbiter*** is a person who is recognized as an authority on some topic and whose advice is regularly sought and followed; an ***arbitrator*** is a person chosen to decide a dispute.

arboretum
▷ has a plural ***arboreta***.

arc
▷ the verb has a past tense ***arced*** and a present participle ***arcing***; the *-c-* is always pronounced hard.

arch-
▷ is a prefix that means 'chief' (eg *archbishop*); the *-ch* is

archae-

always pronounced soft (ie *tsch*), except in **archangel** (pronounced **ark**-*aynjil*).

archae-
▷ is a prefix that means 'of the distant past' (eg *archaeology*); the American spelling is **archeo-**.

arctic
▷ is pronounced **ark**-*tik* and spelt with a *-c-*.

areola
▷ has a plural **areolae**.

argument
▷ is spelt *-ent*.

arise
▷ has a past tense **arose** and a past participle **arisen**.

Arkansas
▷ is pronounced **ar**-*kan-saw*.

arrogance, arrogant
▷ are spelt *-ance, -ant*.

artefact
▷ is spelt with an *-e-*.

---

articles ⓘ

In Grammar, *article* denotes a type of limiting adjective that stands before a noun. In English there are two articles:

○ The definite article ***the***, which is used when the noun it governs is used to refer to a particular item (eg *I don't mean any old cat, I mean the cat we saw here last Thursday*).

○ The indefinite article ***a*** or ***an***, which is used when the noun it governs is not used to refer to a particular item (eg *I can see a cat, but I can't tell whose it is*).
➤ For rules on the use of **a** or **an** see **a / an**.

artist / artiste
▷ an **artist** is a person who is skilled in one of the creative arts (eg writer, painter, musician, ballet dancer) or who shows skill or dexterity in some other way (eg *a real artist with his punt pole*); an **artiste** (pronounced ar-***teest***) is an entertainer (eg juggler, dancer, comedian) in the theatre, circus, or on television. Some speakers think this distinction is snobbish and use **artist** for both groups.

-ary / -ery / -ory
▷ there are no simple rules for deciding which of these endings (which tend to sound the same in speech) a given word has. The vowel ending of the related noun is usually kept (eg *director, directory / baker, bakery*), but there are many exceptions and it is wise to consult a dictionary when in doubt.

as
▷ in formal speech and writing, the two items compared must be in the same case (eg *I am as good as he*, both subjective case; *I don't like him as much as her*, both objective case); but in informal speech and writing the pronoun following the *as* is always put into the objective case (eg *I'm as good a cricketer as him anyday*).

-as / -ae
▷ certain words of Latin origin whose singular ends in *-a* have a plural in *-ae*; the commonest are listed at their alphabetical place in this book. Other words in *-a* make their plural in the usual English way by adding *s*.

ascendancy, ascendant
▷ are spelt *-ancy, -ant*.

ascetic
▷ is spelt *-sc-* and pronounced *a-**set**-ik*.

ashlar

ashlar / ashler
▷ the first spelling is more common.

aspect
▷ denotes those forms of a verb that indicate simple action (eg *he sings, he sang, he will sing*), continued action (eg *she is singing, she was singing, she will be singing*) or completed action (eg *he has sung, he had sung, he will have sung*); in English aspect is expressed by the **simple past tense**, **imperfect tense** and **perfect tense** and these are sometimes called aspects rather than tenses.

asphyxiate
▷ is spelt *-phyx-*.

assent / consent
▷ both mean 'agree to', but **consent** implies a power to refuse (eg *His Majesty has graciously consented to the ship's being named after him / give your assent to the marriage or I'll talk to the police*).

assignation / assignment
▷ an **assignation** is a secret meeting; an **assignment** is a task or post.

assistance, assistant
▷ are spelt *-ance, -ant*.

assurance / insurance
▷ an **assurance** company contracts to pay the customer an agreed sum when a specified inevitable event (eg her 60th birthday or her death if sooner) occurs; an **insurance** company contracts to pay the customer an agreed sum if a specified possible event (eg her house burning down) occurs.

assuredly
▷ is pronounced with four syllables, ie *u-**shawr**-id-li*.

asthma
▷ is spelt *asth-* and pronounced ***as**-mu*.

astrology / astronomy
▷ ***astronomy*** is the scientific study of the stars and planets and their movements; ***astrology*** is the prediction of future events, allegedly from study of the stars.

as well as
▷ introduces a subordinate clause, whose contents do not influence the main verb eg
- ✓ Fred, <u>as well as Bert</u>, wants another cup.
- ✗ My boy, <u>as well as the five next door</u>, go to Scouts.

In both these sentences the main verb should be singular, because its subject is *Fred* or *my boy*, not *Fred + Bert* or *my boy + the five next door*).

-asy / -acy
▷ only four nouns have the *-asy* ending: ***apostasy***, ***ecstasy***, ***fantasy***, ***idiosyncrasy***. All the others end in *-acy*.

ate
▷ is pronounced *et* or *ayt* and is the past tense of the verb ***eat***.

athletics
▷ is singular.

atrium
▷ has plurals ***atria*** and ***atriums***.

attendance, attendant
▷ are spelt *-ance*, *-ant*.

attributive
▷ denotes an adjective or noun that precedes the noun it modifies, as in *the <u>big</u> house has <u>stone</u> walls*.
➤ See also **adjectives**.

aubrietia
▷ is spelt *-ie-* and pronounced *aw-**bree**-shuh*.

audible
▷ is spelt *-ible*.

audience
▷ is a singular noun when thought of as a unified group of people (eg *the audience was shouting for more*) but plural when thought of as a set of individuals (eg *the audience were furious; some catcalled, others attempted to get onto the stage*).

auditor
▷ is spelt *-or*.

auditorium
▷ has plurals ***auditoriums*** and ***auditoria***.

aught / ought
▷ ***aught*** means 'anything'; ***ought*** means 'should'.

auntie / aunty
▷ the first spelling is more common.

aura
▷ has plurals ***auras*** and ***aurae***; the first is in general use.

aural / oral
▷ ***aural*** means 'of the ears or sense of hearing'; ***oral*** means 'of the mouth or by speaking'.

aurora
▷ has a plural ***auroras*** except when it is part (or thought of as being part) of the Latin phrase ***aurora borealis***, when the Latin plural ***aurorae*** is still used.

auspicious / propitious
▷ both mean 'promising or favourable to future success', but ***propitious*** usually implies immediate results (eg *the gods seemed propitious to England, who scored 100 in the first*

hour) and **auspicious** long-term expectations (eg *Lord Megabuck's handsome donation gives an auspicious start to the Building Fund*).

autarchy / autarky
▷ **autarchy** is a form of dictatorship; **autarky** means economic self-sufficiency (eg of a state that refuses to participate in foreign trade).

authoritarian / authoritative
▷ both are spelt *-or-*; **authoritarian** means 'excessively concerned with enforcing obedience' and **authoritative** means 'official, reliable'.

auto-
▷ is a prefix meaning 'self' (eg *automatic, autobiography*) or 'related to cars' (eg *autocross, autocrime*).

automaton
▷ is pronounced *aw-***tom**-*ut-un* and has plurals **automatons** and **automata**.

auxiliary verb
▷ denotes a verb (such as *can, do, has, must, will*) that is placed immediately before another verb to indicate tense (eg *Sheila will have arrived by then*), aspect (eg *he was stroking the dog when it bit him*) or mood (eg *they might be there*).
➤ See also **lexical verb**, **linking verb**.

avenge / revenge
▷ although these verbs are often used as if they were interchangeable, it is best to follow the rule that we **avenge** the wrongs done to others (eg *he set out to avenge his father's murder*) and **revenge** those done to ourselves (eg *at last she could revenge herself upon those who had publicly humiliated her so many years ago*).

averse / adverse
▷ **adverse** means 'unfavourable, hostile, harmful' (eg *train delayed due to adverse weather conditions*); **averse** means 'disliking, disinclined' and is usually found in a negative sentence (eg *not averse to the occasional drink*).

avert / avoid / evade
▷ **avert** means 'prevent or deflect the arrival of something unpleasant' (eg *averted the blow by raising his shield / averted the threatened strike by offering to negotiate*); **avoid** means 'keep away from' (eg *found a route along side roads to avoid the jams / avoided a scandal by settling out of court*); **evade** means 'dodge, sidestep, escape from' and usually involves trickery or deception (eg *evaded his pursuers by hiding in a beer barrel*). An honest accountant shows his client how to **avoid** tax (eg *by claiming all the allowances to which he or she is entitled*), a dishonest one how to **evade** it (eg *by not disclosing all his or her earnings*).

avoidance
▷ is spelt *-ance*.

avowedly
▷ is pronounced with four syllables.

award / reward
▷ an **award** is something symbolic given or received for excellence, merit or bravery, or is a sum of compensation, etc decided by a court (eg *The Queen's Award for Industry / the court awarded her £2,000 damages*); a **reward** is a payment, etc given or received for a specific service performed (eg *£10 reward for finding the dog*).

aware
▷ means 'conscious of, knowing about' and is followed by *that* or *of* (eg *the slam of the door made her aware of their arrival/that they had arrived*); the sense 'well-informed'

(eg *you have to be pretty technically aware to follow her lectures*) is only accepted in informal English.

awesome
▷ is spelt with two *e*s.

awful
▷ is spelt with one *l* and no *e*.

axis
▷ has a plural **axes**.

ay / aye
▷ **aye** is the preferred spelling for both meanings of this word, which denotes
  ○ 'yes', when it is pronounced *iy*.
  ○ 'ever', when it is pronounced *ay*.

Azerbaijan
▷ is spelt *-baij-* and pronounced *az-er-biy-**jahn***.

Azores
▷ is pronounced *uz-**ors***.

b

bacillus / bacterium / virus
▷ doctors know that each of these three words denotes a different sort of germ, but ordinary people use them interchangeably. ***Bacillus*** has a plural ***bacilli***, ***bacterium*** has a plural ***bacteria*** (which must not be treated as a singular) and ***virus*** has a plural ***viruses***.

back-formation
▷ denotes the formation of a word that the speaker imagines must exist as the source of another word he or she already knows: for example, the noun *rate-capping* was formed in the early 1980s from the noun *rate* and the verb *to cap*; but users of *rate-capping* came to think of it as a participle of the (in fact then non-existent) verb *to rate-cap*, which by 1984 had begun a life of its own in sentences such as *The Government threatens to rate-cap Slough and Ealing*.

bad
▷ has a comparative ***worse*** and a superlative ***worst***.

bade
▷ is the past tense of ***bid*** and is pronounced *bad* or *bayd*.

badly
▷ has a comparative ***worse*** and a superlative ***worst***.

baguette
▷ is spelt *-guette* and pronounced *bag-**et***.

Baha'i
▷ is spelt *-ha'i* and pronounced *bah-**hah**-ee*.

bail / bale
▷ ***bail*** denotes the money paid into court to secure the release of a person awaiting trial; to ***bail someone out*** is to obtain their release in this way. A ***bale*** is a bundle of hay and to ***bale out*** is to jump from an aircraft in an emergency, or to scoop water out of a boat.

bain-marie
▷ is pronounced *ban-ma-**ree***.

baited / bated
▷ ***baited*** means 'with bait put in/on it' and is used of a hook or trap; ***bated*** means 'held back' (eg *we listened to the results with bated breath*).

baleful / baneful
▷ ***baleful*** means 'threatening' or 'sad'; ***baneful*** means 'harmful'.

balk / baulk
▷ ***balk*** is the more common spelling.

balmy / barmy
▷ ***balmy*** means 'fragrant, soothing'; ***barmy*** means 'crazy'.

banal
▷ is pronounced *bu-**nahl***.

band
▷ is a singular noun when thought of as a unified group of people (eg *the band was playing a march*) but plural when thought of as a set of individuals (eg *the band were getting out of step*).

banns
▷ is always plural and has no singular form.

barbarian / barbaric / barbarous
▷ the noun **barbarian** denotes a member of a primitive tribe, or a 'civilized' but rude or cultureless person; the adjectives **barbarian** and **barbaric** are both used to describe such tribesmen or acts typical of them, whether approved of by the speaker or not (eg *barbarian greed / barbaric splendour*), but **barbaric** and **barbarous** are particularly used to denote with disapproval the brutality of barbarian tribesmen or of other notoriously cruel persons (eg *Hitler's barbaric treatment of the Jews / a barbarous revenge*). **Barbarous** is also used of mistakes in grammar or usage that are considered crude, though are often widespread.

barbarism / barbarity / barbarousness
▷ all three are nouns: **barbarism** denotes what is considered a crude mistake in grammar or usage; **barbarity** denotes the brutality of primitive tribesmen or other notoriously cruel persons; **barbarism** and **barbarousness** denote generally the state of being, or the acts (good or bad) typical of, a barbarian.

bare infinitive
▷ denotes the form of the infinitive that does not use *to*, as in *let him go*.
➤ See also **'to'-infinitive**.

barmy / balmy
▷ **barmy** means 'crazy'; **balmy** means 'fragrant, soothing'.

baroque
▷ is spelt *-oque* and pronounced *ba-rok*.

barracks
▷ although originally a plural (whose singular survives in such phrases as *barrack room, barrack square*), **barracks** may now be treated as either singular or plural (eg *the bar-*

racks are in the next street / the old barracks was pulled down in 1969).

barracuda
▷ is spelt *-rr-* and has two plurals

   ○ ***barracuda***, when the group is thought of as a whole (eg *saw a large shoal of barracuda on the port bow*).

   ○ ***barracudas***, when the group is thought of as a set of individuals (eg *only two barracudas in the pool, one of which looked pretty sickly*).

basalt
▷ is pronounced

	✓	**ba**-sawlt
or	✓	ba-**sawlt**
not	✗	bay-

basis
▷ has a plural ***bases***.

bass
▷ has two senses

   ○ a deep male singing voice, pronounced *bays* and having a plural ***basses***.

   ○ a sort of fish, pronounced to rhyme with *mass*, and having two plurals, ***bass*** and ***basses***, which follow the rules listed at **barracuda** above.

bated / baited
▷ ***bated*** means 'held back' (eg *we listened to the results with bated breath*); ***baited*** means 'with bait put in/on it' and is used of a hook or trap.

bath / bathe
▷ as verbs ***bath*** means 'wash (usually the whole body) in a bath'; ***bathe*** means 'wash or moisten' or 'go for a swim'.

bathos

bathos / pathos
▷ are both pronounced *-ay-*; **bathos** denotes a sudden change from lofty ideas to trivial ones (eg *he felt deserted, betrayed and unloved — and he had forgotten to put out the cat*); **pathos** denotes a quality in a story, etc that makes the reader feel pity (eg *orphans abandoned on a stormy night — what could have more pathos than that?*).

batman
▷ has a plural **batmen**.

battalion
▷ is spelt with two *t*s and one *l*.

bayonet
▷ the verb has a past tense and past participle **bayoneted**.

BBC English
➤ See under **Standard English**.

be
▷ has a present tense *I am*, *thou art*, *he is*, *we are*, *you are*, *they are*, a past tense *I was*, *thou wast*, *he was*, *we were*, *you were*, *they were* and a past participle **been**; *thou art* and *thou wast* are used as archaic or dialectal forms.

bear
▷ has a past tense **bore**, and past participles **born** and **borne**; **born** is used only in passive sentences where *by* does not follow (eg *she was born in London* / *he was born to rich parents*) and **borne** is used in all other contexts (eg *he was borne along by the waves* / *she has borne him six children*).

beau
▷ is pronounced *boh* and has a plural **beaux** (pronounced *bohz*).

Beaulieu
▷ is pronounced **byuu**-li.

beautiful
▷ is spelt -eau- and -ful.

because of / due to / owing to
▷ may nowadays be used interchangeably.

become
▷ has a past tense **became** and a past participle **become**.

befall
▷ has a past tense **befell** and a past participle **befallen**.

beget
▷ has past tenses **begot** or **begat** and a past participle **begotten**.

beggar
▷ is spelt -ar.

begin
▷ has a past tense **began** and a past participle **begun**.

behold
▷ has a past tense and past participle **beheld**.

beige
▷ is spelt -ei- and pronounced bayj.

bellows
▷ may be treated as either singular or plural eg
    ✓   *the bellows <u>is</u> in the cupboard*
or ✓   *the bellows <u>are</u> in the cupboard*

bellyful
▷ is spelt -ful and has a plural **bellyfuls**.

beloved
▷ is pronounced with three syllables.

bends

bends, the
▷ denotes decompression sickness and may be treated as either singular or plural.

benefactor
▷ is spelt *-or*.

benign / benignant
▷ use **benign** of effects (eg *the whisky began to have a benign influence on their tempers*) and of non-cancerous tumours; use **benignant** of attitudes or intentions (eg *Oxfam's benignant plans for the region have been frustrated by lack of local co-operation*).

Berkshire
▷ is pronounced **bark**-.

berserk
▷ may be accented on either syllable; the *s* may be pronounced *s* or *z*.

Berwick
▷ is pronounced **ber**-*ik*.

beseech
▷ has past tense and past participle **beseeched** or **besought**.

beset
▷ has a past tense and past participle **beset**.

beside / besides
▷ use **beside** for 'at the side of' (eg *she sat down beside me*) and **besides** for 'in addition to' (eg *there's the beds to make, besides the washing up*).

bespeak
▷ has a past tense **bespoke** and a past participle **bespoken**.

bestial
▷ is pronounced **best**-*i-ul*.

bestride
▷ has a past tense **bestrode** and a past participle **bestridden**.

bet
▷ has past tense and past participle **betted** or **bet**.

betake
▷ has a past tense **betook** and a past participle **betaken**.

better / best
▷ **better** is the comparative form, and **best** the superlative form, of both **good** and **well**.

between
▷ between is never followed by a single noun or noun-phrase eg

    ✗   *paused between each sentence*
    ✓   *paused between sentences*

between / among
▷ in sentences of dividing or sharing use **between** when only two persons or groups are involved and **among** when larger numbers are involved (eg *share the clothes out between Fred and Bert/between the boys and the girls/among all the children*). In other senses use **among** when the subject participates in what is described and **between** when it does not (eg *the village is situated between two mountains* — where the implication is that it stands on lower ground apart from the mountains — and *the village is situated among the mountains* — where the implication is that it is itself on the high ground).

between ... and / between ... or
▷ only the first is correct eg

    ✓   *choose between him and me*
    ✗   *choose between him or me;*
    ✓   *will arrive between three and four*

Bewick
▷ is pronounced **byuu**-ik.

biannual / biennial
▷ **biannual** means 'happening twice each year'; **biennial** means 'happening every two years' or (of a plant) 'living for two years'.

biceps
▷ is singular.

bid
▷ the verb has two senses
- 'offer' (a sum of money, etc), which has past tense and past participle **bid**.
- 'tell, order', which has a past tense **bade** and a past participle **bidden**.

bide
▷ has a past tense **bided** or **bode** and a past participle **bided**.

big
▷ has a comparative **bigger** and a superlative **biggest**.

billiards
▷ is singular.

billion
▷ in informal speech **billion** simply means 'a lot' (eg *I've told you a billion times not to talk when I'm reading*). When it is used as a statistic (and always in American English) a **billion** means a thousand million (ie, the unit and nine zeros, or 10^9). However, always check what the speaker or writer means since, in the UK, **billion** was formerly used to represent a million million (ie, the unit and twelve zeros, or 10^{12}).

bimbo
▷ has a plural **bimbos**.

bind
▷ has past tense and past participle **bound**.

binoculars
▷ is plural.

bio-
▷ is a prefix meaning 'life', 'living things', 'biology'.

biodegradable
▷ is spelt *-dable*.

biscuit
▷ is spelt *-cuit*.

bison
▷ has a plural **bison**.

bistro
▷ has a plural **bistros**.

bite
▷ has a past tense **bit** and a past participle **bitten**.

bivouac
▷ has a present participle **bivouacking** and a past tense and past participle **bivouacked**.

bizarre
▷ is spelt with one *z* and two *r*s.

blackguard
▷ is pronounced **blag**-*ard*.

blanch / blench
▷ to **blanch** is to turn white or to immerse vegetables, etc in boiling water; to **blench** is to turn white or to flinch.

blancmange
▷ is spelt *-ncm-* and pronounced *blu-***monj**.

blatant

blatant / flagrant
▷ **blatant** means 'shamelessly obvious' (eg *a blatant liar*); **flagrant** means 'scandalously wicked' (eg *a flagrant abuse of her powers*) and is not used of persons.

bless
▷ has a past tense **blessed** (pronounced *blest*) and past participles **blessed** (pronounced *blest*) and **blest**.

blessed
▷ when used as an adjective is pronounced **ble**-*sid* (eg *take that blessed dog away! / canonization of the Blessed Oliver Plunket*).

bloc / block
▷ a **bloc** is a group of nations, etc that have common interests or policies (eg *the Communist bloc was already crumbling before the fall of the Berlin Wall*); **block** covers the other, more concrete, senses (eg *block of wood, block of flats, road-block*).

blond / blonde
▷ use **blonde** when referring to a woman (eg *she is blonde / she has blonde hair*) and **blond** when referring to a man (eg *he has blond hair*).

blow
▷ has a past tense **blew** and a past participle **blown**.

boatswain / bosun / boson
▷ **boatswain** and **bosun** both mean 'sailor in charge of a lifeboat', and **bosun** is in fact just a respelling of **boatswain** to reflect its current pronunciation (**boh**-*sun*). **Boson**, although looking similar to **bosun**, is in fact unrelated to the other two; it denotes a type of subatomic particle, and is pronounced **boh**-*son*.

bode
➤ See under **bide**.

Boulogne

boil / broil
▷ food is **boiled** by being heated in water, and **broiled** by dry heat (eg on a grill). When used metaphorically (eg *a three-hour tramp under the broiling desert sun*) both simply mean 'very hot'.

bolero
▷ has a plural **boleros**; it denotes
  ○ a Spanish dance, and is pronounced *bu-**le**-roh*.
  ○ a sort of short jacket, and is pronounced ***bol**-u-roh*.

bongo
▷ has plurals **bongos** or **bongoes**.

bonsai
▷ has a plural **bonsai**.

bonus
▷ has a plural **bonuses**.

born / borne
▷ both are past participles of the verb *to bear*
  ○ **born** is used only in passive sentences where *by* does not follow (eg *she was born in London* / *he was born to rich parents*).
  ○ **borne** is used in all other contexts (eg *he was borne along by the waves* / *she has borne him six children*).

boson / bosun / boatswain
▷ **bosun** and **boatswain** both mean 'sailor in charge of a lifeboat', and the first of these is in fact just a respelling of the second to reflect its current pronunciation (***boh**-sun*). **Boson**, although looking similar to **bosun**, is in fact unrelated to the other two; it denotes a type of sub-atomic particle, and is pronounced ***boh**-son*.

Boulogne
▷ is spelt *-ogne* and pronounced *boo-**loyn***.

bouquet

bouquet
▷ is spelt *-quet* and pronounced *boo-kay*; either syllable may be stressed.

bourgeois
▷ is spelt *-geois* and pronounced **boorj**-*wah*.

boutique
▷ is spelt *-ique* and pronounced *boo-***teek**.

bowlful
▷ is spelt *-ful* and has a plural **bowlfuls**.

bowls
▷ is plural.

boycott
▷ is spelt *-tt*.

boxful
▷ is spelt *-ful* and has a plural **boxfuls**.

brackets
➤ See **punctuation**.

bravado / bravery / bravura
▷ **bravado** is a display of daring deeds or words made to impress or to hide fear; **bravery** is another word for *courage*; **bravura** is a display of virtuosic skill in music or other arts.

bravo
▷ has two senses
  ○ a cry of applause, which has a plural **bravos**.
  ○ a daredevil or ruffian, which has plurals **bravos** or **bravoes**.

break
▷ has a past tense **broke** and a past participle **broken**.

bream
▷ has a plural **bream**.

brill
▷ has two plurals
- ○ **brill**, when the group is thought of as a whole (eg *saw a large shoal of brill on the port bow*).
- ○ **brills**, when the group is thought of as a set of individuals (eg *only two brills in the pool, one of which looked pretty sickly*).

brilliance
▷ is spelt *-illi-* and *-ance*.

brimful
▷ is spelt *-ful*.

bring
▷ has a past tense and past participle ***brought***.

Britain
▷ is informally used as an equivalent to **Great Britain**.

British English
▷ is the variety of English grammar, pronunciation and spelling used by native inhabitants of the British Isles.
➤ See also **American English**, **Standard/non-standard English**.

British Isles
▷ denotes the geographical term for the group of islands consisting of Great Britain and Ireland, and all the other smaller islands around them (eg the Hebrides, Channel Islands and Isle of Man).
➤ See also **United Kingdom**, **Great Britain**.

broach / brooch
▷ a ***broach*** is a boring-tool; a ***brooch*** is an ornament attached to clothing by a pin.

broad / wide
▷ in almost all cases either word may be used, but there is a

broadcast

tendency to use **broad** of an object and **wide** of a gap between objects or parts of an object (eg *the wide gateway had been blocked by a pile of broad tree trunks*).

broadcast
▷ has a past tense and past participle **broadcast**.

broil / boil
▷ food is **boiled** by being heated in water, and **broiled** by dry heat (eg on a grill). When used metaphorically (eg *a three-hour tramp under the broiling desert sun*) both simply mean 'very hot'.

bronchus
▷ has a plural **bronchi**.

bronco
▷ has a plural **broncos**.

brother
▷ has two plurals
  ○ **brothers**, used in all senses.
  ○ **brethren**, used of monks.

brother-in-law
▷ has a plural **brothers-in-law**.

browbeat
▷ has a past tense **browbeat** and a past participle **browbeaten**.

Brueghel
▷ is spelt *-uegh-* and pronounced **broy**-*gul*.

brusque
▷ is spelt *-sque* and pronounced *brusk*.

bucket
▷ the verb has a present participle **bucketing** and a past tense **bucketed**.

bucketful
▷ is spelt *-ful* and has a plural **bucketfuls**.

Buddha, Buddhism, Buddhist
▷ are spelt *-ddh-*; their first syllable is pronounced to rhyme either with *mood* or with *foot*.

Buenos Aires
▷ is pronounced **bway**-*nos* **iy**-*rees*.

buffalo
▷ has two plurals
- **buffalo**, when the group is thought of as a whole (eg *saw a large herd of buffalo charging across his path*).
- **buffaloes**, when the group is thought of as a set of individuals (eg *a few buffaloes came past, some limping badly*).

buffet
▷ is pronounced **buu**-*fay* or **bu**-*fay*.

buoy, buoyancy, buoyant
▷ are all spelt *-uo-*; the last two are spelt *-ancy*, *-ant*.

burbot
▷ has two plurals
- **burbot**, when the group is thought of as a whole (eg *saw a large shoal of burbot on the port bow*).
- **burbots**, when the group is thought of as a set of individuals (eg *only two burbots in the pool, one of which looked pretty sickly*).

bureau
▷ is spelt *bur-*, *-eau*, and pronounced **byuu**-*roh*; either syllable may be stressed.

burglar
▷ is spelt *-ar*.

burn

burn
▷ has past tense and past participle **burned** or **burnt**.

burrito
▷ has a plural **burritos**.

business / busyness
▷ **business** means 'trade, commercial company, job', is spelt *-i-*, and pronounced **biz**-*nis*; **busyness** means 'being (fussily) busy', is spelt *-y-*, and pronounced **biz**-*i-nes*.

bust
▷ the verb has past tense and past participle **bust** or **busted**.

by / bye
▷ as a noun **by** is used only in the phrase 'by the by'; **bye** denotes an extra run at cricket, or a free round in knockout competitions, and is also used as a shorter form of 'goodbye'.

Byzantine
▷ is pronounced *bi-**zan**-tiyn* or **biz**-*un-tiyn*.

C

cacao / cocoa / coco / coconut
▷ *cocoa* denotes the hot milky drink, and the ground and roasted seeds of the *cacao* tree from which the drink is made; *coco* denotes the palm tree on which *coconuts* grow.

cactus
▷ has plurals *cacti* and *cactuses*.

caddie / caddy
▷ a *caddie* is a golfer's assistant; a *caddy* is a small container for tea leaves.

caecum
▷ is pronounced **see**-*kum* and has a plural *caeca*.

caffeine
▷ is spelt -*ff*- and -*eine*.

caftan / kaftan
▷ the first spelling is more common.

cagey
▷ is spelt -*ey* but has a comparative *cagier* and a superlative *cagiest*.

cagily
▷ is spelt -*gi*- but pronounced -*ji*-.

calendar / calender
▷ a *calendar* shows the date; a *calender* is a heated press for cloth or paper.

calf

calf
▷ has a plural **calves**.

calculator
▷ is spelt *-or*.

caliph / khaliph
▷ the first spelling is more common.

calliper / callipers
▷ a **calliper** is a metal splint; **callipers** (always plural) are a measuring instrument.

callous / callus
▷ **callous** is an adjective meaning 'ruthless, cruel'; **callus** is a noun denoting a hard pad of skin.

cameo
▷ has a plural **cameos**.

campanile
▷ is pronounced *kam-pan-**ee**-lay*.

candelabrum
▷ has plurals **candelabra** (which some people use as a singular) and **candelabrums**.

canful
▷ is spelt *-ful* and has a plural **canfuls**.

can / may
▷ the traditional distinction was that **can** refers to *ability* (eg *you can't jump as high as a house*) and **may** to *permission* (eg *may I get you another drink?*), but nowadays the verbs are used interchangeably except in the most formal contexts.

cannon / canon
▷ **canon** denotes a rule or a senior clergyman, and has a plural **canons**; **cannon** denotes a large gun and has two plurals

○ ***cannon***, when the guns are thought of as a set (eg *most of the walls had been destroyed by the relentless fire of the enemy cannon*).

○ ***cannons***, when the guns are thought of as a number of individuals (eg *three of the old cannons are covered with rust*).

cantabile
▷ is pronounced *kan-**tah**-bi-lay*.

canvas / canvass
▷ ***canvas*** is a noun and denotes the material used to make tents, etc; ***canvass*** is a verb meaning 'ask for votes or support'.

capability / capacity / ability
▷ ***ability*** means 'being able' or 'competence' (eg *showed above average ability in the practical exam*); ***capability*** refers to an aptitude or potential, mental or physical, to cope with a situation (eg *still amazed at my mother's organizational capabilities*); ***capacity*** has both meanings (eg *the new job was beyond her capacities*).

capercaillie / capercailzie
▷ is pronounced *kap-ur-**kayl**-yee*.

capitalist
▷ is pronounced ***kap**-it-ul-ist*.

capitalization

Capital letters are used:

○ For the first letter of the first word of a sentence or (sometimes) of a line of verse.

○ For the first letter of a proper noun (eg *George, Paris, the Himalayas, Eton College*) and of adjectives derived from a proper noun (eg *Georgian, Parisian, Himalayan, Etonian*).

cappuccino

- For the first letter of the first and each subsequent 'important' word in the titles of books, organizations and jobs (eg *The Taming of the Shrew / Department of Employment / Admiral of the Fleet*).
- For the first letter of brand names (eg *must get the Hoover repaired / she bought a Walkman yesterday*).

NOTE Capitals are not needed when the brand name is used as a verb, as in *must hoover the floor before I go out*.

➤ See also **abbreviations**.

cappuccino
▷ is spelt with two *p*s and two *c*s, and pronounced *kap-oo-cheen-oh*; it has a plural **cappuccinos**.

carburettor
▷ is spelt -*tt*- and -*or*.

carcase / carcass
▷ *carcase* (pronounced **kar**-*kus*) is the preferred spelling.

cardinal number
▷ denotes a number that expresses quantity (eg *two*) rather than sequence (eg *second*).
➤ See also **ordinal number**.

career
▷ is spelt with a single -*r*- in the middle.

Caribbean
▷ is spelt with one *r* and two *b*s.

caribou
▷ has two plurals
- *caribou*, when the group is thought of as a whole (eg *saw a large herd of caribou charging across his path*).
- *caribous*, when the group is thought of as a set of individuals (eg *a few caribous came past, some limping badly*).

carillon
▷ is pronounced *ka-**ril**-yun*.

carousal / carousel
▷ *carousal* means 'drinking bout' and is pronounced *ku-row-zul*; *carousel* means 'rotating luggage conveyor or slide magazine' and is pronounced *ka-ru-sel*.

carp
▷ has two plurals

○ *carp*, when the group is thought of as a whole (eg *saw a large shoal of carp in a shady pool*).

○ *carps*, when the group is thought of as a set of individuals (eg *only a couple of carps in the pool, one of which looked pretty sickly*).

caryatid
▷ is pronounced *ka-ri-**at**-id* and has plurals **caryatids** and **caryatides** (pronounced *-id-eez*).

case
▷ denotes the different forms taken by English pronouns to indicate whether they are the subject (see **subjective case**) or object (see **objective case**) of the verb, such as *she* and *her* in *she hit Fred, but Fred hit her back*; many languages (eg Latin, German and Russian) have an extensive case system in which nouns and adjectives decline as well as pronouns.

casino
▷ has a plural **casinos**.

cast / caste
▷ as a noun *cast* denotes the actors in a play or an act of throwing; as a verb it means 'throw' and has a past tense and past participle *cast*. *Caste* is a noun and means 'social class'. Both words are pronounced *kahst*.

caster / castor
▷ a **caster** is a sugar-sprinkler and a **castor** is a small wheel on a piece of furniture.

castrato
▷ has a plural **castrati**.

cataclysm / catastrophe
▷ both can mean 'disaster', but it is best to use **catastrophe** for this, and reserve **cataclysm** for major social or political upheavals (eg *Europe watched the cataclysm of Hitler's rise to power with mingled fear and admiration*).

catarrh
▷ is spelt *-t-* and *-rrh*.

catechism
▷ is pronounced **kat**-*ek-izm*.

catechumen
▷ is pronounced *kat-ek-***yoo**-*men*.

catharsis
▷ has a plural **catharses** (pronounced *-sees*).

cattle
▷ is plural.

caucus
▷ has a plural **caucuses**.

-cede / -ceed / -sede
▷ although these endings sound alike, it is easy to know which spelling to use: the only words that end in *-ceed* are **exceed**, **proceed**, **succeed**, and the only word that ends in *-sede* is **supersede**; all the others end in *-cede*.

cedilla
▷ denotes the mark or diacritic ¸ written or printed under certain letters in various foreign languages (eg French,

centre

Portuguese and Turkish), or in English words (eg *façade*) borrowed from them, to indicate their pronunciation.

ceilidh
▷ is spelt *-ei-* and *-dh*, and is pronounced ***kay***-*li*.

Celtic
▷ the name of the Glasgow and Belfast football teams is pronounced ***sel***-*tik*; the adjective referring to the ancient Celts and the languages spoken by them is pronounced ***kel***-*tik*.

cement / concrete / mortar
▷ ***cement*** is any material which sets hard to form a building material or to stick other objects together. The commonest building cement is made from clay and limestone; when this is mixed with sand and water it forms ***mortar***, and when mixed with sand, water and small stones it forms ***concrete***. Both mortar and cement are, however, often called 'concrete' in informal speech.

censer / censor / censure
▷ a ***censer*** is a container in which incense is burnt; a ***censor*** bans the publication of material thought harmful to state security or public morality; ***censure*** means 'criticism, blame'.

censorial / censorious
▷ ***censorial*** means 'of or as a censor'; ***censorious*** means 'critical, fault-finding'.

centre / middle
▷ basically both words mean the same, but the information given by ***centre*** is felt to be more precise: for example, the *centre* of a room is a spot roughly (or exactly) measurable from its four walls, while its *middle* is its whole floor area apart from the edges.

centuries

centuries
▷ since the first year of the Christian Era was AD 1 (not AD 0), its first century ended on 31 December 100, and its second century began on 1 January 101; so strictly speaking the millennium should be celebrated on the night of 31 December 2000, and the year 2000 spoken of as part of the twentieth century. Most people, however, think (and speak) of the century ending, and the millennium occurring, at 31 December 1999 when the digital displays flip over to show the 2 (and this *is* of course where the 'nineteen-hundreds' end); this is when the event will be officially celebrated.

cerebrum
▷ has a plural *cerebra*.

ceremonial / ceremonious
▷ *ceremonial* means 'for, suited to, involving, a ceremony'; *ceremonious* means 'excessively formal'.

Chablis
▷ is pronounced ***shab***-*lee*.

chagrin
▷ is pronounced ***shag***-*rin*.

chamois
▷ denotes
  ○ a mountain goat, which is pronounced ***sham***-*wah* and has a plural *chamois*.
  ○ a sort of soft leather, which is pronounced ***sham***-*i*.

changeable
▷ is spelt -*eable*.

chaperon
▷ is spelt -*on* and pronounced ***shap***-*ur-ohn*.

char
▷ the noun denoting a sort of fish is spelt with one *r* and has

chic

two plurals
- ○ ***char***, when the group is thought of as a whole (eg *saw a large shoal of char in a shady pool*).
- ○ ***chars***, when the group is thought of as a set of individuals (eg *only two chars in the tank, one of which looked pretty sickly*).

charade
▷ is pronounced *shu-**rahd***.

charisma
▷ is pronounced *ku-**riz**-mu* and has a plural ***charismata***.

chasm
▷ is spelt *ch-*, *-sm* and pronounced ***kaz**-um*.

chassis
▷ is pronounced ***shas**-i* and has a plural ***chassis*** which is pronounced ***shas**-iz*.

chastise
▷ is spelt *-ise*.

château
▷ is spelt *-â-*, *-eau* and pronounced ***shat**-oh*.

chauffeur
▷ is spelt *-au-*, *-ff-*, *-eur* and pronounced ***shoh**-fur*.

checker / chequer
▷ a ***checker*** is a person who checks; a ***chequer*** (AmE ***checker***) is a pattern of squares of alternating colours, or a piece in the game of Chinese Chequers.

Chianti
▷ is pronounced *ki-**an**-ti*.

chic
▷ is pronounced *sheek* has a comparative ***chicer*** and a superlative ***chicest*** (pronounced ***sheek**-ur* and ***sheek**-ist*).

chide
▷ now has a past tense and a past participle *chided*.

chief
▷ is spelt *-ie-*.

child
▷ has a plural *children*.

childish / childlike
▷ both mean 'of or like a child' and are usually used of adults; the first indicates the speaker's disapproval of what is described (eg *am fed up with her childish tantrums*), while the second indicates approval or pity (eg *his childlike trust is one of the nicest features of his character*).

chilli / chilly
▷ a *chilli* is a sort of pepper, is spelt *-ll-*, and has plurals *chillis* and *chillies*; *chilly* means 'cold'.

chimera
▷ is spelt *-mer-* and pronounced *kiy-**mee**-ru*.

chiropodist
▷ is pronounced *ki-**ro**-pu-dist*.

chirrup
▷ has a present participle *chirruping* and a past tense *chirruped*.

Chiswick
▷ is pronounced ***chiz**-ik*.

choir
▷ is a singular noun when thought of as a unified group of people (eg *this choir always sings flat*) but plural when thought of as a set of individuals (eg *the last choir were hopeless — three old men and a couple of kids*).

choleric
▷ is pronounced ***kol**-ur-ik*.

choose
▷ has a past tense **chose** and a past participle **chosen**.

chord / cord
▷ **cord** is used for ropes, clothing fabric, vocal cords, spinal cord; **chord** is used for the musical and geometrical senses, literal and metaphoric (eg *play that chord again / her face strikes a chord with me / circle subtended by a chord*).

chutzpa
▷ is pronounced **khoot**-*spa*.

cicatrice
▷ is pronounced **sik**-*u-tris*.

Cinque Ports
▷ the first word is pronounced *singk*.

circumcise
▷ is spelt -*ise*.

circumflex accent
▷ denotes the mark or diacritic ˆ written or printed above a letter in certain foreign languages, or in English words (eg *fête*) borrowed from them, to indicate its pronunciation.

cirrus
▷ is pronounced **sir**-*us* and has a plural **cirri**.

clad
▷ is now outdated as a past tense of *clothe* eg
    ✗   *she clad them in the best she could afford*
but is still used as an adjective eg
    ✓   *fishermen clad in oilskins*
    ✓   *snow-clad mountains*.
As a building term eg
    ✓   *we must clad the brickwork with plastic planking*
it is now a verb in its own right (past tense and past participle **cladded**).

clandestine
▷ is pronounced **klan**-des-tiyn or **klan**-des-tin; stress on the second syllable is also correct.

clangour
▷ is pronounced to rhyme with *anger*.

clarinettist
▷ is spelt with one *n* and three *t*s.

classic / classical
▷ as a noun, a **classic** denotes (i) a work of art, literature, music, etc which is generally considered to be of lasting importance; (ii) one of five famous English horse races (eg the Derby). For the plural form (**classics**) (iii) see next entry. As adjectives, **classic** is used for sense (ii) above, and for sense (i) in reference to the work (eg *Thackeray's classic novel Vanity Fair*); but **classical** is used of its creator or of the repertoire of which it becomes a part (eg *Beethoven is a classical composer / Chekhov's plays have established themselves in the international classical repertoire*). **Classical** is also used for sense (iii) (eg *this term the Classical Studies programme will concentrate on Greek Drama*), for styles of design, etc derived from those of ancient Greece or Rome (eg *Bath is full of classical architecture*) and also for any other highly valued culture of past times (eg *she is studying classical Chinese poetry*); **classical** is also used for 'serious' music (as distinguished from pop, folk, etc) of any period, and more narrowly for the 'serious' music composed from about 1750 to 1830 by such composers as Haydn, Mozart and Beethoven. **Classic** is used to mean 'typical' (eg *this is a classic example of her carelessness*) and 'excellent' (eg *the second track features Clapton in a classic display of guitar improvisation*). Either adjective can be used to mean 'pure, simple, austere' (eg *a suit of classic cut / gestures of a classical simplicity*).

clauses and phrases

classics
▷ denotes the study of Ancient Greek and Latin language and literature; although plural in form, **classics** is grammatically a singular noun (eg *Nowadays classics is studied in only a few schools*).
➤ See also previous entry.

clauses and phrases

Both denote groups of words that are part of a sentence and hang together as a unit of meaning (eg *while we were running / a present from Peru*): the basic difference is that a clause usually contains a verb but a phrase usually does not.

NOTE Traditional grammars require a clause to have a subject and a finite verb but many modern authorities simply require a verb to be present in any form (eg participle, infinitive), or even to be merely implied (as in *if possible, get it to us by Thursday*, where *if possible* is said to stand for *if it is possible*).

• **clauses**
There are three types of clause:

○ ***Co-ordinate clauses:*** these are of equal rank with each other and are linked by such words as *and, but, or* (eg *she sat down and he ordered some wine*).

○ ***Main clauses*** (also called ***principal clauses***): these contain the main verb or verbs of a sentence that also contains one or more subordinate clauses (eg *she sat down while he ordered some wine*).

○ ***Subordinate clauses*** (also called ***dependent clauses***): these do not contain the main verb of the sentence but have verbs that are introduced by such words as *because, since, that, though, when, which, while* (eg *she sat down while he ordered some wine*). A sentence that contains subordinate clauses must also have at least one main clause.

NOTE In informal conversation a main clause may often have to be understood from a preceding remark. For example, in '*Why aren't you listening?*' '*Because I'm bored*' the second sentence's main clause (*I'm not listening because...*) has to be understood from the previous sentence.

• **Types of subordinate clause**

There are three types:

○ *Noun clauses*: these perform the same functions in a sentence that a noun would. They may be the subject or object of a verb (eg *how it got there is far from clear / I don't know how it got there*) or they may follow a preposition (eg *they were terrified by what they had seen*).

○ *Adjectival clauses*: these perform the same functions in a sentence that an adjective would (eg *the reason why she did it is still unclear*).

○ *Relative clauses*: many adjectival clauses are also *relative clauses*, ie they are introduced by the relative pronouns *who, whom, which* or *that* (eg *the woman who was here yesterday called again this morning / the man whom I saw in the park was in the race / the cat which sat on the mat didn't eat its tea*). *That* can be used in place of *who, whom* or *which*. *Whom* should be used when the relative pronoun is the object of the clause or if it follows a preposition; however, *who* is often used in this context. The relative pronoun can be omitted when it is the object of the verb or a preposition (eg *the man I saw in the park...*).

➤ *Relative clauses* may be subdivided into *restrictive* (or *defining*) and *non-restrictive* (or *non-defining*) types. A *restrictive relative clause* focuses the meaning of the noun to which it refers (eg a specific woman is identified in the following example: *the woman who was here yesterday called again this*

clearance

morning), whereas a **non-restrictive relative clause** merely adds further information, as in *the woman, whom we saw again this morning, seems to be ideal for the job*.

• Adverbial clauses

These perform the same functions in a sentence that an adverb would (eg *I'll come when I'm ready* (adverbial clause of time) / *I'll dress as I please* (adverbial clause of manner) / *I'll come if I choose* (adverbial clause of condition).

• Phrases

There are five types of phrase:

- **Noun phrases**: these consist of a noun plus any other words directly dependent upon it, as the underlined sections in *a big black car pulled up outside his mother's house*.

- **Verb phrases**: these consist of a group of words that together make up a single verb-unit in a sentence (eg *he must have left before us*).

- **Adjectival phrases**: these consist of an adjective and any adverbs that qualify it (eg *a very big lorry*).

- **Adverbial phrases**: these consist of an adverb plus any other adverbs that qualify it, as in *she ran very quickly but not quickly enough*.

- **Prepositional phrases**: these consist of a preposition plus the words it governs, as in *they ran into the house*.

clean / cleanse

▷ both mean 'remove dirt, germs etc from', but **cleanse** often suggests a deeper or more thorough operation.

clearance

▷ is spelt *-ance*.

cleave

cleave
▷ means
  ○ 'split' or 'cut' and has past tenses **clove**, **cleft** or **cleaved**, and past participles **cloven** (used in *cloven hoof*), **cleft** (used in *cleft palate*, *cleft stick*) or **cleaved**.
  ○ 'stick' and has a past tense and past participle **cleaved**.

cliché
▷ denotes a phrase or combination of words (eg *to coin a phrase* / *at the end of the day* / *at this moment in time*) that was striking and effective when first used but has become stale and feeble through repetition, and is now best avoided.

clientèle
▷ is spelt *-èle*.

clerestory
▷ is spelt *-ere-* and pronounced **kleer**-stur-i.

climactic / climacteric / climatic
▷ **climactic** is an adjective and means 'of or like a climax'; **climacteric** is a noun and denotes the female or male menopause or the ripening of fruit; **climatic** is an adjective and refers to climate, ie weather conditions.

cling
▷ has a past tense and past participle **clung**.

clipped form
▷ denotes words such as **exam**, **deli** and **bus** which began life as abbreviations (of *examination*, *delicatessen* and *omnibus*) but are now treated as words in their own right; in some cases (eg **bus**) they have completely replaced their parent word.

closet
▷ the verb has a present participle **closeting** and a past tense and past participle **closeted**.

club
▷ is a singular noun when thought of as a unified group of people (eg *the club meets on Tuesday evenings*) but plural when thought of as a set of individuals (eg *the club were horrified at the news and voted to expel him*).

Clwyd
▷ is pronounced **kluu**-id.

coalesce
▷ is spelt -*oa*-, -*esce* and is pronounced **koh**-ul-**es**.

coccyx
▷ is pronounced **kok**-siks and has plurals **coccyxes** (now in general use) and **coccyges**.

Cockburn
▷ is pronounced **koh**-burn.

coco / coconut / cocoa / cacao
▷ **coco** denotes the palm tree on which **coconuts** grow; **cocoa** denotes the hot milky drink, and the ground and roasted seeds of the **cacao** tree from which the drink is made.

cod
▷ meaning 'fish' has a plural **cod**.

codex
▷ has a plural **codices** (pronounced **koh**-di-seez).

cognizance
▷ is spelt -*zance* and pronounced **kog**-niz-uns.

cognoscenti
▷ is spelt -*gn*-, -*sc*- and pronounced kog-nu-**shen**-ti.

cohabit
▷ has a present participle **cohabiting** and a past tense **cohabited**.

coherence / cohesion
▷ **coherence** (spelt *-ence*) is used of ideas, etc that 'fit together' logically (eg *ancient musical theory had an inner coherence based upon strict mathematical ratios*) and of social systems, etc that 'gel' or 'work' (eg *the coherence of Inuit life has been destabilized by the arrival of airports and supermarkets*); **cohesion** is used of literal 'sticking together' by glues, etc and of the unanimity of people in a group (eg *the club's cohesion has been torn apart by the controversy*).

coiffeur / coiffure
▷ the first syllable of both words is spelt *coiff-*, pronounced *kwahf*; **coiffeur** (pronounced *-fuhr*) means 'hairdresser' and has a feminine **coiffeuse** (pronounced *-fuhz*); **coiffure** (pronounced *-fyuhr*) means 'hairstyle'.

coincidence
▷ is spelt *-ence*.

collapsible
▷ is spelt *-ible*.

collective noun
▷ denotes a noun that refers to a group of persons or things (eg *audience / baggage*). Those collective nouns (eg *audience*) which may be treated as singular or plural according to their sense are explained at their alphabetical place in this book.
➤ See also **count noun**, **mass noun**, **nouns**.

collector
▷ is spelt *-or*.

collocation
▷ denotes an expression consisting of two or more words that are frequently or usually written or spoken together (eg *black coffee / hammer and tongs*).

colloquial English
➤ See **register**.

colloquium
▷ has a plural *colloquia*.

colon
➤ See **punctuation**.

combat
▷ the verb has a present participle *combating* and a past tense and past participle *combated*.

combo
▷ has a plural *combos*.

come
▷ has a past tense *came* and a past participle *come*.

comic / comical
▷ the traditional rule is that a *comic* person or thing is *intended* to amuse, though in fact it may not do so (eg *Lortzing's comic operas bore me stiff*); a *comical* person or thing *does* amuse, whether intended to or not (eg *old Bloggs was a comical sight as he chased the pig round and round the garden*); many people now use *comic* in both senses.

comma
➤ See **punctuation**.

commandant / commander / commodore
▷ *commandant* (stressed on the first syllable) denotes the officer (of whatever rank) in charge of a barracks or military camp; *commander* denotes the officer (of whatever rank) in charge of a body of troops, and also a rank below captain in the Navy and RAF; *commodore* denotes the president of a yacht club and the senior captain in a fleet of merchant ships, and also a rank above captain in the Navy and RAF.

commando
▷ has a plural *commandos*.

commissioner / commissionaire
▷ a *commissioner* is a government official in charge of a district, or the member of a commission; a *commissionaire* is a uniformed attendant at the door of an hotel, office block, etc.

commitment / committal
▷ *commitment* has two *m*s and one *t*, and denotes

○ dedication (eg *praised his commitment to the cause*).

○ an engagement or undertaking (eg *unable to be with you due to other commitments*).

○ putting someone into prison or a mental institution (eg *his lawyers will appeal against his commitment*).

committal (with two *m*s and two *t*s) denotes

○ putting someone into prison or a mental institution.

○ burying a corpse after a funeral service (eg *committal will follow at Highgate*).

committee
▷ is spelt with two *m*s and two *t*s; it is a singular noun when thought of as a unified group of people (eg *the committee meets on Tuesday evenings*) but plural when thought of as a set of individuals (eg *the committee were horrified at the news and voted to expel him*); in American English both forms of the noun are usually followed by a singular verb (eg, the latter example would be *the committee was horrified at the news*).

common / mutual
▷ the traditional rule to distinguish usage between these two words is that **common** means 'belonging to, used by several/many people' (eg *it's common knowledge that John is a liar / our common interest in gardening prompts*

compare

me to send you this seed catalogue), and **mutual** means 'reciprocal' (eg *though they never became friends, their years in the trenches together forged a strong mutual respect*); many people now use **mutual** (eg *our mutual friend*) as if it meant 'shared'.

common noun
▷ denotes any noun which is not the name of an individual person or place; *cat* and *city* are common nouns; *Robert* and *Paris* are not.
➤ See also **proper noun**, **nouns**.

common sense / common-sense
▷ the noun is written as two separate words (eg *giving your purse to a stranger doesn't show much common sense*), the adjective as a hyphenated compound (eg *the common-sense solution would be to say nothing*).

comparable / comparative
▷ ***comparable*** is pronounced **kom**-*pu-ru-bul* or *kom-**pa**-ru-bul* and means 'of the same sort' (eg *a house here will cost half as much as a comparable one in town*); ***comparative*** means 'judged in the light of something else' (eg *you'll get some comparative peace once the pubs shut, but the traffic goes on all night*).

comparative
▷ denotes that form of adverbs and adjectives that indicates a greater degree of the quality or manner described (eg *bigger, faster, more stupidly*).
➤ See also **superlative**.

compare
▷ we use ***compare to*** when pointing out to others similarities we have already found (eg *in her complaint she compared her treatment at the police station to a Gestapo interrogation*) and ***compare with*** when looking for similarities or assessing relative merit (eg *compare the detail*

comparison of adjectives

of his offer with mine and you'll soon see who's offering you a real bargain).

comparison of adjectives
➤ See **adjectives**.

comparison of adverbs
➤ See **adverbs**.

compass points
▷ are usually written as initialisms (eg *SW, ESE*) but always pronounced as full words.

compendium
▷ has plurals *compendiums* (now more usual) and *compendia*.

compensatory
▷ is usually stressed on the third syllable although stress on the second is also heard.

competence
▷ is spelt *-ence*.

competitor
▷ is spelt *-or*.

compilation
▷ the second syllable is pronounced *-pil-*.

complacent / complaisant / compliant
▷ *complacent* is pronounced *kom-**play**-sunt* and means 'self-satisfied'; *complaisant* is pronounced *kom-**play**-zunt* and, like *compliant*, means 'willing to co-operate'; *complaisant* is more often used of a person of equal rank or power and *compliant* of an inferior who is expected to obey.

complement
▷ denotes a word or phrase that is added after the verb to

complete the predicate of a sentence (eg *dark* in *it grew dark* or *a bit of a fool* in *they all thought him a bit of a fool*).

complement / compliment
▷ a **complement** is something that completes or perfects (eg *a glass of this brandy will be the ideal complement to your meal*); in Grammar it has the technical sense explained in the preceding entry. A **compliment** is a praising or flattering statement (eg *compliments will get you nowhere*).

complexion
▷ is spelt *-x-*.

complex sentence
▷ denotes a type of sentence that consists of a main clause and one or more subordinate clauses (eg *although it rained, the fête was a success*).
➤ See also **simple sentence**, **compound sentence**, **clauses and phrases**.

compose / comprise
▷ **compose** is used only of the parts that make up a whole (eg *the three countries that compose Great Britain are England, Scotland and Wales* / *Great Britain is composed of three countries—England, Scotland and Wales*); **comprise** is used both of the parts and of the whole (eg *the three countries that comprise Great Britain are England, Scotland and Wales* / *Great Britain comprises England, Scotland and Wales*), but should not be used in the passive eg
   ✗ *Great Britain is comprised of England, Scotland and Wales*

compounding
▷ denotes in Grammar the process by which new words (called **compounds**) are formed by joining together two or more other words (eg *blackbird, dining-room, un-get-*

at-able).
➤ See also **derivation**, **inflection**.

compound sentence
▷ denotes a type of sentence that consists of a series of clauses which are linked but not subordinated (eg *she arrived at the house: she parked her car and locked its doors*).
➤ See also **simple sentence**, **complex sentence**, **clauses and phrases**.

comprehensible
▷ is spelt *-ible*.

comprise
▷ is spelt *-ise*.

compromise
▷ is spelt *-ise*.

compulsive / impulsive
▷ *compulsive* means 'unable to stop oneself' (eg *Tom had no use for the 500 tins of dogmeat found in his flat; he was simply a compulsive shoplifter*); *impulsive* means 'likely to act without considering the consequences, done on the spur of the moment' (eg *his action in hitting the burglar had been impulsive, but was none the less an assault*).

concernedness
▷ is pronounced with four syllables.

concertino
▷ has a plural *concertinos*.

concerto
▷ has plurals *concertos* (now usual) and *concerti*.

concord
➤ See **agreement**.

concrete / cement / mortar
▷ *cement* is any material which sets hard to form a building

conditionals

material or to stick other objects together. The commonest building cement is made from clay and limestone; when this is mixed with sand and water it forms **mortar**, and when mixed with sand, water and small stones it forms **concrete**. Both mortar and cement are, however, often called 'concrete' in informal speech.

concrete noun

▷ denotes a noun which names something which has a physical form and existence, eg *dog*, *house*, *London*.
➤ See also **abstract noun**, **nouns**.

conditionals

Conditionals provide a way to talk about what would happen or be the case if something else happens; they refer to hypothetical situations

• Conditional sentences

A *conditional sentence* is one of the 'if *x* then *y*' type (eg *if you don't take more care, you'll cause an accident*); it contains a conditional clause and/or a conditional verb. There are two types of conditional sentence: **real** and **unreal**.

○ A **real conditional sentence** is used when the speaker or writer believes the 'if *x*' event is really likely to happen; in these sentences the verb in the conditional clause is in the indicative (as in the example above).

○ An **unreal conditional sentence** is used when the speaker or writer believes the 'if *x*' event is unlikely to happen; in these sentences the verb in the conditional clause is in the subjunctive, as in *if the boss were ever to find out, we'd all get the sack*.

• Conditional clauses

A *conditional clause* is a sort of adverbial clause (see

conditional tense

clauses and phrases), and usually begins with *if* or *unless* (eg *unless I'm mistaken, we're in for a rough time*).

• Conditional verbs
A *conditional verb* (or *conditional tense*) is the form of verb used in the 'then *y*' part of an unreal conditional sentence (eg *Mick says he has destroyed all the documents, but if they were ever to be found, we would be in real trouble*). For the forms taken by the conditional tense see **conditional tense**.

conditional tense
▷ denotes the form of a verb that is used to express the result in a conditional sentence; it is formed with *would* or *should* (eg *if you came along you would see him too*).

condole / console
▷ **condole** means 'express sympathy with' and is followed by *with*; **console** is a transitive verb and means 'comfort someone in distress'.

confessedly
▷ is pronounced with four syllables.

congeries
▷ is pronounced *kon-**jer**-i-ees* and has a plural **congeries**.

congratulatory
▷ is pronounced *kun-grat-yuu-**layt**-uri*.

conjugal
▷ is pronounced ***kon**-jug-ul*.

conjunctions
▷ are words that link words in a phrase or clauses in a sentence, as in *he sings and dances / I hit him because I felt like it*.

  ○ *co-ordinating conjunctions* link words, phrases or clauses that are equal in rank (eg *Fred and Bert arrived at the same time / she did her best but didn't win*).

consist of

○ **subordinating conjunctions** introduce subordinate clauses (eg *he sat down <u>because</u> he felt tired / she wondered <u>when</u> the bus would come*).

conjunctiva
▷ has plurals **conjunctivas** (now in general use) and **conjunctivae**.

conjuror
▷ is spelt *-or*.

Connecticut
▷ is spelt *-ct-* but pronounced *ku-**net**-i-kut*.

connection / connexion
▷ -ct- is now the more common spelling.

connoisseur
▷ is spelt *-nois-* and *-seur*; it is pronounced *kon-u-**suhr***.

conqueror
▷ is spelt *-or*.

consent / assent
▷ both mean 'agree to', but **consent** implies a power to refuse (eg *His Majesty has graciously consented to the ship's being named after him / give your assent to the marriage or I'll talk to the police*).

consequent / consequential
▷ **consequent** usually means 'following as a result' (eg *there were rumours of food shortages yesterday and consequent riots in many towns*); **consequential** usually means 'important or self-important' (eg *he is quite a consequential figure in these parts*).

consist of / consist in
▷ **consist of** means 'be made of or made up from' (eg *his speech consisted of a long diatribe against the management, larded with a few personal insults*); **consist in** means

consonant

'has as its essential character' (eg *the beauty of her poetry consists in its absolute simplicity*).

consonant
▷ denotes any of the letters of the alphabet except the vowels *a, e, i, o* and *u* and the semi-vowels *w* and *y*; ***consonant*** also denotes any of the speech sounds that the consonant letters, either singly or in combination (eg *c, t, ch, th*), represent.

constrainedly
▷ is pronounced with four syllables.

consummate
▷ the verb is pronounced **kon**-*su*-*mayt*; the adjective **kon**-*su*-*mut* or *kon*-**su**-*mut*.

contemptible / contemptuous
▷ ***contemptible*** is spelt *-ible* and means 'deserving contempt'; ***contemptuous*** is spelt *-ous* and means 'showing contempt'.

content / contents
▷ ***content*** represents two separate words, spelt the same but differing in meaning and stress; ***contents*** belongs in sense to the second of them

  ○ *con-***tent** is an adjective meaning 'pleased, satisfied' and a verb meaning 'please, satisfy' (eg *she was contented with one bar of chocolate*).

  ○ ***con**-tent* is a noun meaning (i) 'subject-matter' (eg *the content of his speech was a tired mixture of slogans and platitudes*) and is singular only; (ii) 'proportion of a particular ingredient' (eg *foods with a low sugar content*) and may be singular or plural.

  ○ ***con**-tents*, belonging in sense to the second meaning, is a plural noun meaning 'things inside' (eg *the contents of*

contiguous / adjacent / adjoining
▷ *adjacent* things may have space between them, but *adjoining* or *contiguous* things do not.

continual / continuous
▷ *continual* means 'constantly repeated or renewed' (eg *the children's continual interruptions gave her little chance to get on with her work*); *continuous* means 'never stopping' (eg *we've had continuous rain for three days now*).

continuous tense
➤ See **progressive tense**.

contractable / contractible
▷ *contractable* means 'able to be caught' (eg *is malaria a contractable disease?*); *contractible* means 'able to be shortened' (eg *difficult to get his camera tripod into the car since the legs aren't contractible*).

contraction
➤ See **abbreviations**.

contractor
▷ is spelt *-or*.

contrary
▷ is pronounced **kon**-*tru-ri* when it means 'opposite', and *kun-***tre**-*ri* when it means 'perverse'.

contrast
▷ the noun is stressed on the first syllable, and the verb on the second.

contributor
▷ is spelt *-or*.

controversy
▷ is now usually stressed on the second syllable.

convalesce
▷ is spelt *-lesce*.

convalescence, convalescent
▷ are spelt *-scence, -scent*.

convertible
▷ is spelt *-ible*.

co-o- / coo-
▷ words of this type (eg *co-operate*, *co-ordinate*) are usually spelt with a hyphen, although a hyphen is not always used (eg *cooperate*, *coordinate*).

co-ordinate clause
➤ See **clauses and phrases**.

copula
▷ denotes any verb that simply serves as a link between the subject of a sentence and its complement, as in *Fred was old and bald / it looks good but it doesn't taste right*.
➤ See also **auxiliary verb**, **lexical verb**.

cord / chord
▷ *cord* is used for ropes, clothing fabric, vocal cords, spinal cord; *chord* is used for the musical and geometrical senses, literal and metaphoric (eg *play that chord again / her face strikes a chord with me / circle subtended by a chord*).

cornflour / cornflower
▷ *cornflour* is a sort of maize flour; *cornflower* is a plant with blue flowers.

corona
▷ has plurals *coronae* and *coronas*.

corps
▷ is pronounced *kawr* and has a plural *corps* (pronounced *kawrz*).

corpus
▷ has a plural *corpora*.

correspond to / correspond with
▷ *correspond to* means 'be the equivalent of' (eg *this button must correspond to the carriage return lever on ordinary typewriters*); *correspond with* means 'be consistent with' (eg *his treatment of his staff scarcely corresponds with his political principles*).

correspondence, correspondent
▷ are spelt *-ence*, *-ent*.

correspondent / co-respondent
▷ a *correspondent* is a writer; a *co-respondent* is the person alleged to have committed adultery with the spouse being sued in a divorce case.

corrigendum
▷ has a plural *corrigenda*.

cortex
▷ has a plural *cortices*.

cosset
▷ has a present participle *cosseting* and a past tense *cosseted*.

cost
▷ has a past tense and past participle *cost* in all senses except 'estimate', where they are *costed* (eg *the planners had initially costed the whole project at £50,000, but the final accounts showed it had cost at least 25% more*).

could / might
▷ *could* is used to indicate permission (eg *she said they*

council

could all go provided they behaved themselves) and **might** to indicate possibility (eg *if we get a move on we still might catch the 2.30 train*).

council / counsel
▷ a **council** is a group of people who meet to make decisions (eg how a town, etc is to be run) or to advise a ruler, etc; **counsel** means 'advice' or 'a lawyer'.

councillor / counsellor
▷ both are spelt *-llor*; a **councillor** is an elected member of a council; a **counsellor** is a person who gives advice, or is a lawyer.

counterfeit
▷ is spelt *-feit*.

countersink
▷ has a past tense **countersank** and a past participle **countersunk**.

count noun
▷ is a noun that has a plural and denotes something of which more than one instance may exist eg
    ✓   *cat, woman, man*
but not
    ✗   *furniture, information*
➤ See also **collective noun**, **mass noun**, **nouns**.

coup / coupe / coupé
▷ a **coup** (pronounced *kuu*) is a successful move, or the sudden and usually violent overthrow of a government (in full, **coup d'etat**; eg *the dictator was toppled in a dawn coup*); a **coupe** (pronounced *kuup*) is a sort of pudding; a **coupé** (pronounced **kuu**-*pay*) is a sort of car.

court-martial
▷ the noun has plurals **courts-martial** (in formal use) and **court-martials** (in informal use).

coxswain
▷ is usually pronounced **kok**-sun, though **kok**-swayn is also used.

coyote
▷ is pronounced **koy**-oht or koy-**oh**-ti; it has two plurals
- **coyote**, when the group is thought of as a whole (eg *the coyote kept on howling through the night*).
- **coyotes**, when the group is thought of as a set of individuals (eg *saw a couple of coyotes in the headlights*).

coypu
▷ is pronounced koy-puu or koy-pyuu, with stress on either syllable; it has two plurals
- **coypu**, when the group is thought of as a whole (eg *the breeding of coypu for profit*).
- **coypus**, when the group is thought of as a set of individuals (eg *saw a couple of coypus in the headlights*).

cranium
▷ has two plurals
- **craniums**, which is in general use.
- **crania**, which is used in technical writing.

crayfish
▷ has a plural **crayfish**.

creator
▷ is spelt -or.

credible / creditable
▷ **credible** means 'believable, likely' (eg *it is scarcely credible that he could have got there so soon*); **creditable** means 'praiseworthy' (eg *just to get into the first ten is a creditable performance*).

credo
▷ is pronounced **kray**-doh and has a plural **credos**.

creep
▷ has a past tense and past participle **crept**.

crematorium
▷ has plurals **crematoria** and **crematoriums**; the latter is now in general use.

crème de menthe
▷ is spelt -è- and *menthe* and is pronounced *krem du* **month**.

crêpe
▷ is spelt -ê- and pronounced *krayp* or *krep*.

crevasse / crevice
▷ a **crevasse** is a crack in a glacier and is pronounced *kriv-as*; a **crevice** is a narrow opening and is pronounced **krev**-*is*.

Crichton
▷ is pronounced **kriy**-*tun*.

crisis
▷ has a plural **crises**.

criterion
▷ has a plural **criteria**, which should not be used as a singular noun eg
    ✗ *the criteria is whether he can get here fast enough*
should be
    ✓ *the criterion is whether…*
but
    ✓ *the five criteria for the project have all been taken into account*
is correct.

crochet
▷ is spelt *-chet* and pronounced **kroh**-*shay*; the verb has a present participle **crocheting** and a past tense and past participle **crocheted**.

crooked
▷ is pronounced with two syllables.

crosier / crozier
▷ the first spelling is more common.

crotch / crutch
▷ **crotch** denotes the place where the body forks into the two legs; a **crutch** is a support.

croûton
▷ is spelt -oû- and pronounced **kruu**-ton.

cruel
▷ has a comparative **crueller** and a superlative **cruellest** (AmE **crueler, cruelest**).

crumby / crummy
▷ **crumby** means 'full of crumbs'; **crummy** means 'shabby, dirty'.

crux
▷ has a plural **cruces**.

-ction / -xion
▷ the -ction spelling is now acceptable for almost all of these words; the few that are still spelt -xion are listed at their alphabetical place in this book.

cue
▷ has a present participle **cueing** and a past tense **cued**.

cul-de-sac
▷ has a plural **culs-de-sac**.

cumulus
▷ has a plural **cumuli**.

cupful
▷ is spelt -ful and has a plural **cupfuls**.

curio
▷ has a plural *curios*.

currant / current
▷ a *currant* is a sort of fruit (eg *put currants in the apple pie*); *current* is a noun that means 'flow' (eg *hard to swim against the current / the lamp will come on when the current is restored*) and an adjective that means 'belonging to the present' (eg *have you got the current copy of <u>Radio Times</u>?*).

curriculum vitae
▷ is pronounced *ku-**rik**-yoo-lum **vee**-tiy* and is often abbreviated to *CV*; the plural forms (*curricula vitae* for copies of one person's details, and *curricula vitarum* for copies of several persons' details) are unwieldy and best avoided. Use
    ✓   *fifty copies of my curiculum vitae*
    ✓   *have got to read through fifty CVs to decide the shortlist*
instead of
    ✗   *fifty curricula vitae*
    ✗   *have got to read through fifty curricula vitarum to decide the shortlist*

cussed, cussedly, cussedness
▷ are pronounced with 2, 3 and 3 syllables respectively.

cut
▷ has a past tense and past participle *cut*.

Cyclops
▷ has a plural *Cyclopes* (pronounced *siy-**kloh**-peez*).

cygnet / signet
▷ a *cygnet* is a young swan and a *signet* is a sort of seal-stamp for official documents; both are pronounced ***sig**-nit*.

czar / tsar

▷ the spelling **tsar** is now standard and correctly reflects the Russian spelling and pronunciation of this word, which was first anglicized as **czar**; in English, both spellings are pronounced *zahr*.

d

Dáil Eireann
▷ is spelt *-áil* and *-eann* and pronounced *doyl **ayr**-un*.

dam / damn
▷ *dam* denotes a barrier built to hold back water; ***damn*** is an expression of annoyance.

dangling participle
▷ denotes the error in such misleading sentences as
  - ✗ *while driving through the farm a cow ran into his car*

where the wording implies that *the cow* was doing the driving. The subject of the main verb in a sentence (here 'a cow') is always assumed to be the subject of any subordinate clauses in it (here 'while driving through the farm'), unless they have a subject of their own; so the sentence is corrected by changing the dangling participle into a verb with its own subject: *while he was driving through the farm a cow ran into his car*.

darts
▷ is singular when used of the game (eg *darts needs more skill than people think*), but is plural (and has a singular *dart*) when used of several of the missiles (eg *two darts were embedded in the window frame*).

dash
➤ See **punctuation**.

data / datum

▷ strictly speaking, ***datum*** is the singular of a noun meaning 'item of information', which has a plural ***data*** (eg ✓*all our planning must take into account this basic datum: we can expect no more help from Bill* / ✓*the data used below were collected by Smith during field work in 1915*); but many people now use ***data*** as a mass noun (eg ✓*useful data has been obtained*). But ***data*** is never a count noun (✗ *a data* / ✗ *some datas*).

dates

The following rules are mostly concerned with avoiding clutter or misunderstandings with the written forms.

- **Sequence**
  - Use the order *day-month-year* for both all-figure and written-out forms (eg *11/6/95, 11 June 1995*).
  - No comma is needed after the month in the written-out form although some people do use one.
    NOTE In American usage *11/6/95* means 6 November 1995, not 11 June, and is written by Americans as November 6, 1995.
  - In figure-sequences of days or years repeat the fewest figures possible (eg *1923–4, 1923–35, 23–4 June, 18–25 August*); but sequences in the range 10–19 are always written out in full, as are year sequences that span a century (eg *1895–1925*) and BC sequences (*259–252BC*).

- **Eras**

When referring to dates, CE (*Common Era*) can be used to mean the same as AD (*Anno Domini* or *in the year of our Lord*); BCE (*Before Common Era*) can be used to mean the same as BC (*Before Christ*). AD precedes the year-number; BC, BCE and CE follow it.

dative case

dative case
▷ is another name for the **objective case of the indirect object**, which denotes the form taken by pronouns which are the indirect object (see under **object**) of a verb, such as *him* in *she gave him the book*.

daughter-in-law
▷ has a plural ***daughters-in-law***.

deal
▷ the verb has a past tense and past participle ***dealt***.

debacle / débâcle
▷ is now usually spelt without any accents and is pronounced *day-**bah**-kul*.

debatable
▷ is spelt *-table*.

debut / début
▷ is now usually spelt without any accents and is pronounced ***day**-byuu*.

débutante
▷ is spelt *dé-* and *-tante* and pronounced ***day**-byoo-tont*.

deca- / deci-
▷ ***deca-*** is pronounced *deka* and denotes 'ten, ten times' (so a *decathlon* is a sports competition with 10 events and a *decalitre* is a unit of capacity equal to 10 litres); ***deci-*** is pronounced *desi* and denotes 'a tenth' (so a *decimetre* is a unit of length equal to 0.1 metres).

décor
▷ is spelt *dé-*.

deep-freeze
▷ the verb has a past tense ***deep-froze*** and a past participle ***deep-frozen***.

defective / deficient
▷ ***defective*** means 'faulty, needing repair' (eg *the crash was caused by defective wiring in the signal box*); ***deficient*** means 'inadequate' (eg *the islanders' diet was deficient in vitamin C*).

defector
▷ is spelt *-or*.

defendant
▷ is spelt *-ant*.

defensible
▷ is spelt *-ible*.

defiance, defiant
▷ are spelt *-ance, -ant*.

defining relative clause
➤ See **clauses and phrases**.

definite article
➤ See **article**.

deign
▷ is spelt *-ei-* and *-gn* and pronounced *dayn*.

delphinium
▷ has plurals ***delphiniums*** (in general use) and ***delphinia***.

delusion / illusion
▷ a sane person has an ***illusion*** when the light, etc plays tricks upon him or her (eg *the successive still pictures flashed upon the cinema screen give an illusion of motion*); ***delusions*** are false ideas that arise in the minds of people who are mentally ill (eg *has this delusion that everyone is trying to kill her / that she is the Queen of the Fairies*).

demise
▷ is spelt *-ise*.

demonstrative adjective

demonstrative adjective
➤ See **adjectives**.

demonstrative pronoun
➤ See **pronouns**.

denouement
▷ is spelt without accents and pronounced *day-**noo**-mo^ng*.

deny / refute
▷ to **deny** a fact or statement is to *claim* it is not true; to **refute** a statement or theory is to *prove* it is not true. **Refute** should not be used to mean 'deny strongly'.

dependant / dependent
▷ *-ant* is the noun and *-ent* is the adjective.

dependent clause
➤ See **clauses and phrases**.

depositary / depository
▷ *depositary* denotes a *person* with whom things may be left for safekeeping; *depository* denotes a *place* where things may be left for safekeeping.

deprecate / depreciate
▷ *deprecate* means 'disapprove of, express disapproval of' (eg *issued a statement dissociating himself from his brother's actions which, he said, he strongly deprecated*); *depreciate* means 'fall in value, speak of as unimportant' (eg *lack of confidence in the government caused the pound to depreciate yet further in world markets / in reply to their praise she spoke depreciatingly of her achievements*).

derisive / derisory
▷ *derisive* means 'mocking' (eg *peals of derisive laughter greeted the minister's claim that the economy was improving*); *derisory* means 'deserving mockery' or 'insulting', especially because it is particularly small (eg

diacritic

after the management's derisory offer of 1% a strike seems inevitable).

descendant / descendent
▷ *-ant* is the noun and *-ent* is the adjective.

descriptive adjective
➤ See **adjectives**.

desiccated
▷ is spelt with one *s* and two *c*s.

desideratum
▷ has a plural ***desiderata***.

desperado
▷ has plurals ***desperados*** and ***desperadoes***.

despise
▷ is spelt *-ise*.

destructible
▷ is spelt *-ible*.

detente / détente
▷ is often spelt without an accent and pronounced *day-to^{ng}t*.

determiner
▷ is another term for *limiting adjective*; see **adjectives**.

deterrable
▷ is spelt with two *r*s and ends in *-able*.

deterrence
▷ is spelt with two *r*s and ends in *-ence*.

devise
▷ is spelt *-ise*.

diacritic
▷ denotes any of the marks put above a letter (eg grave accent in French and Italian), below a letter (eg the cedilla

diaeresis

in French) or through a letter (eg the Danish *ø*) to show how it is pronounced. They are not used in native English, but are often retained in borrowed foreign words (eg *blasé, façade*).

diaeresis
▷ denotes the pair of dots placed over a vowel (eg the *ï* in *naïve*) to show that it is to be pronounced separately from the vowel that precedes it.
➤ See also **umlaut**.

diagnosis
▷ has a plural *diagnoses*.

dialysis
▷ has a plural *dialyses*.

diarrhoea
▷ is spelt *-rrhoea*.

dice
➤ See under **die**.

dicey
▷ is spelt *-ey* and has a comparative *dicier* and a superlative *diciest*.

dictator
▷ is spelt *-or*.

dictum
▷ has a plural *dicta*.

die
▷ the verb has a present participle *dying*; the noun means
  ○ a sort of metal stamp and has a plural *dies*.
  ○ a small cube with a different number of spots on each face and has a plural *dice* which is now also used as the singular in informal contexts (eg *found a dice on the floor when I was cleaning up*).

differ from / differ with
▷ to **differ from** means 'to be different from' (eg *this one differs from yours in being bigger*); to **differ with** means 'to disagree with' (eg *I'm afraid I must differ with you—I still think Liz is the better applicant*).

different from / different to / different than
▷ the first two are both now acceptable, but **different than** is more common in American English and is best avoided in British English.

dig
▷ has a past tense and past participle **dug**.

digestible
▷ is spelt *-ible*.

digraph
▷ denotes a pair of letters that represent a single sound (eg *th* as in *threw*, *ch* as in *church*, *ee* as in *seek*, *oo* as in *room*).

dike / dyke
▷ **dyke** is the most common spelling in all senses.

dildo
▷ has a plural **dildos**.

dilettante
▷ is spelt with one *l* and three *t*s; it is pronounced *dil-et-**an**-ti* and has plurals **dilettantes** and **dilettanti**.

diminuendo
▷ has a plural **diminuendos**.

diminutive
▷ denotes a suffix (eg *-let*) that is added to a word to indicate smallness (eg *booklet*), or the word so formed (eg *the diminutive of book is booklet*).

dinghy / dingy
▷ **dinghy** is a noun, is pronounced with a hard *g* and means

diphthong

'small sailing boat'; ***dingy*** is an adjective, is pronounced with a soft *g* and means 'dark and dirty'.

diphthong

▷ is pronounced **dif**-*thong* and denotes a pair of vowels that preserve their separate sounds when the word containing them is pronounced slowly, although in quick speech they seem to be a single sound (eg when spoken slowly *cow* unpacks into the sounds *kah-oo*).

direct object

➤ See **object**.

director

▷ is spelt *-or*.

direct speech

▷ denotes the method of recording what someone has said in which their words are repeated exactly as they said them, as in

> *'The cat is dead,' he said*

and not as in

> *he said that the cat was dead*

➤ See also **indirect speech**.

dirigible

▷ is spelt *-ible*.

dis- / dys

▷ ***dis-*** means 'not' and is used in all the common words that begin with this syllable (eg *disappointed*, *dissatisfied*); ***dys-*** means 'badly' and is used in a few medical and technical terms (eg *dysentery*, *dysfunction*, *dyslexia*).

disappearance

▷ is spelt *-ance*.

disassociate / dissociate

▷ these verbs are interchangeable but the second, being shorter, is more often heard.

disastrous
▷ there is no *e* in this word.

disc / disk
▷ a computer has **disks**; for all other senses of the word (eg medical, gramophone) use **disc**. In American English **disk** is used for all senses.

discernible
▷ is spelt -*sc*- and -*ible*.

disciplinary, discipline
▷ are spelt -*sc*-.

discreet / discrete
▷ **discreet** means 'prudent, cautious, avoiding embarrassment' (eg *it wasn't very discreet of her to gossip about her husband's tax fiddles*); **discrete** means 'separate' (eg *why we should go and how we are to get there are two discrete issues which I will deal with in turn*).

discrepancy / disparity
▷ **discrepancy** denotes a failure of two things to match up as they morally should (eg *there was an alarming discrepancy between the number of gallons sold and the amount of cash in the till / there are several discrepancies between his account and yours*); **disparity** denotes a distance or gap of any kind (eg *the year's figures show a depressing disparity between projected and actual income*).

disguise
▷ is spelt -*guise*.

disinterested / uninterested
▷ **disinterested** means 'fair, unbiased'; **uninterested** means 'not interested, bored'.

disk / disc
▷ a computer has **disks**; for all other senses of the word

disobedience

(eg medical, gramophone) use **disc**. In American English **disk** is used for all senses.

disobedience
▷ is spelt *-ence*.

dispirit
▷ has a past tense and past participle **dispirited**.

dissociate / disassociate
▷ these verbs are interchangeable but the second, being shorter, is more often heard.

distinct / distinctive
▷ **distinct** means 'definite, clear' (eg *there was a distinct smell of alcohol about him when he came back from lunch*); **distinctive** means 'characteristic, special' (eg *you can recognize her voice anywhere; she has a distinctive way of rolling her rs*).

distribute
▷ should be stressed on the second syllable.

distributive adjective
➤ See **adjectives**.

distributive pronoun
➤ See **pronouns**.

distributor
▷ is spelt *-or*.

disturbance
▷ is spelt *-ance*.

dither
▷ has a past tense **dithered**.

ditto
▷ has a plural **dittos**.

divers / diverse

▷ **divers** means 'assorted, many different' (eg *divers sorts and conditions of men*); it is stressed on the first syllable and is now almost obsolete. **Diverse** means 'assorted, dissimilar' (eg *though they pursued similar policies, Major's and Thatcher's styles of governing were totally diverse*) and is usually stressed on the second syllable.

dividers

▷ is plural.

divisible

▷ is spelt *-ible*.

do

▷ the noun has a plural **dos**; the verb has a third person singular present **does**, a present participle **doing**, a past tense **did** and a past participle **done**.

doctor

▷ is spelt *-or*.

dodo

▷ has a plural **dodos**.

dogged

▷ is pronounced with two syllables.

doily / doyley

▷ both spellings are correct; their respective plurals are **doilies** and **doyleys**.

dolour

▷ is pronounced in the same way as *dollar*.

domesday / doomsday

▷ use **domesday** for the book and **doomsday** for the end of the world; both are pronounced ***duumz***-*day*.

dominance

▷ is spelt *-ance*.

dominate

dominate / domineer
▷ **dominate** means 'be the most powerful or important, have a commanding influence' (eg *though he seldom spoke, his wealth and prestige enabled him effectively to dominate any committee on which he sat*); **domineer** means 'dominate in an arrogant or aggressive way' (eg *the chairman's domineering manner has lost us many members*).

dominoes
▷ is singular when used of the game (eg *dominoes needs more skill than people think*), but is plural (and has a singular *domino*) when used of several of the pieces with which the game is played (eg *two dominoes were found under the carpet*).

doner / donor
▷ use **doner** for the kebab and **donor** for a person who gives something.

dopey
▷ is spelt *-ey* and has a comparative **dopier** and a superlative **dopiest**.

doubling of final consonants
➤ See **inflection** under **verbs**.

doubtful / dubious
▷ **doubtful** means 'uncertain' (eg *the result remained doubtful until the last ten minutes when Arsenal finally established control / I'm still doubtful about the weather*); **dubious** means 'suspicious, unconvinced, unconvincing, morally suspect' (eg *despite her assurances I remain dubious as to whether we shall really get a free trip / some of the talent on display at the concert was pretty dubious / she hangs about with a pretty dubious bunch*).

dour
▷ is pronounced to rhyme with *poor*.

douse / dowse
▷ *douse* means 'throw water over, throw into water, extinguish'; *dowse* means 'search for water with a divining-rod'.

doyley / doily
▷ both spellings are correct; their respective plurals are **doyleys** and **doilies**.

dozen
▷ is followed by a singular verb when thought of as a single unit (eg *a dozen is enough for the moment*), but by a plural verb when thought of as a group of items (eg *he inspected the tins; a dozen were dented, but the rest were OK*).

drachm
▷ is pronounced *dram*.

drachma
▷ is spelt -*ch*- and pronounced ***drak**-mu*.

draft / draught
▷ *draft* means 'rough outline' (eg *circulated a draft of the letter for their comments*) or 'order to a bank for payment of money' (eg *handed the solicitor a draft for the purchase price*); *draught* means 'suction or movement of water or air' (eg *you'll catch cold if you sit in that draught / beer on draught / drank it off in a single draught*). Both are pronounced *drahft*.

dramatics
▷ the noun is singular.

draughts
▷ is singular when used of the game (eg *draughts needs more skill than people think*).

draw

draw
▷ has a past tense **drew** and a past participle **drawn**.

dray / drey
▷ a **dray** is a sort of cart; a **drey** is a squirrel's nest.

dregs
▷ is always plural and has no singular form.

drive
▷ has a past tense **drove** and a past participle **driven**.

dubious / doubtful
▷ **dubious** means 'suspicious, unconvinced, unconvincing, morally suspect' (eg *despite her assurances I remain dubious as to whether we shall really get a free trip / some of the talent on display at the concert was pretty dubious / she hangs about with a pretty dubious bunch*); **doubtful** means 'uncertain' (eg *the result remained doubtful until the last ten minutes when Arsenal finally established control / I'm still doubtful about the weather*).

due to / because of / owing to
▷ may nowadays be used interchangeably.

duffel / duffle
▷ the first spelling, which reflects the original Dutch form of this word, is most common.

Dulwich
▷ is pronounced ***dul**-ij*.

duly
▷ has no *e* in it.

dumbo
▷ has a plural **dumbos**.

duo
▷ has a plural **duos**.

dutiful
▷ is spelt *-iful*.

dwarf
▷ has a standard plural **dwarfs**; however, **dwarves** has become popular through its use by J R Tolkien in his children's novels.

dwell
▷ has past tense and past participle **dwelt** (the most common) or **dwelled**.

dye
▷ has a present participle **dyeing**.

Dyfed
▷ is pronounced **duv**-*id*.

dyke / dike
▷ **dyke** is the most common spelling in all senses.

dynamics
▷ is singular when referring to the scientific study of motion (eg *dynamics is taught next term*), but plural in all other senses.

dynamo
▷ has a plural **dynamos**.

dys- / dis-
➤ See **dis-**.

e

-e- / -ae-
▷ except for ***medieval*** and ***encyclopedia***, British English (unlike American) prefers the *-ae-* spelling.

each
▷ when ***each*** is the subject (or part of the subject) of a sentence or clause, the verb of that sentence or clause will be singular (eg *each has his own cupboard / each child has his own cupboard / each of the children has his own cupboard*); when it appears elsewhere, ***each*** does not influence the verb (eg *the children each have their own cupboard*).

each other / one another
▷ the traditional rule is that ***each other*** is used to refer to two persons and ***one another*** to larger numbers; but nowadays the phrases are interchangeable.

earful
▷ has a plural ***earfuls***.

earnest
▷ unlike the name, the adjective is spelt *ear-*.

earring
▷ is spelt *-rr-*.

earthly / earthy
▷ ***earthly*** means 'of or in this world' (eg *haven't an earthly chance of winning*); ***earthy*** means 'like soil' or 'crude' (eg

the potatoes were freshly dug and still had an earthy smell / his earthy humour won't appeal to Aunt Edna).

eat
▷ has a past tense **ate** (pronounced *et* or *ayt*) and a past participle **eaten**.

eatable / edible
▷ many people use these words as if they were interchangeable, but the difference between their meanings can sometimes be important. **Eatable** (spelt *-able*) means 'possible to eat' or 'nice to eat'; **edible** (spelt *-ible*) means 'safe to eat'. So grass is (for humans) *edible* but not *eatable* (unless one is starving) and a poisonous but nice-tasting mushroom is *eatable* but not *edible*.

economic / economical
▷ *economic* means 'to do with the study of economics' or 'giving a reasonable profit' (eg *studied economic history / just isn't economic to keep the station open*); **economical** means 'careful, thrifty' (eg *economical use of limited supplies*).

ecstasy
▷ is spelt *-cs-*.

eczema
▷ is spelt *ecze-* and pronounced **ek**-*si-mu*.

-ed / -t
➤ See **inflection**.

editor
▷ is spelt *-or*.

educable / educible
▷ *educable* means 'capable of being educated'; *educible* means 'able to be educed'.

effect / affect

▷ **effect** is a noun meaning 'result, impression' (*repeated warnings have had no effect upon him*) and a verb meaning 'bring about' (*tried to effect a reconciliation between her parents*); **affect** is a verb meaning 'to cause a change in, have influence upon' (*the accident has affected his eyesight*).

effective / effectual / efficacious / efficient

▷ although there is a broad overlap in meaning between the first three words, their differences in sense and usage are worth preserving

- **effective** means (i) 'successful', 'likely to be successful' (eg *the only effective way of keeping them out is to block up the entrance*); (ii) 'powerful, impressive' (eg *despite his small stature Mussolini was an effective speaker*); (iii) 'in force' (eg *the regulations become effective in the new year*); (iv) 'in fact but not in name' (eg *the king is a fool and his brother has been the effective ruler for many years*).

- **effectual** means (i) 'actually successful' (eg *the police have now taken effectual measures and muggings have been halved over the last six months*); (ii) 'valid' (eg *but is this old permit still effectual?*).

- **efficacious** also means 'successful', but is used only of medical treatments (eg *the Salk vaccine has proved efficacious against polio*).

- **efficient** means 'producing the desired results with a minimum of effort, expense, etc' (eg *halved costs by introducing efficient methods throughout the company*).

effluent / affluence / affluent

▷ **effluent** is a noun meaning 'outflow'; **affluence** is a noun meaning 'riches'; **affluent** is an adjective meaning 'rich'. All three words are spelt *-en-*.

-efy / -ify
▷ most of these verbs end in *-ify*; those that do not are listed at their alphabetical place in this book.

ego
▷ has a plural *egos*.

egoist / egotist
▷ an *egotist* is selfish and self-centred; an *egoist* is the same, but believes his or her way of life is justified by moral or philosophical principles.

egregious
▷ is spelt *-gious* but pronounced *i-****gree****-jus*.

-ei- / -ie-
▷ the traditional rule '*i* before *e* except after *c*' is useful as a rule of thumb although it does have many exceptions; these are all noted at their alphabetical place in this book.

eighth
▷ is spelt by adding a final *h* to *eight*; in pronunciation the *t* does double duty (*ayt-th*).

eisteddfod
▷ is spelt *-dd-* and *-d*, and is pronounced *iy-****sted****-fud* or (more authentically Welsh) *iy-****stedh****-vod*; it has plurals *eisteddfods* and *eisteddfodau* (pronounced *iy-****stedh****-vod-iy*).

either
▷ is spelt *ei-* and pronounced ***iy****-dhur* or ***ee****-dhur*.

either ... or
▷ use the following rules to decide whether the following verb should be singular or plural
  ○ if the alternatives are both singular, the verb is singular (eg *either John or Mary is wrong*).
  ○ if one of the alternatives is plural, the verb is plural (eg *either John or his friends are wrong*).

élan

- if both the alternatives are plural, the verb is plural (eg *either his dogs or our cats <u>have</u> done this*).
- if the alternatives differ in person, the verb agrees with the nearest one (eg *either you or I <u>am</u> wrong*); but such sentences often sound better if rephrased (eg *either <u>you are</u> wrong or <u>I am</u>*).

élan
▷ is spelt *é-*.

eland
▷ has two plurals
- ***eland***, when the group is thought of as a whole (eg *saw a large herd of eland charging across his path*).
- ***elands***, when the group is thought of as a set of individuals (eg *a few elands came past, some limping badly*).

elder, eldest / older, oldest
▷ ***older***, ***oldest*** are always correct; they may be replaced by ***elder***, ***eldest*** only when
- the topic is relative age within a family and
- the adjective is immediately followed by its noun (eg *Fred's <u>elder brother</u> came in*) or immediately preceded by a limiting adjective such as *the*, *my*, *his* (eg *she is <u>my elder</u> by three years*).

electable
▷ is spelt *-able*.

elegance, elegant
▷ are spelt *-ance*, *-ant*.

elegiac
▷ is pronounced *e-le-**jiy**-ak*.

elephant
▷ has two plurals

ellipsis

○ ***elephant***, when the group is thought of as a whole (eg *saw a large herd of elephant charging across his path*).

○ ***elephants***, when the group is thought of as a set of individuals (eg *a few elephants came past, some limping badly*).

elevator
▷ is spelt *-or*.

elf
▷ has a plural ***elves***.

eligible
▷ is spelt *-ible*.

eliminable
▷ is spelt *-able*.

elision
▷ denotes the omission of a vowel or syllable in speech (eg *he's stupid* instead of *he is stupid*).

elite / élite
▷ is now usually spelt without an accent; its first syllable may be pronounced *e-*, *ay-* or *i-*.

elk
▷ has two plurals

○ ***elk***, when the group is thought of as a whole (eg *saw a large herd of elk charging across his path*).

○ ***elks***, when the group is thought of as a set of individuals (eg *a few elks came past, some limping badly*).

ellipsis
▷ has a plural ***ellipses*** and denotes

○ the omission from a sentence of words which the hearer or reader is expected to supply or understand (eg *morning!* for *good morning!* or *I don't want to go, but I must* for *I don't want to go, but I must go*).

embryo

○ the set of three dots used to indicate the omission of several words from a quoted passage.
➤ See **full stop** at **punctuation**.

embryo
▷ has a plural *embryos*.

emend / amend
▷ *emend* means 'correct the mistakes (eg spellings, miscopyings) in'; *amend* means 'change (the style or content of a document) in order to improve'.

émigré
▷ has an acute accent on its first and last letter and is pronounced *ay*-mee-gray.

emphasis
▷ has a plural *emphases*.

emporium
▷ has plurals *emporiums* and *emporia*.

-ence / -ance
▷ there are no easy rules to find which ending is used by a given word; all the commonest *-ance* and *-ence* words are listed at their alphabetical place in this book.

encomium
▷ has plurals *encomiums* and *encomia*.

encyclopaedia / encyclopedia
▷ the second spelling is now preferred.
➤ See **-e-**.

endeavour
▷ is spelt *-deav-* and *-our*.

endurable, endurance
▷ are spelt *-able*, *-ance*.

enforceable
▷ is spelt *-eable*.

enfranchise
▷ is spelt *-ise*.

enjoyable
▷ is spelt *-able*.

ennui
▷ is pronounced *o^{ng}-nwee*.

enquire, enquiry / inquire, inquiry
▷ the traditional rule is that the first pair are used of ordinary questions (eg *enquired whether she had slept well*) and the second of formal investigations (eg *the inquiry into the train crash starts today*); many people now use them interchangeably.

enrolment
▷ has one *-l-*.

ensure / insure
▷ ***ensure*** means 'make sure' (eg *ensure that the doors are locked before you leave*); ***insure*** means 'contract with an insurance company to be paid an agreed sum if a specified possible event occurs' (eg *is the house insured against fire?*).

-ent / -ant
▷ there are no easy rules to find which ending is used for a given word; all the commonest *-ant* and *-ent* words are listed at their alphabetical place in this book.

enterprise
▷ is spelt *-ise*.

entirety
▷ is pronounced *en-**tiyr**-ut-ee*.

entrails
▷ is plural.

entrecôte

entrecôte
▷ is spelt -tre- and côte and pronounced **o**^{ng}-tru-koht.

entrée
▷ is spelt -trée and pronounced **on**-tray.

entrepôt
▷ is spelt -pôt and pronounced **o**^{ng}-tru-poh.

envelop / envelope
▷ **envelop** is a verb meaning 'wrap, conceal' and is pronounced en-**vel**-up; **envelope** is a noun meaning 'paper packet, glass cover of light bulb' and is pronounced **en**-vel-ohp.

enviable
▷ is spelt -iable.

epaulette / epaulet
▷ is pronounced **ep**-ul-et; the first spelling is more common.

épée
▷ is spelt with two és and pronounced **ay**-pay.

ephemera
▷ is plural.

ephemeris
▷ has a plural **ephemerides**.

epitome
▷ is pronounced e-**pi**-tu-mi.

equable / equitable
▷ **equable** means 'moderate, without extremes, even-tempered'; **equitable** means 'fair, just'. Both words are stressed on the first syllable.

-er / -ar / -or
▷ these suffixes denote 'doers' (eg *runner, actor, beggar*); the *-er* form is by far the most common and is used on

all new coinings. All words ending in *-ar* and *-or* are listed at their alphabetical place in this book.

erotica
▷ is plural.

erratum
▷ has a plural **errata**.

-ery / -ary / -ory
▷ there are no simple rules for deciding which of these endings (which tend to sound the same in speech) a given word has. The vowel ending of the related noun is usually kept (eg *director, directory / baker, bakery*), but there are many exceptions and it is wise to consult a dictionary when in doubt.

escallop / escalope
▷ an **escallop** is a sort of shellfish; an **escalope** is a thin slice of meat.

Eskimo
▷ has plurals **Eskimos** and **Eskimo**; although **Eskimo** is the established English name for this people, it is now often considered offensive and the people themselves prefer the name **Inuit**.

especially / specially
▷ **especially** means 'particularly' (eg *this sort are expensive, especially the red ones*); **specially** means 'solely for' (eg *I made this specially for you*).

espresso
▷ has a plural **espressos**.

etiquette
▷ is spelt *-quette* and pronounced **et**-*i-ket*.

étude
▷ is spelt *é-* and pronounced *ay-***tuud**.

eucalyptus

eucalyptus
▷ has plurals *eucalyptuses* and *eucalypti*.

eugenics
▷ is singular.

euphemism
▷ denotes the use of an inoffensive word or phrase in place of one considered rude or blunt (eg *are you sure?* instead of *are you telling the truth?*, *he passed away* instead of *he died*, or *spend a penny* instead of *go to the lavatory*), or a word or phrase that is used in this way.

evade / avert / avoid
▷ *avert* means 'prevent or deflect the arrival of something unpleasant' (eg *averted the blow by raising his shield / averted the threatened strike by offering to negotiate*); *avoid* means 'keep away from' (eg *found a route along side roads to avoid the jams / avoided a scandal by settling out of court*); *evade* means 'dodge, sidestep, escape from' and usually involves trickery or deception (eg *evaded his pursuers by hiding in a beer barrel*). An honest accountant shows his client how to *avoid* tax (eg by claiming all the allowances to which he or she is entitled), a dishonest one how to *evade* it (eg by not disclosing all his or her earnings).

ever
▷ is joined to *when*, *why*, *where*, etc in statements or commands, but remains a separate word in questions (eg *the lamb followed wherever she went / do whatever he tells you / why ever did you say that?*).

every
▷ is followed by a singular verb (eg *every room has a sea view*).

every one / everyone
▷ *every one* means 'each individual in the group mentioned' (eg *God bless us every one / she had a present for*

every one of them); ***everyone*** means 'everybody' (eg *everyone expects polite treatment when they go to a restaurant*).

evoke / invoke
▷ **evoke** means 'cause' or 'bring into the mind' (eg *his accusations evoked an angry response / that scent always evokes fond memories*); ***invoke*** means 'appeal to', 'call up (a spirit)', 'bring (a law, etc) into operation' (eg *invoked God as his witness / in his desperation Saul made the witch invoke the dead prophet Samuel and ask his advice / if our case fails in the national courts we will invoke the European Declaration on Human Rights*).

exalt / exult
▷ ***exalt*** means 'raise', 'praise' (eg *exalted to the rank of cabinet minister after only six months in parliament / will exalt the Lord with my whole heart*); ***exult*** means 'rejoice, triumph over' (eg *were just exulting over their victory when news of a fresh invasion arrived*).

excavator
▷ is spelt *-or*.

exceed
▷ is spelt *-ceed*.

exceedingly / excessively
▷ ***exceedingly*** means 'very much'; ***excessively*** means 'too much'.

excellent
▷ is spelt *-ent*.

exceptionable / exceptional
▷ ***exceptionable*** is spelt *-able* and means 'likely to cause, or deserving, disapproval or objection' (eg *the only exceptionable part is his proposal to keep all the profits*);

exceptional means 'outstanding' or 'outside the general rule' (eg *his exceptional achievement in winning*).

excerpt
▷ is spelt -*xc*-.

excise
▷ is spelt -*ise*.

exclamation / interjection
▷ both are followed by exclamation marks, but an *exclamation* gives some information about the outside world (eg *you silly little fool!* / *I must find those keys!*) whilst an *interjection* merely gives vent to the speaker's feelings (eg *ouch!* / *good Lord!* / *phew!*).

exclamation mark
➤ See **punctuation**.

execrable
▷ is spelt -*able* and pronounced **ex**-*e-kru-bul*.

executrix
▷ has plurals *executrices* and *executrixes*.

exercise
▷ is spelt -*ise*.

exhaustible
▷ is spelt -*ible*.

existence, existent
▷ are spelt -*ence*, -*ent*.

exordium
▷ has a plural *exordia*.

exotica
▷ is plural.

expatriate
▷ is spelt -*ate*.

expendable
▷ is spelt *-able*.

expense
▷ is spelt *-se*.

expo
▷ has a plural ***expos***.

exposé
▷ is spelt *-é*.

expressible
▷ is spelt *-ible*.

extempore
▷ is pronounced *ex-**tem**-paw-ray*.

extendable / extendible / extensible
▷ all mean the same.

extravagance / extravagant
▷ are spelt *-ance*, *ant*.

extravert, extrovert
▷ both spellings are correct; the second is the more common and is to be preferred.

extricable
▷ is spelt *-able* and pronounced with the stress on ***ex-*** or on ***-trik-***.

exuberance
▷ is spelt *-ance*.

exult / exalt
▷ ***exult*** means 'rejoice', often with undertones of pleasure at the failure of others (eg *exulted over their failure*); ***exalt*** means 'praise' or 'promote to a higher rank' (eg *found himself exalted to the rank of Admiral*).

f

façade
▷ is spelt -*çade* and pronounced *fu-**sahd***.

facsimile
▷ is pronounced *fak-**sim**-i-li*.

faeces
▷ is spelt *fae-* (AmE *fe-*), pronounced ***fee**-seez* and is plural.

faience
▷ is spelt *-aie-* and pronounced ***fah**-yo^{ng}s*.

fait accompli
▷ is pronounced *fayt u-**kom**-plee*; it has a plural **faits accomplis** which is pronounced *fayz u-**kom**-plee*.

faker / fakir
▷ a **faker** is a person who fakes (eg *made millions as a faker of 'undiscovered' Picassos*); a **fakir** is a Muslim or Hindu holy man (eg *the fakir sat on his bed of nails*).

fall
▷ the verb has a past tense **fell** and a past participle **fallen**.

fallible
▷ is spelt *-ible*.

falsetto
▷ has a plural **falsettos**.

fandango
▷ has a plural **fandangos**.

fantasy
▷ is spelt *-asy*.

Far East
▷ denotes China, Korea, Japan, Mongolia and eastern Siberia. It may also be taken to include the Philippines, Vietnam, Laos, Kampuchea, Thailand, Burma (Myanmar), Malaysia, Singapore and Indonesia.

farrago
▷ has plurals **farragos** and **farragoes**.

farther / further
▷ as an adjective or adverb **further** is now correct in all senses; it may be replaced by **farther** only when physical distance is involved eg

    ✓   *I can't walk any farther*
    ✗   *I have a couple of farther questions*

The verb is always **further** (eg *this win will further our chances of promotion*).

fat
▷ has a comparative **fatter** and a superlative **fattest**.

fatal / fateful
▷ **fatal** means 'causing death or disaster' (eg *a widow since her husband was involved in a fatal accident* / *it would be fatal to bring Rover to the interview—the boss hates dogs*); **fateful** means 'important, having important consequences' (eg *at last the fateful day of the audition arrived*).

faun / fawn
▷ a **faun** is a mythical creature whose body has an upper half like a man's but a lower half like a goat's; **fawn** is a noun denoting a young deer or a buff colour and a verb meaning 'to flatter'.

fauna

fauna
▷ has plurals **faunas** (in general use) and **faunae** (in scientific and technical use).

feasible
▷ is spelt *-ible*.

feed
▷ the verb has a past tense and past participle **fed**.

feel
▷ the verb has a past tense and past participle **felt**.

female / feminine
▷ as adjectives, **female** means 'of that sex that gives birth or produces eggs or seeds' (eg *a female pig is called a sow*) and **feminine** means 'womanish' (eg *he has a feminine voice*); for its grammatical sense see next entry.

feminine
▷ denotes the grammatical gender to which the nouns denoting female people, animals, etc belong; this distinction does not exist in English Grammar (see **gender**).

ferment / foment
▷ both verbs are used of stirring up trouble; **foment** is used of agitators' deliberate activity and takes a direct object of the type of trouble eg

    ✓ *he was arrested because he fomented discontent among the miners*

    ✗ *arrested because he fomented the miners into discontent*

ferment can be used with or without an object and does not imply deliberate agitation eg

    ✓ *three bad harvests have fermented discontent throughout the kingdom*

    ✓ *after three bad harvests discontent was fermenting throughout the kingdom*

ferret
▷ the verb has a past tense **ferreted**.

fervent / fervid
▷ both mean 'keen, eager'; **fervid** often has a tone of disapproval and cannot be applied to people eg
- ✓ *Smith is fervent in his support of Labour*
- ✗ *Smith is fervid in his support of Labour*
- ✓ *managers soon grew wary of this fervid and inflexible trade-unionist*

fetal, fetid, fetus / foetal, foetid, foetus
▷ the *fe-* forms are now the most popular and correctly reflect the word's Latin origins; but the *foe-* forms are still acceptable in non-technical use.

fête / fete
▷ is usually spelt with an *-ê-*.

fewer / less
▷ when speaking or writing of a number of individuals or separate units, use **fewer** followed by a plural noun (eg *fewer boys than girls sat the exam*); when speaking or writing of a single amount or quantity, use **less** followed by a singular noun (eg *put less tonic in next time*).

fez
▷ has a plural **fezzes**.

fiancé, fiancée
▷ are both spelt with *é*.

fiasco
▷ has plurals **fiascos** and **fiascoes**.

fibula
▷ has plurals **fibulae** and **fibulas**.

fictional / fictitious
▷ **fictional** means 'existing only in literature' (eg *Sherlock*

Holmes is a purely fictional character); **fictitious** means 'made up, having no real existence', 'lying' (eg *the police soon established that his address and alibi were fictitious*).

fidget
▷ has a present participle **fidgeting** and a past tense and past participle **fidgeted**.

figure of speech
▷ denotes any expression in which words are used in a striking or unusual way for special effect (eg *her smile is about as friendly as <u>a slap round the face with a wet kipper</u>* / *I see Fred's started to <u>hit the bottle</u> again*).
➤ See **litotes**, **metaphor**, **metonymy**, **simile**, **synecdoche**.

filet mignon
▷ is pronounced **fee-lay meen-yon**.

fillet
▷ the verb has a present participle **filleting** and a past tense and past participle **filleted**.

finite verb
▷ denotes a verb that is in a form that is governed by the subject of its sentence; so in *she <u>likes</u> him <u>to write</u> every day* the first underlined verb is finite, but the second is not.
➤ See also **non-finite verb**, **clauses and phrases**.

first person
➤ See **persons**.

fish
▷ has plurals **fish** and **fishes**.

fistful
▷ is spelt *-ful* and has a plural **fistfuls**.

flagellum
▷ has a plural **flagella**.

flagrant / blatant
▷ **blatant** means 'shamelessly obvious' (eg *a blatant liar*); **flagrant** means 'scandalously wicked' (eg *a flagrant abuse of her powers*) and is not used of persons.

flambé
▷ is spelt *-é*; the verb has a present participle **flambéing** and a past tense and past participle **flambéed**.

flamenco
▷ has a plural **flamencos**.

flamingo
▷ has plurals **flamingos** and **flamingoes**.

flammable / inflammable
▷ both are spelt *-able* and both mean 'able or likely to catch fire'; the first is used in technical contexts, the second in everyday speech.

flaunt / flout
▷ **flaunt** means 'to show off proudly' (eg *he found Millie at the front, flaunting her new dress to an admiring circle of young executives*); **flout** means 'ignore, deliberately disobey' (eg *he drove through the town at a steady 50, flouting speed limits and ignoring traffic lights*).

fledgling / fledgeling
▷ the first spelling is most common.

flee
▷ has a past tense and past participle **fled**.

flexible
▷ is spelt *-ible*.

fling
▷ has a past tense and past participle **flung**.

flora

flora
▷ has plurals **floras** and **florae**.

flotation / floatation
▷ the first spelling is more common.

floury / flowery
▷ **floury** means 'with or like flour' (eg *if it still tastes too floury, put some more lard in*); **flowery** means 'with flowers' or 'fancy' (eg *flowery meadows / paid the Queen many a flowery compliment in his speech*).

fly
▷ the verb has a past tense **flew** and a past participle **flown**.

fo'c'sle
▷ is spelt -*'c'*- and *sle* and pronounced **fohk**-*sul*.

focus
▷ the noun has plurals **focuses** (in general use) and **foci** (in scientific and technical contexts); the verb has past participles **focusing** or **focussing** and past tenses and past participles **focused** or **focussed**, of which the -*s*- forms are more common.

foetal, foetid, foetus / fetal, fetid, fetus
▷ the *fe*- forms are now the most popular and correctly reflect the word's Latin origins; but the *foe*- forms are still acceptable in non-technical use.

fogey / fogy
▷ the first spelling is most common.

folio
▷ has a plural **folios**.

folk
▷ is a plural noun when meaning 'people in general' or 'relatives' (eg *folk tend to get annoyed if they see someone jumping the queue / though we've been married now for*

twenty years, my folk have never accepted her); is singular when meaning 'a people or tribe' (eg *the entire Lebongo folk was exterminated in the Zulu Wars*); and is a mass noun when meaning 'folk music' (eg *folk has never been part of her repertoire*).

foment / ferment

▷ both verbs are used of stirring up trouble; **foment** is used of agitators' deliberate activity and takes a direct object of the type of trouble eg

  ✓ *he was arrested for fomenting discontent among the miners*

  ✗ *arrested for fomenting the miners into discontent*

ferment can be used with or without an object and does not imply deliberate agitation eg

  ✓ *three bad harvests have fermented discontent throughout the kingdom*

  ✓ *after three bad harvests discontent was fermenting throughout the kingdom*

foot

▷ has a plural **feet**.

for- / fore-

▷ **for-** words generally have a sense of loss or deprivation (eg *forbid, forfeit*); **fore-** words generally have a sense of anticipation (eg *forewarn, forearm*). Some words with these prefixes can be spelt either way (eg **forfend** and **forgather**; see also **forbear**, **forgo**).

forbear / forebear

▷ as a noun meaning 'ancestor' either spelling can be used and stress is on the first syllable; the verb meaning 'to abstain, to refrain' is spelt **forbear**, is stressed on the second syllable, has a past tense **forbore** and a past participle **forborne**.

forbid

forbid
▷ has past tenses **forbade** (recommended by some authorities) and **forbad** and a past participle **forbidden**.

forceful / forcible
▷ both mean 'powerfully done' and 'persuasive, influential' (eg *gave a forceful performance as Macbeth / the gory accident was a forcible reminder to keep to the speed limit*); **forcible** also means 'violent, by force' (eg *bailiffs burnt down the protesters' huts in a forcible attempt to evict them*).

forceps
▷ is plural.

forecast
▷ has a traditional past tense and past participle **forecast**; however, **forecasted** is now often heard.

forecastle
▷ is pronounced **fohk**-*sul*.

forego / forgo
▷ as a verb meaning 'to do without, or abstain from' either spelling can be used with past tenses **forwent** or **forewent** and past participles **forgone** or **foregone**; the verb meaning 'to precede' is spelt **forego** and has a past tense **forewent** and past participle **foregone**.

foreign, foreigner
▷ are spelt *-eig-*.

foresee
▷ has a past tense **foresaw** and a past participle **foreseen**.

foreseeable
▷ is spelt *-able*.

foretell
▷ has a past tense and past participle **foretold**.

for ever / forever
▷ *for ever* is most common for all meanings, but *forever* is also correct.

forfeit
▷ is spelt *-feit*.

forget
▷ has a past tense *forgot* and a past participle *forgotten*.

forgive
▷ has a past tense *forgave* and a past participle *forgiven*.

forgo / forego
▷ as a verb meaning 'to do without, or abstain from' either spelling can be used with past tenses *forwent* or *forewent* and past participles *forgone* or *foregone*; the verb meaning 'to precede' is spelt *forego* and has a past tense *forewent* and past participle *foregone*.

formal English
➤ See **register**.

formula
▷ has plurals *formulas* (in general use) and *formulae* (in scientific and technical use).

forsake
▷ has a past tense *forsook* and a past participle *forsaken*.

forswear
▷ has a past tense *forswore* and a past participle *forsworn*.

forte
▷ is pronounced *fawr-ti*.

fowl
▷ has plurals *fowls* and *fowl*.

fracas
▷ is pronounced *fra-kah*; its plural is spelt the same but pronounced *fra-kahz*.

fragrance

fragrance
▷ is spelt *-ance*.

franchise
▷ is spelt *-ise*.

fräulein
▷ is spelt *-au-* and *-ei-* and pronounced *froy-liyn*.

free
▷ the adjective has a comparative *freer* (pronounced *free-ur*) and a superlative *freest* (pronounced *free-ist*).

freeze
▷ has a past tense *froze* and a past participle *frozen*.

friar / frier
▷ a *friar* is a sort of monk; a *frier* is a person or machine that fries.

frolic
▷ the verb has a present participle *frolicking* and a past tense *frolicked*.

fuchsia
▷ is pronounced *fyuu-shu*.

fulcrum
▷ has plurals *fulcrums* (now in general use) and *fulcra*.

fulfil, fulfilment
▷ have only two *l*s.

full stop
➤ See **punctuation**.

fulsome
▷ has only one *l*.

fungous / fungus
▷ *fungous* is the adjective and *fungus* (plural *fungi*) the noun.

furnishing / furnishings
▷ *furnishing* is singular and is derived from the verb *to furnish* which means 'to stock something with furniture' (eg *furnishing the whole house was an expensive business*); *furnishings* means 'furniture' and is plural (eg *the flat was nicely situated but its furnishings were tatty and tasteless*).

further / farther
▷ as an adjective or adverb *further* is now correct in all senses; it may be replaced by *farther* only when physical distance is involved eg

  ✓ *I can't walk any farther*
  ✗ *I have a couple of farther questions*

The verb is always *further* (eg *this win will further our chances of promotion*).

future perfect tense
▷ denotes that tense of verbs that is used to describe an action that will already have taken place by the time some other mentioned event occurs (eg *he will have left before you get there*); it is formed from *will have* plus the past participle of the verb.

future tense
▷ denotes that tense of verbs that is used to describe an action that will take place, or a situation that will exist, after the time of speaking or writing; it is formed from *will* or *shall* and the infinitive form of the verb, eg *John will arrive at 6pm / I shall leave tomorrow.*

g

gallop
▷ has a present participle **galloping**, and a past tense and past participle **galloped**.

gallows
▷ is singular.

galore
▷ always follows its noun (eg *whisky galore at the manse tonight*).

gamble / gambol
▷ *gamble* means 'bet' and *gambol* means 'dance about'.

games
▷ the names of games that end in *-s* are treated as singular nouns (eg *skittles is boring*). In some games (eg skittles and darts) the same word is used for the game and for the pieces with which it is played; when used for the pieces the word is singular or plural in the usual way (eg *a dart was stuck in the wall and three skittles were on the floor*).

ganglion
▷ has plurals **ganglions** (in general use) and **ganglia** (in scientific and technical use).

gaol / goal / jail
▷ *gaol* and *jail* are different spellings of a single word which means 'prison' and is pronounced *jayl*; the spelling *gaol* is now only used in official documents. *Goal* is a dif-

gender

ferent word; it is pronounced *gohl* and means 'scoring-place, point scored' or 'purpose'.

garda
▷ has a plural **gardai**.

gasworks
▷ may be treated as either singular or plural eg
- ✓ the gasworks <u>is</u> in the next street
- ✓ the gasworks <u>are</u> in the next street

gâteau
▷ is spelt *-â-* and *-eau* and pronounced **gat**-*oh*; it has plurals **gâteaux** and **gâteaus** which are both pronounced *gat-ohz*.

gauge
▷ is spelt *-au-*.

gazebo
▷ is pronounced *gu-**zee**-boh* and has plurals **gazebos** and **gazeboes**.

gazelle
▷ has two plurals
- ○ **gazelle**, when the group is thought of as a whole (eg *saw a large herd of gazelle charging across his path*).
- ○ **gazelles**, when the group is thought of as a set of individuals (eg *a few gazelles came past, some limping badly*).

gecko
▷ has plurals **geckos** and **geckoes**.

geisha
▷ is pronounced **gay**-*shu* and has plurals **geishas** (in general use) and **geisha**.

gender
▷ grammatical gender, by which (in such languages as

French, German and Latin) 'feminine', 'masculine' and 'neuter' nouns each take different forms, does not exist in English nouns or adjectives; so when we speak of the English word 'boy' being 'a masculine noun', 'laundress' being 'a feminine noun' or 'table' being 'a neuter noun' we are referring to the *sex* (or lack of it) of the person or thing to which that noun refers, not to the grammatical gender of the noun itself.

generator
▷ is spelt *-or*.

genesis
▷ has a plural ***geneses***.

genetics
▷ is singular.

genie
▷ has plurals ***genies*** (now in general use) and ***genii***.

genitive case
▷ is another way of describing the ***possessive*** form of nouns, adjectives and pronouns (eg *John's, mine, hers*).

genius
▷ has two plurals
  ○ ***genii*** when it means 'guardian spirit'.
  ○ ***geniuses*** for all other senses.

genre
▷ is pronounced ***zhon***-*ruh*.

gentry
▷ is plural.

gents
▷ is singular when it means 'men's public lavatory' (eg *the gents is the third door on the right*) and plural when it

means 'men' (eg *a couple of old gents were nattering in the corner of the snug*).

genus
▷ has a plural **genera**.

gerund
➤ See **verbal noun**.

get
▷ has a present participle **getting** and a past tense and past participle **got**; in American English **gotten** is used as well as **got**.

ghetto
▷ is spelt *gh*- and has plurals **ghettos** and **ghettoes**.

gibbet
▷ the verb has a present participle **gibbeting** and a past tense and past participle **gibbeted**.

gibe / gybe / jibe
▷ for 'mock' use **gibe** and for the sailing terms use **gybe**; **jibe** is a non-recommended alternative spelling for both and in American English also means 'agree with'.

giblets
▷ is plural.

gigolo
▷ has a plural **gigolos**.

gild / guild
▷ **gild** means 'cover with gold' and has a past tense and past participle **gilded** or **gilt**; **guild** means 'club, association' and is spelt *gui*-.

gill
▷ the fish's breathing organ is pronounced with a hard *g*, the liquid measure with a soft one.

gillie

gillie / ghilly
▷ is pronounced *gil*-ee; the first spelling is more common.

gipsy / gypsy
▷ both spellings are correct, but the second is more common.

gird
▷ has a past tense and past participle *girded* or *girt*; the second is more common.

giro
▷ has a plural *giros*.

give
▷ has a past tense *gave* and a past participle *given*.

glacé
▷ is spelt with a final *é*.

gladiolus
▷ has plurals *gladioli* and *gladioluses*.

glasses
▷ is plural, even when meaning 'pair of spectacles'.

glissando
▷ has a plural *glissandi*.

glottis
▷ has plurals *glottises* (in general use) and *glottides* (in scientific and medical use).

Gloucester
▷ is spelt *-ou-* and *-ces-* and pronounced *glo*-stur.

gnaw
▷ has past participles *gnawed* (in general use) and *gnawn*.

gnocchi
▷ is a plural noun and pronounced *nyok*-ee.

gnu

▷ is pronounced *noo* or (humorously) *gnoo* and has two plurals

- ○ **gnu**, when the group is thought of as a whole (eg *saw a large herd of gnu charging across his path*).
- ○ **gnus**, when the group is thought of as a set of individuals (eg *a few gnus came past, some limping badly*).

go

▷ the verb has a third person singular present **goes**, a past tense **went** and a past participle **gone**.

goal / gaol / jail

▷ **gaol** and **jail** are different spellings of a single word which means 'prison' and is pronounced *jayl*; the spelling **gaol** is now only used in official documents. **Goal** is a different word; it is pronounced *gohl* and means 'scoring-place, point scored' or 'purpose'.

gobbledygook / gobbledegook

▷ the first spelling is more common.

goldfish

▷ has plurals **goldfish** and **goldfishes**.

gonorrhoea

▷ is spelt *-rrhoea* and pronounced *gon-uh-***ree***-u*.

good

▷ has a comparative **better** and a superlative **best**.

goods

▷ is always plural and has no singular form.

goose

▷ the noun has a plural **geese** for all senses except 'pinch on the bottom', where the plural is **gooses**.

gorilla

gorilla / guerilla / guerrilla
▷ a *gorilla* is a large ape; a *guerrilla* (the spelling with two rs is more common) is a resistance fighter.

gossip
▷ the verb has a present participle *gossiping* and a past tense *gossiped*.

got / gotten
▷ *got* is the past tense and past participle form of *get*; in American English *gotten* is used as well as *got*.

gourmand / gourmet
▷ a *gourmand* is a glutton; a *gourmet* is an expert on food.

govern
▷ a verb or preposition is said to *govern* the noun or pronoun that is its object (eg *I saw him with you*, where *saw* governs *him* and *with* governs *you*); it is also said to *govern* (ie control) *the case* of such nouns and pronouns, since it makes them go into the *objective case* eg

      ✓ *I saw <u>him</u>*

not

      ✗ *I saw <u>he</u>*

government
▷ is a singular noun when thought of as a unified group of people (eg *this government has been in power too long*) but plural when thought of as a set of individuals (eg *the government are at loggerheads over the European single currency*).

governor
▷ is spelt *-or*.

graffito
▷ has a plural *graffiti*.

gram / gramme
▷ *gram* has always been the preferred spelling in scientific

graphics

and technical contexts and is now replacing **gramme** in general use.

grammatical word
▷ denotes a word that is defined not only by its sound or spelling but also by its grammatical function: so in the sentences *Where have you put it?* and *Put it down!* the *put*s, although exactly the same in spelling and sound, are two different **grammatical words** because the first is a past participle and the second an imperative.

➤ See also **lexeme, orthographic word, phonological word**.

gramophone
▷ has an *o* in the middle.

grandad / granddad
▷ the most common spelling is with only one *d* in the middle.

grandchild
▷ has a plural **grandchildren**.

granddaughter
▷ has two *d*s in the middle.

grannie / granny
▷ the first spelling is preferred in Scotland, the second in England.

grapefruit
▷ has plurals **grapefruit** and **grapefruits**.

graphics
▷ is singular when referring to the art of design, etc (eg *graphics is taught by Mr Squeers*), but plural when referring to a number of actual designs, etc (eg *are the graphics all ready for the next issue?*); there is no singular in this sense (eg ✗ *one graphic is still missing*).

grave
▷ is pronounced *grayv* when it means 'tomb' and *grahv* when it means 'a sort of accent'.

grave accent
▷ denotes the mark or diacritic ` written or printed above a letter in certain foreign languages, or in English words (eg *Gruyère*) borrowed from them, to indicate its pronunciation or stress.

gray / grey
▷ a **gray** is a unit of radiation; **grey** (AmE **gray**) is the name of a colour.

Great Britain
▷ denotes the largest island in Europe containing England, Scotland and Wales and forming, together with Northern Ireland, the United Kingdom.
➤ See also **United Kingdom**, **British Isles**.

greenfly
▷ has two plurals
  ○ **greenfly**, when the group is thought of as a whole (eg *saw a dense cloud of greenfly*).
  ○ **greenflies**, when the group is thought of as a set of individuals (eg *swatted a couple of greenflies crawling up his shirt*).

Greenwich
▷ is pronounced **gren**-*ich*.

griffin / griffon
▷ a **griffin** is a mythical monster; a **griffon** is a sort of dog or vulture.

grilse
▷ has two plurals
  ○ **grilse**, when the group is thought of as a whole (eg *saw a large shoal of grilse on the port bow*).

○ ***grilses***, when the group is thought of as a set of individuals (eg *only two grilses in the pool, one of which looked pretty sickly*).

gringo
▷ has a plural ***gringos***.

grisly / gristly / grizzly
▷ ***grisly*** means 'horrible' and is pronounced ***griz***-li; ***gristly*** means 'full of gristle' and is pronounced ***gris***-li; ***grizzly*** means 'greying' or 'grizzly bear' and is pronounced ***griz***-li.

Grosvenor
▷ is pronounced ***grohv***-nur.

grotto
▷ has plurals ***grottos*** and ***grottoes***.

group possessive
▷ is the name given to phrases such as that underlined in the sentence *the man we were talking to's car caught fire*, where the *'s* is attached not to a noun (as it is in *the man's car caught fire*) but to a whole noun phrase.
➤ See also **possessive**.

grouse
▷ when meaning 'sort of bird' has a plural ***grouse***; when meaning 'complaint' has a plural ***grouses***.

grow
▷ has a past tense ***grew*** and a past participle ***grown***.

guarantee / guaranty
▷ as nouns ***guarantee*** means 'promise to repair, etc a faulty article' and ***guaranty*** means 'agreement to take responsibility if another person fails to repay debt, etc' or the security given for this.

gubbins
▷ is singular.

guerrilla

guerrilla / guerilla / gorilla
▷ a **gorilla** is a large ape; a **guerrilla** (the spelling with two *r*s is most common) is a resistance fighter.

guesstimate / guestimate
▷ the *-ss-* spelling is most common.

guidance
▷ is spelt *-ance*.

guild / gild
▷ **gild** means 'cover with gold' and has past tense and past participle **gilded** or **gilt**; **guild** means 'club, association' and is spelt *gui-*.

guilder
▷ the modern Dutch coin has plurals **guilder** and **guilders**; the former Dutch and German gold piece has a plural **guilders**.

guinea fowl
▷ has a plural **guinea fowl**.

gullible
▷ is spelt *-ible*.

gunwale
▷ is pronounced to rhyme with *tunnel*.

Gwynedd
▷ is pronounced **gwin**-*edh*.

gybe / gibe / jibe
▷ for 'mock' use **gibe** and for the sailing terms use **gybe**; **jibe** is a non-recommended alternative spelling for both and in American English also means 'agree with'.

gymkhana
▷ is spelt *gymkh-*.

gymnasium
▷ is spelt *gym-* and has plurals **gymnasiums** (now in general use) and **gymnasia**.

gymnastics
▷ is singular.

gynaecology
▷ is spelt *gynae-*.

gypsy / gipsy
▷ both spellings are correct, but the first is more common.

h

haddock
▷ has a plural *haddock*.

haemorrhage
▷ is spelt *haem-* and *-rrhage* and pronounced **hem**-*ur-ij*.

haemorrhoid
▷ is spelt *haem-* and *-rrhoid* and pronounced **hem**-*ur-oyd*.

Hague, the
▷ is spelt *-gue* and pronounced *hayg*.

haiku
▷ has a plural *haiku*.

hairdo
▷ has a plural *hairdos*.

hake
▷ has two plurals
  ○ *hake*, when the group is thought of as a whole (eg *saw a large shoal of hake on the port bow*).
  ○ *hakes*, when the group is thought of as a set of individuals (eg *only two hakes in the pool, one of which looked pretty sickly*).

half
▷ has plurals *halves* (used in all senses) and *halfs* (used in all senses *except* 'one of two equal parts'; eg
  ✓ *three more halfs of Burton, please*

but

    ✗   *cut the cake into two halfs*

halleluia / alleluia / alleluya
▷ the first spelling is most common.

hallo / hello
▷ the second spelling is more common; **hallo** is used informally.

halo
▷ has plurals **halos** and **haloes**.

hamstring
▷ the verb has past tenses and past participles **hamstringed** and **hamstrung**.

handkerchief
▷ is spelt *-dk-* and *-chief* and has plurals **handkerchieves** and **handkerchiefs**.

hang
▷ the verb has a past tense and past participle
- ○ **hanged** for senses 'execute with a rope' (eg *Crippen was hanged in 1910*) and 'damn' (eg *I'm hanged if I'll do all his dirty work*).
- ○ **hung** for all other senses.

hangar / hanger
▷ a **hangar** is a shelter for aircraft; a **hanger** is a frame for clothes storage.

hankie / hanky
▷ the second spelling is more common.

Hants
▷ is an abbreviation for Hampshire, the English county, and has no full stop after it (except when it ends a sentence).

harangue
▷ is spelt *-gue* but pronounced *hu-**rang***.

harass
▷ is spelt with one *r* and two *s*s and pronounced **ha**-*rus*.

hard consonant
▷ the consonants *c* and *g* are said to be **hard** when they are pronounced as in the starts of *cat* and *get* (and **soft** when they are pronounced as in the starts of *centre* and *gentle*).

harem
▷ is pronounced **hah**-*reem* or *huh*-**reem**.

Hartford / Hertford
▷ the first is a city in America, the second a town in England.

Harwich
▷ is pronounced **ha**-*rij*.

have
▷ has a third person singular present **has** and a past tense and past participle **had**.

he or she ?
➤ See **political correctness**.

headquarters
▷ may be treated as a singular or a plural eg
  ✓ the headquarters <u>is</u> in the next street
  ✓ the headquarters <u>are</u> in the next street

hear
▷ has a past tense and past participle **heard**.

heave
▷ has a past tense and past participle **heaved**, except in nautical senses when **hove** is used (eg *as soon as the ship <u>hove</u> to he <u>heaved</u> the bundle over its side*).

hegemony
▷ is pronounced *hi*-**jem**-*un*-*i*.

Hegira
▷ is pronounced *hi-**jiy**-ru*.
height
▷ is spelt *-ei-*.
helix
▷ has plurals **helixes** (now in general use) and **helices** (pronounced ***hel**-i-seez*).
hello / hallo
▷ the first spelling is more common; **hallo** is used informally.
herbarium
▷ has a plural **herbaria**.
Herculean / herculean
▷ begins with an upper-case *h* when referring to the mythical Greek hero and with a lower-case *h* in the senses 'extremely difficult or dangerous' or 'requiring an enormous effort'; it is stressed on the second or third syllable.
heroin / heroine
▷ the first denotes a sort of drug, the second a woman who is noted for bravery or who is the subject of a story, etc.
herring
▷ has two plurals
  ○ **herring**, when the group is thought of as a whole (eg *saw a large shoal of herring on the port bow*).
  ○ **herrings**, when the group is thought of as a set of individuals (eg *only two herrings in the pool, one of which looked pretty sickly*).
Hertford / Hartford
▷ the first is a town in England, the second a city in America.
hertz
▷ has a plural **hertz**.

hew

hew
▷ has a past tense *hewed* and a past participle *hewn*.

hiatus
▷ has a plural *hiatuses*.

hibiscus
▷ has a plural *hibiscuses*.

hiccup / hiccough
▷ the first spelling is now standard; the verb has a present participle *hiccuping* and a past tense and past participle *hiccuped*.

hide
▷ has a past tense *hid* and a past participle *hidden*.

Himalayas
▷ is pronounced hi-mu-**lay**-uz or (less commonly) hi-**mah**-li-uz.

hindrance
▷ is spelt *-ance*.

hippo
▷ has a plural *hippos*.

hireable
▷ is spelt *-eable*.

historic / historical
▷ *historic* means 'famous or important in history' (eg *nearby is the site of the historic Battle of Hastings*); *historical* means 'about history' or 'that actually happened or lived' (eg *a volume of historical essays / the historical Macbeth gained his throne by conquest, not murder*).

hit
▷ has a past tense and past participle *hit*.

hoard / horde
▷ a *hoard* is a hidden store (eg *found the hoard of silver*

coins under a tree root); a **horde** is a crowd of people (eg *a horde of rioters turned into the side streets, looting shops as they went*).

hoe
▷ the verb has a present participle **hoeing**.

hold
▷ the verb has a past tense and past participle **held**.

holeable
▷ is spelt *-eable*.

holey / holy
▷ the first means 'full of holes', the second 'sacred'; both have a comparative **holier** and a superlative **holiest**.

homeo- / homoeo- / homo-
▷ **homeo-** is the American spelling of **homoeo-**; both mean 'like, similar' (eg *homoeopathy*, the treatment of a disease by substances that induce similar symptoms); **homo-** means 'the same' (eg *homosexuality*, sexual desire for persons of the same sex).

homogeneous / homogenous
▷ **homogeneous** means 'made of the same stuff throughout' (eg *stir thoroughly to ensure a homogeneous mixture*); **homogenous** means 'similar because of having a common descent or origin' (eg *ultimately all mammals must be homogenous*).

homograph
▷ denotes a word that is spelt the same as another word but is pronounced differently from it, such as *tear* (in cloth, pronounced *ter*; in the eye, pronounced *teer*).

homonym
▷ denotes a word which has the same spelling and pronunciation as some other word but has a different meaning, such as *light* (which can mean 'not heavy' or 'dark').

homophone

▷ denotes a word that sounds the same as some other word but is spelt differently and has a different meaning, eg *brooch* ('ornament') and *broach* ('break into'), both of which are pronounced *brohch*.

honorarium

▷ has plurals **honorariums** (now in general use) and **honoraria**.

hoof

▷ has plurals **hooves** (now in general use) and **hoofs**.

hoorah, hooray / hurrah, hurray

▷ the *-urr-* spellings are best, except for **hooray Henry**.

hopefully

▷ the use of this word to mean 'with luck' (eg *hopefully I shall be finished by 3 pm*) should be limited to informal contexts.

horde / hoard

▷ a **horde** is a crowd of people (eg *a horde of rioters turned into the side streets, looting shops as they went*); a **hoard** is a hidden store (eg *found the hoard of silver coins under a tree root*).

horsey / horsy

▷ the first spelling is more common; in either case the comparative is **horsier** and the superlative **horsiest**.

hospitable

▷ is now usually stressed on the second syllable; stress on the first is also correct.

hotel

▷ is now usually pronounced *hoh-**tel***, but *oh-**tel*** is also correct.

how ever / however
▷ always use the one-word form, except in emphatic questions (eg *how ever did you manage to climb up there?*).

Huguenot
▷ is pronounced **hyuu**-ge-noh.

human / humane
▷ *human* means 'belonging to people (as opposed to animals, machines, etc)' (eg *must allow 10% for human error*); *humane* means 'kindly, civilized' (eg *it was scarcely humane to tell him of the accident so abruptly*).

humerus
▷ has a plural *humeri*.

hummus / humous / humus
▷ *hummus* is a chick-pea spread; *humous* means 'of rich soil'; *humus* is a rich soil made from leaf-mould, etc.

humorist, humorous
▷ are both spelt -*mor*-.

hundred / hundreds
▷ when preceded by a numeral, use *hundred* (eg *three hundred quid to you, squire*); when just meaning 'a lot' use *hundreds* (eg *I've spend hundreds of pounds on it and it still doesn't work*).

hundredweight
▷ is singular (eg *three hundredweight of sand*).

hurrah, hurray / hoorah, hooray
▷ the -*urr*- spellings are best, except for *hooray Henry*.

hurt
▷ has a past tense and past participle *hurt*.

hussy / huzzy
▷ use the -*ss*- spelling.

hydro

hydro
▷ has a plural **hydros**.

hygiene, hygienic
▷ are spelt *-gie-*.

hyper- / hypo-
▷ **hyper-** means 'excessive', as in *hypercorrection* (see previous entry) or 'very big', as in *hypermarket*; **hypo-** means 'under', as in *hypodermic* (meaning 'under the skin') or 'insufficient', as in *hypothermia* (the condition of having insufficient body-heat).

hypercorrection
▷ means 'over-correction' and is used in Grammar to describe an excessive correction of an error (for example, where a person who has been warned about dropping aitches puts an aitch in front of every word that begins with a vowel).

hyphens

The hyphen is a punctuation mark (-) in the form of a short line half the length of a **dash** (see under **punctuation**) and is used for three main purposes:

○ To link words that form a grammatical unit in a sentence, usually to clarify the meaning.

○ To join into a hyphenated compound a group of words that represents a single idea.

○ To mark the division of a word at the end of a line in print, when there is not room for the whole word.

• The hyphen as a grammatical link
This is used

○ To link word-groups that act as an adjective when they precede the noun they modify (eg *an up-to-date report, a balance-of-payments problem, a two-year-old child, a*

hyphens ...

kind-faced man). Phrases of this type should not be hyphenated in other positions in the sentence (eg *The report is completely up to date / a problem with the country's balance of payments*).

NOTE Word-groups that consist of an adverb and an adjective should not normally be linked by a hyphen (eg *a beautifully written book*). Examples of hyphenation in this position are not uncommon where the meanings of the adverb and adjective are felt to be closely bound together (eg *the problems of mentally-handicapped children*), although strictly speaking a hyphen is only necessary to avoid misunderstanding.

○ To avoid misunderstanding, as in *twenty-odd people / twenty odd people, extra-marital sex / extra marital sex*.

○ With numbers from 21 to 99 when expressed in words (eg *twenty-three*) and with fractions (eg *three-quarters*).

• The hyphen in compounds

Most compounds of this type start life as two words (eg *bus company*), develop with use into a hyphenated compound (eg *knock-on*) and finally become single words (eg *hangover*). Those that are most used tend to develop the fastest but there is little agreement among speakers or dictionaries as to which stage a given word-group of this type has currently reached: for example, *break-up* is recommended below, but *breakup* is not 'wrong'. As a basic rule, use a hyphen:

○ When there is an implied grammatical relationship between the two parts. For example, *taxi-driver, concrete-mixer, ice-skating* (where the first part of the compound is felt to be a noun 'object' of the second, which is looked on as a verb), *break-up, passer-by* (which are looked on as phrasal verbs) and *home-made* (which is looked on as an adjective–adverb pair). However,

hypnosis

some better established or more familiar compounds are already written as one word (eg *firefighter*, *bookmaker*, *breakthrough*, *ladylike*).

○ When the first of a pair of nouns qualifies the second, rather like an adjective, they are not usually hyphenated but written as a single word or as two words, eg *fire alarm*, *fireguard*, *pay bed*, *payphone*, *pipe dream*, *pipeline*.

○ After a prefix like *re-*, to warn that a one-word combination is being used with a different meaning, eg *re-cover* (meaning 'cover again') / *recover* (meaning 'get back'), *re-sign* (meaning 'sign again') / *resign* (meaning 'give up job'), etc.

○ When the compound represents a combination of two things: *shampoo-conditioner*, *major-general*.

• **The hyphen marking word division**
This is a problem mainly for printers since word-division is flexible in hand-written notes or letters and is provided automatically by most word-processing packages. Further guidance is given in the *Chambers Dictionary of Spelling and Word Division*.

hypnosis
▷ has a plural ***hypnoses***.

hypo
▷ has a plural ***hypos***.

hypocrisy
▷ has first syllables that are spelt *hypo-* but pronounced ***hi**-po-*.

hypocrite
▷ has first syllables that are spelt *hypo-* but pronounced ***hi**-po-*.

hypothesis
 ▷ has a plural *hypotheses*.

hysterics
 ▷ is plural.

i

-i / -oes / -os
▷ certain words of Italian origin whose singular ends in *-o* have a plural in *-i*; most other words whose singular ends in *-o* have plurals in *-os* or *-oes*. There are no simple universal rules for deciding the plural of a particular *-o* word and the commonest ones are listed at their alphabetical place in this book.

iambus
▷ has plurals ***iambuses*** and ***iambi***.

ibex
▷ has three plurals
- ***ibex***, when the group is thought of as a whole (eg *a herd of ibex charging across the veldt*).
- ***ibexes***, when the group is thought of as a set of individuals (eg *a couple of ibexes came past, one of them limping*).
- ***ibices*** (pronounced ***iy***-*bi-seez*), now seldom used.

ibis
▷ has two plurals
- ***ibis***, when the group is thought of as a whole (eg *the lakeside was crowded with ibis and other waders*).
- ***ibises***, when the group is thought of as a set of individuals (eg *only two ibises by the pool, one of which looked pretty sickly*).

Ibiza
▷ is pronounced *i-**bee**-thu*.

-ible / -able
▷ although the second of these suffixes is the more common, there are no simple rules for remembering which a particular word will take. All the commonest *-able* and *-ible* words are listed at their alphabetical place in this book.

icon / ikon
▷ the first spelling is more common.

Ides
▷ is plural.

idiom
▷ denotes an expression used in informal speech or writing (eg *sowed his wild oats / kick the bucket / can't put up with her*) whose meaning cannot be worked out from the meanings of the words that make it up; common idioms are usually listed in dictionaries.

idiosyncrasy
▷ is spelt *-syn-* and *-crasy*.

idyll
▷ is pronounced ***i**-dil*.

idyllic
▷ is pronounced *i-**dil**-ik*.

-ie- / -ei-
▷ the traditional rule '*i* before *e* except after *c*' is useful as a rule of thumb although it does have many exceptions; these are all noted at their alphabetical place in this book.

-ify / -efy
▷ most of these verbs end in *-ify*; those that do not are listed at their alphabetical place in this book.

ignominy

ignominy
▷ is stressed on the first syllable.

ignoramus
▷ has a plural *ignoramuses*.

ignorance
▷ is spelt *-ance*.

ikon / icon
▷ the second spelling is more common.

il- / ill-
▷ if the *il-* sound means 'not' or 'in, into, on', the first syllable will be spelt *il-* and combine with the word it prefixes (eg *illegal, illegible*); but if the *il-* sound means 'badly' it will be spelt *ill-* and remain a separate hyphenated syllable (eg *ill-advised, ill-tempered*).

il- / im- / in- / ir-
▷ these prefixes mean 'not' (eg *illegal* = not legal) or 'in, into, on' (eg *innate* = inborn, *irradiate* = put radiation into).

ilium
▷ has a plural *ilia*.

illegal / illicit / illegitimate
▷ *illegal* means 'not allowed by law or the rules' (eg *it's illegal to park on double yellow lines*); *illicit* means 'not allowed' and usually also denotes secrecy (eg *police discovered illicit photographs in the outhouse*); *illegitimate* means 'born out of wedlock' (eg *the Duchess of Portsmouth bore many of Charles II's illegitimate children*) or 'unjustified' (eg *illegitimate claims for compensation*).

illegible
▷ is spelt *-ible*.

illiterate
▷ has only one *t* in the middle and ends *-ate*.

illusion / delusion
▷ a sane person has an **illusion** when the light, etc plays tricks upon him or her (eg *the successive still pictures flashed upon the cinema screen give an illusion of motion*); **delusions** are false ideas that arise in the minds of people who are mentally ill (eg *has this delusion that everyone is trying to kill her / that she is the Queen of the Fairies*).

imago
▷ has plurals **imagos** (in general use) and **imagines** (in scientific use).

imbroglio
▷ is spelt *-glio*, pronounced im-***brohl***-*yoh* and has a plural **imbroglios**.

im- / il- / in- / ir-
▷ these prefixes mean 'not' (eg *illegal* = not legal) or 'in, into, on' (eg *innate* = inborn, *irradiate* = put radiation into).

im- / imm-
▷ the prefix itself is always *im-*; so spell *imm-* only when the word to which the prefix is added itself begins with *m* (eg *immoral* = *im* + *moral*).

immanence / immanent / imminence, imminent
▷ all are spelt *-nen-*; the first pair mean 'being present everywhere' and the second 'being about to happen'.

immoral / amoral
▷ an **amoral** person believes that there are no moral rules; an **immoral** person accepts that there are such rules, but disobeys them.

immunity / impunity
▷ **immunity** means 'freedom from' (eg *his diplomatic status gives him immunity from prosecution*) or 'resistance to' (eg *the vaccination will give you immunity from measles*);

impala

impunity means 'freedom from punishment' (eg *don't think you can flout the law with impunity*).

impala
▷ has two plurals
  ○ *impala*, when the group is thought of as a whole (eg *saw a large herd of impala charging across his path*).
  ○ *impalas*, when the group is thought of as a set of individuals (eg *a few impalas came past, some limping badly*).

impassable / impassible
▷ *impassable* means 'that cannot be travelled through' (eg *to the east the town was protected by impassable swamps*); *impassible* means 'incapable of feeling pain or emotion' (eg *the Docetists argued that since Christ was God he was impassible and so suffered no pain during the Crucifixion*).

imperative
▷ denotes in Grammar the **mood** of the verb used to give orders such as *leave him alone!* or *don't do that*.

imperfect tense
▷ is sometimes called the *imperfect aspect* and denotes verb forms that are used to describe a continuing or incompleted action or state (eg *he was eating his dinner when the roof fell in*); in English it is usually called the *progressive tense* and is formed from the appropriate part of the past tense of the verb *to be* plus the present participle of the verb.

impersonator
▷ is spelt *-or*.

imperturbable
▷ is spelt *-able*.

impetus
▷ has a plural *impetuses*.

impi
▷ has plurals *impi* and *impies*.

impious
▷ is pronounced *im-pi-us*.

implacable
▷ is spelt *-able*.

implausible
▷ is spelt *-ible*.

imply / infer
▷ the traditional rule is that *infer* means 'deduce from known facts' eg
> ✓ *from your sneers I infer that you are no friend of ours*

and *imply* means 'hint at, indicate' eg
> ✓ *I took his sneers to imply that he was no friend of ours*

use of *infer* for *imply* eg
> ✗ *her smiles inferred that she liked the idea*

is common, but thought by many to be incorrect.

importance
▷ is spelt *-ance*.

importune
▷ is stressed on the second or third syllable.

impostor
▷ is spelt *-or*.

impotent
▷ is stressed on the first syllable.

impracticable / impractical
▷ *impracticable* is spelt *-able*, stressed on the second syllable and means 'not able to be done or used' (eg *closure of the straits by ice has made the route impracticable*);

impregnable

impractical means 'not sensible or efficient' (eg *the development of the railways had made canal transport impractical by the mid-nineteenth century / impractical dresses seen only in fashion magazines are the ones I like best*).

impregnable
▷ is spelt *-able*.

impresario
▷ has a plural *impresarios*.

improbable
▷ is spelt *-able*.

improvise
▷ is spelt *-ise*.

impulsive / compulsive
▷ *compulsive* means 'unable to stop oneself' (eg *Tom had no use for the 500 tins of dogmeat found in his flat; he was simply a compulsive shoplifter*); *impulsive* means 'likely to act without considering the consequences, done on the spur of the moment' (eg *his action in hitting the burglar had been impulsive, but was none the less an assault*).

impunity / immunity
▷ *impunity* means 'freedom from punishment' (eg *don't think you can flout the law with impunity*); *immunity* means 'freedom from' (eg *his diplomatic status gives him immunity from prosecution*) or 'resistance to' (eg *the vaccination will give you immunity from measles*).

in- / il- / im- / ir-
▷ these prefixes mean 'not' (eg *illegal* = not legal) or 'in, into, on' (eg *innate* = inborn, *irradiate* = put radiation into).

in- / inn-
▷ the basic rule is to write *inn-* only when the word to which *in-* is prefixed itself begins with *n* (eg *innumerable* = in +

numerable, inactive = in + active); but there are many exceptions and in cases of doubt it is wise to consult a dictionary.

inadvertence, inadvertent
▷ are spelt *-ten-*.

inadvisable
▷ is spelt *-visable* but pronounced *-**viyz**-ubl*.

inapplicable
▷ is spelt *-able*.

inapt / inept
▷ both mean 'unsuitable, out of place' (eg *pretty inept/inapt of you to talk of motor accidents a week after her husband died in one*) and 'unskilful' (eg *his inept/inapt efforts at steering rammed the boat into the bank*); **inept** also means 'silly, absurd' (eg *the more she drank the louder and more inept her conversation became*).

inaudible
▷ is spelt *-ible*.

inchoate
▷ is stressed on the second syllable.

incise
▷ is spelt *-ise*.

incoherence
▷ is spelt *-ence*.

incommensurable
▷ has two *m*s and ends *-able*.

incomparable
▷ is spelt *-able* and stressed on the second syllable.

incompatible
▷ is spelt *-ible*.

incompetence, incompetent
▷ are spelt *-en-*.

incomprehensible
▷ is spelt *-ible*.

inconceivable
▷ is spelt *-able*.

inconsolable
▷ is spelt *-able*.

incontinence, incontinent
▷ are spelt *-nen-*.

incontrovertible
▷ is spelt *-ible*.

incorrigible
▷ is spelt *-ible*.

incorruptible
▷ is spelt *-ible*.

incredible / incredulous
▷ ***incredible*** is spelt *-ible* and means 'unbelievable' (eg *find his claims to have cycled up Snowdon blindfold somewhat incredible*) or 'remarkable' (eg *to be turned back by storms within a hundred yards of the summit was incredible bad luck*); ***incredulous*** is spelt *-ous* and means 'refusing to believe' (eg *his claims to have cycled up Snowdon blindfold met with an incredulous reception down at the club*).

incubus
▷ has plurals ***incubuses*** (now in general use) and ***incubi***.

incurable
▷ is spelt *-curable*.

incus
▷ has a plural ***incudes***.

indecent
▷ is spelt *-ent*.

indecipherable
▷ is spelt *-able*.

indefatigable
▷ is spelt *-able* and stressed on the third syllable.

indefinable
▷ is spelt *-finable* but pronounced *-fiyn-*.

indefinite adjective
➤ See **adjectives**.

indefinite article
➤ See **article**.

indefinite pronoun
➤ See **pronouns**.

indelible
▷ is spelt *-ible*.

independence, independent
▷ are both spelt *-den-*.

indescribable
▷ is spelt *-cribable* and pronounced *-kriyb-*.

indestructible
▷ is spelt *-ible*.

indeterminable
▷ is spelt *-able*.

index
▷ has plurals ***indexes*** (in general use) and ***indices*** (in technical use).

indicative
▷ denotes in Grammar the **mood** of a verb used to state

indict

facts or ask questions. For the standard inflections of this mood with English verbs see **verbs**.

indict, indictable, indictment
▷ are spelt *-dict* but pronounced *-**diyt***.

indifference, indifferent
▷ are spelt *-ren-*.

indigestible
▷ is spelt *-ible*.

indigo
▷ has plurals *indigos* and *indigoes*.

indirect object
➤ See **object**.

indirect speech
▷ denotes the method of recording what someone has said in which their words are altered to fit the point of view of the person repeating them (eg *we will come* becomes *they said they would come*). Also called **reported speech**.
➤ See also **direct speech**.

indiscernible
▷ is spelt *-ible*.

indispensable
▷ is spelt *-able*.

indivisible
▷ is spelt *-ible*.

indolence, indolent
▷ are spelt *-len-*.

indomitable
▷ is spelt *-able*.

indubitable
▷ is spelt *-able*.

indulgence, indulgent
▷ are spelt -gen-.

inedible
▷ is spelt -ible.

ineducable
▷ is spelt -able.

ineffable
▷ is spelt -able.

ineffective / ineffectual
▷ both mean 'failing to produce results'; but **ineffectual**, when said of a person, also suggests that the failure is due to that person's lack of ability or determination (eg *Edith gave an ineffectual push to the tiller—to her mind, the boat was lost already*).

inept / inapt
▷ both mean 'unsuitable, out of place' (eg *pretty inept/inapt of you to talk of motor accidents a week after her husband died in one*) and 'unskilful' (eg *his inept/inapt efforts at steering rammed the boat into the bank*); **inept** also means 'silly, absurd' (eg *the more she drank the louder and more inept her conversation became*).

inequitable
▷ is spelt -able.

ineradicable
▷ is spelt -able.

inestimable
▷ is spelt -able.

inevitable
▷ is spelt -able.

inexcusable
▷ is spelt -able.

inexhaustible
▷ is spelt *-ible*.

inexorable
▷ is spelt *-able*.

inexpedience, inexpedient
▷ are spelt *-dien-*.

inexperience
▷ is spelt *-ence*.

inexplicable
▷ is spelt *-able*.

inexpressible
▷ is spelt *-ible*.

inextinguishable
▷ is spelt *-able*.

inextricable
▷ is spelt *-able* and stressed on the second or third syllable.

infallible
▷ is spelt *-ible*.

infamous
▷ is stressed on the first syllable.

infer / imply
▷ the traditional rule is that **infer** means 'deduce from known facts' eg
    ✓ *from your sneers I infer that you are no friend of ours*
and **imply** means 'hint at, indicate' eg
    ✓ *I took his sneers to imply that he was no friend of ours*
use of **infer** for **imply** eg
    ✗ *her smiles inferred that the liked the idea*
is common, but thought by many to be incorrect.

ingenious

inferable / inferrable
▷ the first spelling is more common.

inferno
▷ has a plural *infernos*.

infinitive
▷ denotes the form of a verb which is used to express an action or event without limiting it to a particular subject or time (eg *to err is human / she told him to go / let her go*).
➤ See also **bare infinitive**, **'to'-infinitive**.

inflammable / flammable
▷ both are spelt *-able* and both mean 'able or likely to catch fire'; the first is used in everyday speech, the second in techical contexts.

inflatable
▷ is spelt *-flatable*.

inflection / inflexion
▷ is usually spelt *-ct-*; it denotes the changed form of a verb, noun or pronoun that is used to indicate a past tense, plural, objective case, etc. For example, the verb *walk* inflects into *walks* in the third person singular present and into *walked* in the past tense; the noun *child* inflects into *children* in the plural, and the pronoun *she* into *her* in the objective case.
➤ See also **compounding**, **derivation**, **nouns**, **verbs**.

inflexible
▷ is spelt *-ible*.

informal English
➤ See **register**.

ingenious / ingenuous
▷ *ingenious* means 'clever' or 'cleverly made' (eg *an ingenious contraption that not only peels and washes the vegetables but boils them too*); *ingenuous* means 'naïve,

childishly trustful' (eg *pretty ingenuous of her not to realize he was after her money*).

inhibitor
▷ is spelt *-or*.

inhuman / inhumane
▷ both are used only of humans and the first is the strongest.
  ○ ***inhuman*** means 'so cruel or brutal as to make the doer unfit to be called a human being' (eg *many prisoners died under the new camp commandant's inhuman regime*).
  ○ ***inhumane*** means 'unkindly, unfeeling' (eg *it's a bit inhumane to shut the cat out when you know it's ill*).

inimitable
▷ is spelt *-able*.

initialism
➤ See **abbreviations**.

inlay
▷ the noun is stressed on the first syllable; the verb may be stressed on either syllable and has a past tense and past participle ***inlaid***.

innings
▷ the usage varies according to the game
  ○ in cricket ***innings*** is both singular and plural (eg *his last innings was a disaster—out for a duck* / *Somerset could only total 150 over both innings*).
  ○ in baseball ***innings*** is plural only and has a singular ***inning***.

innuendo
▷ is spelt *-innu-* and has plurals ***innuendos*** and ***innuendoes***.

innumerable
▷ is spelt *innu-* and *-able*.

inoperable
▷ is spelt *inop-* and *-able*.

inquire, inquiry / enquire, enquiry
▷ the traditional rule is that the second pair are used of ordinary questions (eg *enquired whether she had slept well*) and the first of formal investigations (eg *the inquiry into the train crash starts today*); many people now use them interchangeably.

inscrutable
▷ is spelt *-able*.

insensible
▷ is spelt *-ible*.

inset
▷ the noun is stressed in the first syllable; the verb is stressed on the second and has a past tense and past participle **inset**.

insignia
▷ has plurals **insignia** and **insignias**.

insolence, insolent
▷ are spelt *-len-*.

install
▷ has two *l*s.

instalment
▷ has one *l* (AmE **installment**).

instigator
▷ is spelt *-or*.

insufferable
▷ is spelt *-able*.

insuperable
▷ is spelt *-able*.

insupportable
▷ is spelt *-able*.

insurable
▷ is spelt *-able*.

insurance / assurance
▷ an ***assurance*** company contracts to pay the customer an agreed sum when a specified inevitable event (eg her 60th birthday or her death if sooner) occurs; an ***insurance*** company contracts to pay the customer an agreed sum if a specified possible event (eg her house burning down) occurs.

insure / ensure
▷ ***ensure*** means 'make sure' (eg *ensure that the doors are locked before you leave*); ***insure*** means 'contract with an insurance company to be paid an agreed sum if a specified possible event occurs' (eg *is the house insured against fire?*).

insurmountable
▷ is spelt *-able*.

intaglio
▷ has a plural ***intaglios***.

intangible
▷ is spelt *-ible*.

intelligible
▷ is spelt *-ible*.

intense / intensive
▷ ***intense*** means 'very great' (eg *flowers withered in the intense heat*); ***intensive*** means 'thorough, very careful' (eg *kept in the intensive care unit until the fever subsided*).

interbreed
▷ has a past tense and past participle ***interbred***.

interceptor
▷ is spelt -or.

intercessor
▷ is spelt -or.

interchangeable
▷ is spelt -geable.

interdependence, interdependent
▷ are spelt -den-.

interference
▷ is spelt -ence.

interjection / exclamation
▷ both are followed by exclamation marks, but an ***exclamation*** gives some information about the outside world (eg *you silly little fool!* / *I must find those keys!*) whilst an ***interjection*** merely gives vent to the speaker's feelings (eg *ouch!* / *good Lord!* / *phew!*).

interment / internment
▷ ***interment*** means 'burial'; ***internment*** means 'imprisonment'.

intermezzo
▷ has plurals ***intermezzi*** and ***intermezzos***.

interminable
▷ is spelt -able.

internecine
▷ is pronounced *in-tur-**nee**-syn*.

interpret
▷ has a past tense and past participle ***interpreted*** and a present participle ***interpreting***.

interregnum
▷ has plurals ***interregnums*** (now in general use) and ***interregna***.

interrogation mark
▸ See **punctuation**.

interrogative
▷ in Grammar denotes a word that is used to ask a question, such as *interrogative adjectives*, *interrogative adverbs* and *interrogative pronouns*.
▸ See **adjectives**, **adverbs**, **pronouns**.

interrogator
▷ is spelt *-or*.

intolerable
▷ is spelt *-able*.

intolerance, intolerant
▷ are spelt *-an-*.

intransitive
▷ denotes those verbs that do not govern a direct object, as in
> *this meat stinks*
> *Fred is stupid*

but not as in
> *Jane kicked the cat*

intravert, introvert
▷ the second spelling is more common.

intrusive / obtrusive
▷ *intrusive* means 'pushing in where not wanted, prying' (eg *I am fed up with his intrusive questions about my private life*); *obtrusive* means 'sticking out, catching the eye when not wanted' (eg *painting the garden shed dark brown will make it less obtrusive*).

intuit
▷ has a past tense *intuited*.

invaluable
▷ is spelt *-able*.

invariable
▷ is spelt -*able*.

inventor
▷ is spelt -*or*.

inverted commas
▷ is another name for **quotation marks**; see **punctuation**.

invigilator
▷ is spelt -*or*.

invincible
▷ is spelt -*ible*.

inviolable
▷ is spelt -*able*.

invisible
▷ is spelt -*ible*.

invoke / evoke
▷ ***invoke*** means 'appeal to', 'call up (a spirit)', 'bring (a law, etc) into operation' (eg *invoked God as his witness / in his desperation Saul made the witch invoke the dead prophet Samuel and ask his advice / if our case fails in the national courts we will invoke the European Declaration on Human Rights*); ***evoke*** means 'cause' or 'bring into the mind' (eg *his accusations evoked an angry response / that scent always evokes fond memories*).

invulnerable
▷ is spelt -*able*.

ir- / il- / im- / in-
▷ these prefixes mean 'not' (eg *illegal* = not legal) or 'in, into, on' (eg *innate* = inborn, *irradiate* = put radiation into); the *ir*- form is used only before words that themselves begin with *r* (eg *irreverent* = *ir* + *reverent*).

irascible

irascible
▷ is spelt *-scible*.

ironworks
▷ may be treated as either singular or plural eg
  ✓ *the ironworks <u>is</u> in the next street*
  ✓ *the ironworks <u>are</u> in the next street*

irreconcilable
▷ is spelt *-lable* and stressed on the second or the fourth syllable.

irredeemable
▷ is spelt *-able*.

irreducible
▷ is spelt *-ible*.

irrefragable
▷ is spelt *-gable* and stressed on the second syllable.

irrefutable
▷ is spelt *-table* and stressed on the second or third syllable.

irregular
▷ is used to describe a word or construction that does not follow the standard grammatical rules (eg it is regular in English to form the plural of a noun by adding *s* to the singular as in *book, books*, but **irregular** plurals such as *child, children* also exist).

irrelevance, irrelevant
▷ are spelt *-van-*.

irremediable
▷ is spelt *-able* and pronounced *i-re-**meed**-i-ubl*.

irremovable
▷ is spelt *-vable*.

irreparable
▷ is spelt *-rable* and pronounced *i-**rep**-ur-ubl*.

irreplaceable
▷ is spelt *-ceable*.

irrepressible
▷ is spelt *-ible*.

irreproachable
▷ is spelt *-able*.

irresistible
▷ is spelt *-ible*.

irresponsible
▷ is spelt *-ible*.

irretrievable
▷ is spelt *-vable*.

irreversible
▷ is spelt *-versible*.

irrevocable
▷ is spelt *-cable* and pronounced *i-**rev**-uk-ubl*.

irrigable
▷ is spelt *-able*.

irritable
▷ is spelt *-able*.

-ise / -ize
▷ generally *-ize* is used almost exclusively in American English while both *-ise* and *-ize* are found in British English; there are a number of verbs which are always spelt *-ise* in both American and British English and all the commonest ones are listed at their alphabetical place: there is no simple rule for deciding which verbs have only the *-ise* spelling.

Islay
▷ is pronounced ***iy**-lu*.

isthmus
▷ has a plural ***isthmuses***.

its / it's
▷ spell ***its*** for 'of it' (eg *the cat was mewing for its kittens*) and ***it's*** for 'it is' or 'it has' (eg *it's brightening up now / it's gone nine o'clock*).

j

jackknife
▷ is spelt with two *k*s.

jail / gaol / goal
▷ *jail* and *gaol* are different spellings of a single word which means 'prison' and is pronounced *jayl*; the spelling *gaol* is now only used in official documents. *Goal* is a different word; it is pronounced *gohl* and means 'scoring-place, point scored' or 'purpose'.

jailor
▷ is spelt *-or*.

jardinière
▷ is spelt *-ère*.

jeans
▷ is plural when referring to denim trousers (eg *my jeans are torn*); the singular (*jean*) is used of the twilled cotton cloth from which they were formerly made (eg *jean is on special offer*); however, nowadays the material is described as *denim*, or *jean material*.

jeopardise, jeopardy
▷ both have a first syllable pronounced *jep*; the verb is spelt *-ise*.

jewellery / jewelry
▷ the first spelling is in British use, the second American; both are pronounced *juul-ri*.

jibe / gibe / gybe
▷ for 'mock' use **gibe** and for the sailing terms use **gybe**; **jibe** is a non-recommended alternative spelling for both and in American English also means 'agree with'.

jodhpurs
▷ is spelt *-dhp-*, is pronounced **jod**-*puhrz* and is plural.

judgement / judgment
▷ the first spelling is the preferred one.

judicial / judicious
▷ **judicial** means 'done by judges or law courts' (eg *to hang him on such flimsy evidence was nothing short of judicial murder*); **judicious** means 'careful, prudent' (eg *although he refused to award a first prize, by his judicious choice of words he avoided disheartening the competitors*).

jugful
▷ is spelt *-ful* and has a plural **jugfuls**.

junction / juncture
▷ a **junction** is a point where things (eg roads, wires, railway lines) meet; a **juncture** is a point in time, especially a critical one (eg *He rose to begin his speech, but at this juncture his voice failed him*).

junta
▷ should be pronounced as written, with the stress on the first syllable.

k

kaftan / caftan
▷ the second spelling is the preferred one.

kamikaze
▷ is spelt *-kaze* and pronounced *ka-mi-**kah**-zi*.

karaoke
▷ is spelt *-oke* and pronounced *ka-ri-**oh**-ki*.

Keswick
▷ is pronounced ***kes**-ik*.

Keynes
▷ the place-name (*Milton Keynes*) is pronounced *keenz*, the surname of the economist *kaynz*.

khaliph / caliph
▷ the second spelling is more common.

kibbutz
▷ has a plural ***kibbutzim***.

kilometre
▷ is pronounced *ki-**lom**-i-tur* or ***kil**-u-mee-tur*.

kimono
▷ has a plural ***kimonos***.

Kirkcudbright
▷ is pronounced *kir-**kuu**-bri*.

kissagram / kissogram
▷ the second spelling is more common.

kneel

kneel
▷ has past tenses and past participles **kneeled** or **knelt**.

knickers
▷ is plural.

knife
▷ has a plural **knives**.

knight errant
▷ has a plural **knights errant**.

knoll
▷ is pronounced *nohl*.

know
▷ has a past tense **knew** and a past participle **known**.

knowable
▷ is spelt *-able*.

knowledgeable
▷ is spelt *-eable*.

kopeck / kopek
▷ the second spelling is more common.

Koran / Qur'an
▷ the first spelling is more common.

krona / króna / krone
▷ **krona** is a Swedish currency unit and has a plural **kronor**; **króna** is an Icelandic currency unit and has a plural **krónur**; **krone** is a Danish and Norwegian currency unit and has a plural **kroner**.

kudos
▷ is singular and is pronounced **kyuu**-*dos*.

l

labium
▷ has a plural **labia**.

laboratory
▷ is pronounced lu-**bor**-ut-or-i or lu-**bor**-ut-ri.

lacquer
▷ is spelt -cqu-.

lacuna
▷ has plurals **lacunae** and **lacunas**.

ladies
▷ is singular when it means 'women's public lavatory' (eg *the ladies is the third door on the right*) and plural when it means 'women' (eg *a couple of old ladies were nattering in the corner of the snug*).

ladleful
▷ is spelt -*ful* and has a plural **ladlefuls**.

ladyfy
▷ is spelt -*dy*-.

lama / llama
▷ a **lama** is a Tibetan monk; a **llama** is a South American pack animal.

lamella
▷ has a plural **lamellae**.

lamentable
▷ is spelt -*able* and stressed on the first syllable.

larva
▷ has a plural *larvae*.

later / latter
▷ *later* means

- 'at some time after' or 'in the near future' (eg *they'll be here later on*).
- it is also the comparative of the adjective *late* (eg *she got there even later than I did*).

latter means

- 'second of two previously mentioned things' (eg *of the two we much preferred the latter*).
- 'nearer the end' (eg *the latter part of the holiday*).
- 'recent' (eg *the loose morals of these latter days*).

latex
▷ has plurals *latexes* (now in general use) and *latices*.

lath / lathe
▷ a *lath* is a strip of wood; a *lathe* is a cutting and polishing machine.

laudable
▷ is spelt *-able*.

laughable
▷ is spelt *-able*.

launderette / laundrette
▷ the first spelling is more common; it is pronounced as three syllables.

lawful / legal / legitimate
▷ *legal* means 'connected with the law' (eg *the legal profession*) or 'permitted by law or the rules' (eg *is it legal to capture that pawn?*); *legitimate* means 'honest, law-abiding' (eg *unlike the border rustlers, O'Toole was a legitimate livestock importer who filled in Customs forms and*

leaf

kept accounts), 'justified' (eg *in view of his past failures their caution is perfectly legitimate*) or 'born in wedlock'; **lawful** also means 'permitted by the law or rules', but is now used mostly in religious or moral contexts.

lay / lie

▷ as verbs, **lay** means 'place, set out', has a past tense and past participle **laid** and is transitive (eg *lay the clothes on the bed, please / she laid the table for supper / has the table been laid?*); **lie** is intransitive and has two senses

○ 'be in a flat position, remain, etc', when it has a present participle **lying**, a past tense **lay** and a past participle **lain** (eg *the books lay scattered across the floor / the topic has lain dormant for many years*).

○ 'tell lies', when it has a present participle **lying** and a past tense and past participle **lied**.
Do not use *laid* as a past tense of *lie* eg
    ✗   *the children laid asleep in the cave*

lea / lee

▷ a **lea** is a sort of field; **lee** means 'shelter, sheltered side' (eg *we will anchor in the lee of those cliffs until the storm blows out*).

lead

▷ two separate word-families share this spelling

○ those pronounced *leed* have a basic meaning 'guide by going in front of'; the verb has a past tense and past participle **led** and a present participle **leading**.

○ those pronounced *led* refer to the soft heavy grey metal; the verb means 'put lead on to' and has regular inflections (ie **leaded, leading**).

leaf

▷ has a plural **leaves**.

lean

lean
▷ the verb has past tenses and past participles **leant** (pronounced *lent*) and **leaned**.

lean-to
▷ has a plural **lean-tos**.

leap
▷ the verb has past tenses and past participles **leapt** (pronounced *lept*) and **leaped**.

learn
▷ has past tenses and past participles **learnt** and **learned** (pronounced as one syllable).

learned
▷ the adjective meaning 'knowing a lot' is pronounced as two syllables.

leave
▷ the verb has a past tense and past participle **left**.

ledger line / leger line
▷ the first spelling is more common.

legal / lawful / legitimate
▷ **legal** means 'connected with the law' (eg *the legal profession*) or 'permitted by law or the rules' (eg *is it legal to capture that pawn?*); **lawful** also means 'permitted by the law or rules', but is now used mostly in religious or moral contexts; **legitimate** means 'honest, law-abiding' (eg *unlike the border rustlers, O'Toole was a legitimate livestock importer who filled in Customs forms and kept accounts*), 'justified' (eg *in view of his past failures their caution is perfectly legitimate*) or 'born in wedlock'.

legible
▷ is spelt *-ible*.

lend / loan
▷ **lend** is a verb and has a past tense and past participle

lent; *loan* is both a noun and a verb, but many consider its use as a verb (eg *can you loan me £5?*) an Americanism.

lengthy / long
▷ both mean 'of great length', but *lengthy* is used mostly of speech and writing and often means 'boring because too long'.

less / fewer
▷ when speaking or writing of a number of individuals or separate units, use *fewer* followed by a plural noun (eg *fewer boys than girls sat the exam*); when speaking or writing of a single amount or quantity, use *less* followed by a singular noun (eg *put less tonic in next time*).

let
▷ has a past tense and past participle *let*.

lexeme
▷ denotes a word when considered purely as a unit of meaning: for example, in the sentences *he will go* and *he'll go* the letter-groups *will* and *'ll* both represent the same lexeme, while in the sentence *Joan lies in bed reading books that are full of lies* the two identical letter-groups *lies* represent two separate lexemes ('be flat out' and 'untruths').
➤ See also **grammatical word, orthographic word, phonological word**.

lexical verb
▷ denotes any verb, or phrase containing a verb, that describes an action, state or event eg
✓ *I think he was beginning to recognise his failings*
➤ See also **auxiliary verb, linking verb**.

liable / apt / likely / prone
▷ *apt* means 'tending to, in the habit of' (eg *grandma is apt*

to nod off after supper); **prone** is similar in meaning, but should only be used of persons or of things composed of persons (eg *the motor industry is prone to wildcat strikes*) and usually refers to what is considered to be bad actions. **Likely** means 'will probably' (eg *since he's a keen music-lover you're likely to see him at the concert*). **Liable** means 'runs the risk of, will probably' and usually refers to an unpleasant consequence of the subject of the sentence's previous action (eg *children who play in the road are liable to end up in hospital*).

liar
▷ is spelt *-ar*.

libel / slander
▷ in English law both terms refer to making an untrue statement which damages the reputation of a living person; **libel** is uttered publicly and deliberately (eg in print, on stage or in a broadcast), whereas **slander** occurs casually (eg in conversation). Neither term exists in Scottish law.

liberator
▷ is spelt *-or*.

libido
▷ has a plural **libidos**.

libretto
▷ has plurals **libretti** and **librettos**.

licence / license
▷ in British English the noun is spelt *-ce* and the verb *-se* (AmE uses *-se* for both).

lido
▷ is pronounced **lee**-*doh* and has a plural **lidos**.

lie / lay
▷ as verbs, **lay** means 'place, set out', has a past tense and

past participle **laid** and is transitive (eg *lay the clothes on the bed, please / she laid the table for supper / has the table been laid?*); **lie** is intransitive and has two senses

○ 'be in a flat position, remain, etc', when it has a present participle **lying**, a past tense **lay** and a past participle **lain** (eg *the books lay scattered across the floor / the topic has lain dormant for many years*).

○ 'tell lies', when it has a present participle **lying** and a past tense and past participle **lied**.

Do not use *laid* as a past tense of *lie* eg

      ✗ *the children laid asleep in the cave*

Liebfraumilch
▷ is pronounced **leeb**-*frow-milkh*.

lied
▷ the noun meaning 'song' is pronounced *leed* and has a plural **lieder**.

lieutenant
▷ in British English the first syllable is pronounced *lef-* and spelt *lieu-*; in American English the first syllable is pronounced *loo-* and spelt *lieu-*.

life
▷ has a plural **lives**.

light
▷ the verb has past tenses and past participles **lit** and **lighted**.

likeable
▷ is spelt *-eable*.

likely / apt / liable / prone
▷ **apt** means 'tending to, in the habit of' (eg *grandma is apt to nod off after supper*); **prone** is similar in meaning, but should only be used of persons or of things composed of persons (eg *the motor industry is prone to wildcat*

limbo

strikes) and usually refers to what is considered to be bad actions. **Likely** means 'will probably' (eg *since he's a keen music-lover you're likely to see him at the concert*). **Liable** means 'runs the risk of, will probably' and usually refers to an unpleasant consequence of the subject of the sentence's previous action (eg *children who play in the road are liable to end up in hospital*).

limbo
▷ has a plural *limbos*.

limiting adjective
➤ See **adjectives**.

limo
▷ has a plural *limos*.

linage / lineage
▷ *linage* means 'number of lines in a piece of printed matter' and is pronounced *liyn-ij*; *lineage* means 'ancestry' and is pronounced *lin-i-ij*.

linctus
▷ has a plural *linctuses*.

lineal, lineament
▷ are both pronounced *lin-i-a-*.

ling
▷ the noun, denoting a sort of cod, has two plurals:
  - ○ *ling*, when the group is thought of as a whole (eg *saw a large shoal of ling on the port bow*).
  - ○ *lings*, when the group is thought of as a set of individuals (eg *only two lings in the pool, one of which looked pretty sickly*).

lingerie
▷ is pronounced *la^{ng}-jer-ee*.

lingo
▷ has a plural **lingos**.

lingua franca
▷ has a plural **lingua francas**.

linguistics
▷ denotes the scientific study of language and is singular.

linking verb
▷ denotes any verb that simply serves as a link between the subject of a sentence and its complement, as in *Fred was old and bald* | *it looks good but it doesn't taste right*.
➤ See also **auxiliary verb, lexical verb**.

lino
▷ has a plural **linos**.

liquefy
▷ is spelt *-efy*.

liqueur / liquor
▷ **liqueur** is spelt *-queur* and denotes a drink made from spirits and flavoured with fruit essences, etc; **liquor** denotes any alcoholic drink.

literally
▷ means 'really, exactly as the word says' eg
    ✓ *as a result of the civil war and droughts, thousands in Ethiopia were literally starving to death*

not 'almost, as good as, metaphorically' eg
    ✗ *by the end of his 'short walk' I was literally at my last gasp*

litho
▷ has a plural **lithos**.

litotes
▷ is a figure of speech which uses deliberate under-

liveable

▷ is spelt *-eable*.

ll

▷ is pronounced *thl* in Welsh words, eg *Llangollen* is pronounced *thlan-**goth**-len*.

llama / lama

▷ a *llama* is a South American pack animal; a *lama* is a Tibetan monk.

loaf

▷ has a plural *loaves*.

loan / lend

▷ *lend* is a verb and has a past tense and past participle *lent*; *loan* is both a noun and a verb, but many consider its use as a verb (eg *can you loan me £5?*) an Americanism.

loan translation

▷ denotes a word or phrase that has been created by translating a foreign word or phrase that has the same meaning (eg *motorway* from German *Autobahn*).

loanword

▷ denotes a word or phrase (eg *blitzkrieg, mañana*) that is borrowed from a foreign language.

loath / loathe

▷ *loath* is an adjective that means 'reluctant' (eg *am loath to ask him to pay me now he has lost his job*); *loathe* is a verb that means 'feel disgust at' (eg *loathe her patronizing attitude*).

loco

▷ the noun has a plural *locos*.

luxuriant

locus
▷ has a plural *loci*.

logistics
▷ may be used as a singular or a plural.

logo
▷ is pronounced *loh*-goh or *log*-oh and has a plural *logos*.

-logy
▷ is a suffix which usually denotes some academic subject or study (eg *sociology, Kremlinology*).

lone
▷ must always precede its noun eg
  - ✓ *a lone sheep crossed the road*
  - ✗ *the sheep was lone in the field*

long / lengthy
▷ both mean 'of great length', but *lengthy* is used mostly of speech and writing and often means 'boring because too long'.

loose / lose
▷ as verbs, *loose* is pronounced *loos* and means 'untie', and *lose* is pronounced *looz* (which has a past tense and past participle *lost*) and means 'mislay', 'fail to get', 'be deprived of'.

lough
▷ is pronounced *lokh*.

louse
▷ has a plural *lice*.

lumen
▷ has plurals *lumina* and *lumens*.

luxuriant / luxurious
▷ *luxuriant* means 'growing profusely' (eg *a luxuriant crop*

-ly

of weeds greeted the gardener's return from holiday); ***luxurious*** *means 'very comfortable'.*

-ly
▷ is a suffix used to
   - form adverbs from adjectives (eg *clever, cleverly*).
   - form adverbs and adjectives with the sense 'at intervals of' (eg *daily*).
   - form adjectives meaning 'like a…' (eg *brotherly love*).

m

machete
▷ is pronounced *mu-**shet**-i*.

machismo
▷ is pronounced *mu-**chiz**-mo* or *mu-**kiz**-mo*.

macho
▷ is pronounced ***mach**-oh*.

mackerel
▷ has two plurals
  - ○ ***mackerel***, when the group is thought of as a whole (eg *saw a large shoal of mackerel on the port bow*).
  - ○ ***mackerels***, when the group is thought of as a set of individuals (eg *only two mackerels in the pool, one of which looked pretty sickly*).

macramé
▷ is pronounced *mu-**krah**-mi*.

macro
▷ has a plural ***macros***.

macro- / mega-
▷ both prefixes mean 'large'; ***macro-*** also means 'long' (eg *macrobiotic*, 'life-prolonging') and 'excessively large' (eg *macrocephaly*, 'having an over-large head'); when prefixed to units of measurement ***mega-*** means 'million' (eg *megawatt*, *megaton*), except in computing, where a *megabyte* denotes 1048576 (or 2^{100}) bytes.

macula
▷ has a plural *maculae*.

madam / madame
▷ these are basically the English and French forms of the same word, but their forms and meanings in current English need some disentangling

○ *madam* is a polite form of address to a woman (eg *can I help you, madam?*), is stressed on the first syllable and has in this sense no plural.

○ *madam* may also be used before a job-title when the holder is a woman (eg *Madam Chairman, I beg leave to propose the motion*).

○ *madam* is also used as a noun meaning 'arrogant woman' and 'female brothel-keeper'; in these senses it has a plural *madams*.

○ *madame* (pronounced *ma-dahm*) is used instead of *Mrs* before the surnames of French women and is usually abbreviated to **Mme**; its plural **mesdames** (pronounced *may-dahm*) is also used in English business reports, etc to refer by surname to a number of women and is equivalent in use to the male form *Messrs* (eg *present: Mesdames Jones, Smith and Forbes; Messrs McPherson and O'Donovan* which can also be written as *present: Mrs Jones, Mrs Smith, Mrs Forbes, Mr McPherson and Mr O'Donovan*).

Madeira
▷ is spelt *-ei-*.

maestro
▷ is pronounced **miy**-*stroh* and has plural *maestros* (now in general use) and *maestri*.

Mafioso
▷ has a plural *Mafiosi*.

maisonette

magazine
▷ is usually stressed on the third syllable; stress on the first is also correct.

Magdalen / Magdalene
▷ the first is the name of an Oxford college, the second of a Cambridge college; both are pronounced **mawd**-*lin*. When used as a woman's name **Magdalen** is pronounced as it is written.

magic / magical
▷ both mean 'done by, to do with, magic'; **magical** also means 'enchanting, spellbinding' (eg *as an encore she gave a magical rendering of a Strauss song*).

magma
▷ has plurals **magmas** and **magmata**.

magus
▷ has a plural **magi** (pronounced **may**-*jiy*).

maharaja / maharajah
▷ the second spelling is more common.

maharanee / maharani
▷ the second spelling is more common.

Mahomet / Mohammed / Muhammad
▷ the second spelling is more common.

main clause
➤ See **clauses and phrases**.

maintenance
▷ is spelt *-ance*.

main verb
▷ denotes the principal verb in a sentence, which will be in the indicative or imperative mood.

maisonette / maisonnette
▷ the first spelling is more common.

make

make
▷ has a past tense and past participle *made*.

majority
▷ is singular, but is usually followed by a plural verb when the reference is to a number of items, etc (eg *the majority of her paintings have been lost*).

male / masculine
▷ as adjectives, *male* means 'of that sex that begets young or has similar sexual characteristics' (eg *a male pig is called a boar*) and *masculine* means 'mannish' (eg *she has a masculine voice*); for the grammatical sense of masculine see separate entry.

malign / malignant
▷ both words refer to a disease, especially cancer, which if left untreated may cause death; *malign* also refers to being evil in nature or influence (eg *the malign influence of the spell began to take hold*) and *malignant* also refers to having an attitude or intention to harm another (eg *the witch's malignant glare made my blood run cold*).

mall
▷ is now usually pronounced *mal*; the pronunciation *mawl* is also correct.

man
▷ has a plural *men*; see also **political correctness**.

manageable
▷ is spelt *-eable*.

mandatory
▷ is spelt *-ory* and pronounced *man*-du-tu-ri.

mango
▷ has plurals *mangos* and *mangoes*.

maniacal
▷ is pronounced mu-*niy*-u-kul.

manifesto
▷ has plurals *manifestos* and *manifestoes*.

mankind
▷ is plural.

manoeuvrable
▷ is spelt *-oeuvr-* and *-able*.

manoeuvre
▷ is spelt *-oeuvre*.

manservant
▷ has a plural *menservants*.

mantis
▷ has plurals *mantises* (in general use) and *mantes*.

margarine
▷ is spelt *-gar-* but pronounced *-jur-*.

marihuana / marijuana
▷ the second spelling is more common.

martello
▷ has a plural *martellos*.

masculine
▷ denotes the grammatical gender to which the nouns denoting male people, animals, etc belong; this distinction does not exist in English Grammar (see **gender**).

masculine / male
▷ as adjectives, **male** means 'of that sex that begets young or has similar sexual characteristics' (eg *a male pig is called a boar*) and **masculine** means 'mannish' (eg *she has a masculine voice*); for **masculine**'s grammatical sense see previous entry.

mass noun or uncountable noun
▷ is a noun (such as *furniture*) that cannot be counted eg
    ✗   *two furnitures*

mat

has no plural and cannot be used with the indefinite article eg

    ✗   *a furniture*

➤ See also **collective noun**, **count noun**, **nouns**.

mat / matt
▷ for the adjective the second spelling is more common.

matey / maty
▷ the first spelling is more common.

mathematics
▷ is singular.

matins / mattins
▷ the first spelling is more common; the word may be treated as a singular or a plural.

matrix
▷ has plurals *matrices* and *matrixes*.

maximum
▷ has a plural *maxima*; strictly speaking, the singular *maximum* should always be followed by a singular verb (eg *the maximum is 30 tons*); but when *maximum* is followed by a plural noun phrase that defines it (eg *a maximum of 30 persons*), the verb tends to be 'attracted' into the plural (eg *a maximum of 30 persons are permitted to use the lift at any one time*) and nowadays most people accept this as correct English.

may / can
▷ the traditional distinction was that *can* refers to *ability* (eg *you can't jump as high as a house*) and *may* (which has a past tense *might*) to *permission* (eg *may I get you another drink?*), but nowadays the verbs are used interchangeably except in the most formal contexts.

mean
▷ the verb has a past tense and past participle *meant*.

means
▷ the noun has two senses

○ 'method or way of achieving' and is singular or plural eg
- ✓ *this is just <u>a</u> means to our end*
- ✓ *there <u>are</u> various means of achieving that*

○ 'financial resources' and is plural eg
- ✓ *our means <u>are</u> insufficient to fund our present lifestyle*

measles
▷ is singular.

media
▷ is plural in all senses, including that of 'the press'; so
- ✗ *the media <u>is</u>*

is always wrong.
➤ See also **medium**.

mediator
▷ is spelt *-or*.

mediaeval / medieval
▷ the second spelling is more common.

medicine
▷ is spelt *-dic-* but pronounced ***med**-sun* or ***med**-i-sin*.

Mediterranean
▷ has one *t* and two *r*s.

medium
▷ has two plurals

○ ***media*** when referring to the press, TV, etc (eg *at first, local radio was the only <u>medium</u> that reported on his progress, but since his London win all the <u>media</u> are taking an interest*); see also **media**.

meet

○ ***mediums*** in all other senses (eg *exhibition shows work in several mediums / 300 mediums attended a Spiritualist conference at Harrogate*).

meet
▷ the verb has a past tense and past participle ***met***.

mega- / macro-
▷ both prefixes mean 'large'; when prefixed to units of measurement ***mega-*** means 'million' (eg *megawatt, megaton*), except in computing, where a *megabyte* denotes 1048576 (or 2^{100}) bytes; ***macro-*** also means 'long' (eg *macrobiotic*, 'life-prolonging') and 'excessively large' (eg *macrocephaly*, 'having an over-large head'.

mélange
▷ is spelt *mél-* and pronounced *may-lahnzh*.

mêlée
▷ is spelt *mêl-* and *ée* and pronounced ***me**-lay* or *me-**lay***.

memento
▷ has plurals ***mementos*** and ***mementoes***.

memo
▷ has a plural ***memos***.

mendacity / mendicity
▷ the first means 'lying', the second 'beggary'.

meninx
▷ has a plural ***meninges***.

meniscus
▷ has plurals ***meniscuses*** (in general use) and ***menisci*** (in scientific and technical writing).

-ment
▷ is a suffix denoting action (eg *repayment, treatment*) or state or condition (eg *enjoyment, merriment*).

merchandise
▷ the noun and verb are both spelt *-ise*.

meringue
▷ is spelt *-ingue* but pronounced *mu-**rang***.

merino
▷ has a plural ***merinos***.

Messrs
▷ is pronounced ***mes***-*uz* and is the plural of *Mr*; it is usually used in English business reports, etc to refer by surname to a list of men (eg *present: Messrs McPherson and O'Donovan* which can also be expanded out to *present: Mr McPherson and Mr O'Donovan*).
➤ See also **Mesdames** at **madame**.

metamorphosis
▷ may be stressed on the third or fourth syllables; it has a plural ***metamorphoses***.

metaphor
▷ denotes a figure of speech in which the person or thing described is spoken of as if it actually were the thing it in fact only resembles (eg *she is a pig* instead of *she is like a pig*).

metastasis
▷ is stressed on the second syllable and has a plural ***metastases***.

meteorological, meteorologist, meteorological
▷ are spelt *-teor-*.

meter / metre
▷ a ***meter*** is a measuring and recording instrument; a ***metre*** is a unit of length.

métier
▷ is spelt *méti-* and pronounced ***me***-*ti-ay*.

metonymy
▷ denotes a figure of speech in which an element is used instead of the whole (eg *the bottle*, meaning 'hard drinking', *the turf*, meaning 'horse-racing').

mews
▷ is singular and has plurals *mews* and *mewses*.

mezzanine
▷ is spelt with two *z*s and two (not three) *n*s; it is pronounced *met*-sun-een.

miasma
▷ has plurals *miasmata* and *miasmas*.

Michigan
▷ is pronounced *mish*-ig-un.

micro
▷ has a plural *micros*.

micro- / milli-
▷ *micro-* means 'very small' (eg *microchip, microbore*); *milli-* means 'a thousand' (eg *millipede*) or 'a thousandth' (eg *millisecond*).

midday, midnight
▷ the traditional rule is to use **12pm** for midday (and *11.59am* and *12.01pm* for the minute before and after midday) and **12am** for midnight (and *11.59pm* and *12.01am* for the minute before and after midnight); to avoid any danger of misunderstanding use **noon**, **midday**, **midnight** or **12 noon**, **12 midnight**.

middle / centre
▷ basically both words mean the same, but the information given by **centre** is felt to be more precise: for example, the *centre* of a room is a spot roughly (or exactly) measur-

able from its four walls, while its *middle* is its whole floor area apart from the edges.

Middle East
▷ denotes the Arabic-speaking countries situated in the Arabian Peninsula and round the eastern end of the Mediterranean, together with Turkey, Cyprus, Iran and North Africa.

midshipman
▷ has a plural **midshipmen**.

midwife
▷ has a plural **midwives**.

mien
▷ is pronounced *meen*.

might / could
▷ **could** is used to indicate permission (eg *she said they could all go provided they behaved themselves*) and **might** to indicate possibility (eg *if we get a move on we still might catch the 2.30 train*).

mileage / milage
▷ the first spelling is more common.

mileometer / milometer
▷ the first spelling is more common.

milieu
▷ is spelt *-lieu*, pronounced *meel-**yuh*** and has plurals **milieux** and **milieus**.

militate / mitigate
▷ **militate** means 'act upon, influence' and is usually followed by *for* or *against* (eg *the fog warnings militated against our going out that night*); **mitigate** means 'excuse, make less serious' (eg *this lotion will mitigate the*

millennium

soreness). The two words are not interchangeable and *mitigate against* is always wrong.

millennium
▷ is spelt with two *l*s and two *n*s; it has a plural ***millennia***. Since the first millennium began with the year 1 (not 0), strictly speaking, the forthcoming millennium should be celebrated on the night of 31 December 2000 and the year 2000 spoken of as part of the nineteenth century. Most people, however, think (and speak) of the century ending and the millennium occurring, at 31 December 1999 when the digital displays flip over to show the 2 (and this *is* of course where 'the nineteen-hundreds end'); and this is when the event will be officially celebrated.

milli- / micro-
▷ ***milli-*** means 'a thousand' (eg *millipede*) or 'a thousandth' (eg *millisecond*); ***micro-*** means 'very small' (eg *microchip*, *microbore*).

million / millions
▷ when preceded by a numeral use ***million*** (eg *three million unemployed*); when just meaning 'a lot' use ***millions*** (eg *I've told you millions of times I don't like toffees*).

minimum
▷ has plurals ***minimums*** and ***minima***; strictly speaking, the singular noun should always be followed by a singular verb (eg *the minimum is 30p*); but when ***minimum*** is followed by a plural noun phrase that defines it (eg *a minimum of 5 persons*), the verb tends to be 'attracted' into the plural (eg *a minimum of 5 persons constitute a quorum*) and nowadays most people accept this as correct English.

miniscule / minuscule
▷ the second spelling is the correct one.

mink
▷ has a plural *mink*.

minority
▷ is singular, but is usually followed by a plural verb when the reference is to a number of items, etc (eg *a sizeable minority of the voters <u>have</u> deliberately spoiled their ballots in protest*).

mis-
▷ is a prefix forming words meaning 'wrongly, badly' (eg *misuse*) or 'lack of' (eg *mistrust*).

mischief
▷ is spelt *-chie-*.

mischievous
▷ is spelt *-chie-* and *-vous* and pronounced **mis**-*chiv-us*.

miscible
▷ is spelt *-scible* and pronounced **mis**-*ibl*.

mishit
▷ is spelt with one *s*, pronounced *mis*-**hit** and has a past tense and past participle **mishit**.

mislay
▷ has a past tense and past participle **mislaid**.

mislead
▷ has a past tense and past participle **misled**.

misread
▷ has a past tense and past participle **misread** (pronounced *mis*-**red**).

misrelated participle
➤ See **dangling participle**.

Mississippi
▷ has four *ss*, four *is* and two *ps*.

misspell

misspell
▷ is spelt with two *ss* and two *ls* and has past tenses and past participles **misspelt** and **misspelled**.

misspend
▷ is spelt with two *ss* and has a past tense and past participle **misspent**.

mistake
▷ has a past tense **mistook** and a past participle **mistaken**.

mistletoe
▷ is spelt *-stle-*.

misunderstand
▷ has a past tense and past participle **misunderstood**.

misuse / abuse
▷ **abuse** tends to refer to the use of things for the wrong purposes (eg *the President's abuse of his powers in giving Government posts to all his friends*), **misuse** to the use of things in the wrong way (eg *years of misuse finally made the handle drop off*).

mitigate / militate
▷ **mitigate** means 'excuse, make less serious' (eg *this lotion will mitigate the soreness*); **militate** means 'act upon, influence' and is usually followed by *for* or *against* (eg *the fog warnings militated against our going out that night*). The two words are not interchangeable and *mitigate against* is always wrong.

mnemonic
▷ is spelt *mne-* but pronounced *nee-*.

modal
▷ in Grammar denotes a verb (also called **modal auxiliary** or **modal verb**) such as *can, dare, may, need, ought to* which is used with another verb to express condition, possibility or obligation (eg *we still might get there in time*

more than

/ *you <u>ought to be</u> more polite*).
➤ See also **primary auxiliary verb**.

modifier
▷ denotes a word or phrase that modifies or identifies the meaning of another word in the sentence (eg *she was <u>very</u> angry* | *the man <u>in the green hat</u>*).

Mohammed / Mahomet / Muhammad
▷ the first spelling is more common.

Mohammedan / Moslem / Muslim
▷ both **Moslem** and **Muslim** are correct; the second is now more common. **Mohammedan** is thought offensive by some Muslims and should be avoided.

Mojave
▷ is pronounced *moh-**hah**-vi*.

momentarily, momentary
▷ both should be stressed on the first syllable.

money
▷ is a mass noun except in the commercial and legal sense 'sum of money', where it has plurals **moneys** or **monies**.

mood
▷ denotes in Grammar one of the sets of forms taken by a verb. In English there are 3 moods:

○ ***indicative***, used to state or ask about facts (eg *the cat <u>sat</u> on the mat*).

○ ***imperative***, used to give orders (eg *go away!*).

○ ***subjunctive***, used to express uncertainty or wishes (eg *if that <u>be</u> so* / *God <u>grant</u> us success!*)
➤ See also **conditionals**.

more than
▷ is singular, but is usually followed by a plural verb when the number, etc exceeded is itself plural (eg *more than <u>one</u>*

morello

company <u>has</u> crashed this week / more than <u>five</u> companies <u>have</u> crashed this week).

morello
▷ has a plural **morellos**.

mortar / cement / concete
▷ **cement** is any material which sets hard to form a building material or to stick other objects together. The commonest building cement is made from clay and limestone; when this is mixed with sand and water it forms **mortar** and when mixed with sand, water and small stones it forms **concrete**. Both mortar and cement are, however, often called 'concrete' in informal speech.

mortgage
▷ is spelt *mort-*.

Moslem / Mohammedan / Muslim
▷ both **Moslem** and **Muslim** are correct; the latter is now more common. **Mohammedan** is thought offensive by some Muslims and should be avoided.

motto
▷ has plurals **mottos** and **mottoes**.

moussaka
▷ has two *ss* and is pronounced *moo-**sah**-ka*.

movable / moveable
▷ the first spelling is more common.

mow
▷ has a past tense **mowed** and a past participle **mown**.

much
▷ has a comparative **more** and a superlative **most**.

mucous / mucus
▷ the first is the adjective, the second the noun.

Muhammad / Mohammed / Mahomet
▷ the second spelling is more common.

multi-
▷ is a prefix that means 'many' (eg *multiracial, multicultural*).

mumps
▷ is singular (eg *mumps is nasty*).

Munich
▷ is pronounced ***myuu***-*nik* and is the English version of the German *München*.

Muscadet
▷ is pronounced ***mus***-*ku-day*.

mutable
▷ is spelt *-table*.

mutual / common
▷ the traditional rule is that **common** means 'belonging to, used by several/many people' (eg *it's common knowledge that John is a liar / our common interest in gardening prompts me to send you this seed catalogue*) and **mutual** means 'reciprocal' (eg *though they never became friends, their years in the trenches together forged a strong mutual respect*); but many people now use **mutual** (eg *our mutual friend*) as if it meant 'shared'.

myna / mynah
▷ the first spelling is more common.

n

nadir
▷ is pronounced *nay*-deer or *na*-deer.

naevus
▷ has a plural ***naevi***.

naiad
▷ has plurals ***naiads*** and ***naiades*** (pronounced ***niy***-ad-eez).

naïve / naive
▷ the first spelling is closer to the original French and is preferred by some; the word is pronounced niy-***eev*** or nah-***eev***.

naïvety / naivety
▷ the first spelling is closer to the original French and is preferred by some; the first two syllables are pronounced as in the preceding entry and are followed by either *-e-ti* (making four syllables in all) or by *-ti* (making three).

nameable
▷ is spelt *-eable*.

naphtha
▷ is spelt *-phtha*.

narcissus
▷ has plurals ***narcissuses*** and ***narcissi***.

narcosis
▷ has a plural ***narcoses***.

naturalist / naturist
▷ a *naturalist* studies animal and plant life; a *naturist* is a nudist.

naught / nought
▷ *naught* means 'nothing' (eg *naught for your comfort*); *nought* means 'the figure zero' (eg *knock a couple of noughts off the price and I might consider it*).

Neanderthal
▷ is pronounced *ni-**an**-dur-tahl*.

nebula
▷ has plurals **nebulae** and **nebulas**.

necessarily
▷ is usually stressed on the first syllable but can also be stressed on the third syllable.

neckerchief
▷ is spelt *-chief* and has plurals **neckerchiefs** and **neckerchieves**.

necrosis
▷ had a plural **necroses**.

née
▷ is spelt *-ée* and pronounced *nay*.

---

negatives

A **negative** is a word such as *no, not, never, nobody* which can be put into a simple sentence, or into a clause or phrase of a complex or compound sentence, to make it mean the opposite of what it did before (eg *he said that / he never said that*): such a sentence, clause or phrase is called a **negative sentence** (or clause or phrase).

• Double negative
When two negatives are used in a simple sentence or within a

négligée

single clause in a longer sentence (eg *he didn't do nothing*) the meaning of the sentence, etc differs radically according to whether the speaker or writer is using Standard or non-standard English:

- In Standard English the two negatives cancel each other out, so that *he didn't do nothing* would mean 'he did (*or* he must have done) something': this can be useful for hinting at opinions one does not wish to state directly; another example is *he didn't not come* meaning 'he did come'. Double negatives are often considered to be bad style.
- In non-standard English the two negatives strengthen each other, so that *'he didn't do nothing'* would mean *'he didn't do anything at all'*.

négligée / negligee
▷ the first spelling is more common.

negligence
▷ is spelt *-ence*.

negligible
▷ is spelt *-gible* (pronounced *-jibl*).

negotiable
▷ is spelt *-able*.

negotiator
▷ is spelt *-or*.

neighbour
▷ is spelt *neigh-* and *bour* (AmE **neighbor**).

neither
▷ is spelt *nei-* and pronounced **niy**-*dhur* or **nee**-*dhur*.

neither ... nor
▷ use the following rules to decide whether the verb should be singular or plural

nicety

- when both alternatives are third-person and singular, the verb is singular (eg *neither John nor Bill has a clue about navigation*); in informal speech or writing, however, the plural is often found (eg *I've asked around and neither Alison nor Jane have seen it*).
- when one alternative is singular and the other is plural, the verb is plural (eg *neither Mary nor her parents have arrived*).
- when the alternatives are both singular but not both third-person, the verb should either agree with the nearest (eg *neither I nor he has any idea where it is*) or be put into the plural (eg *neither I nor he have any idea where it is*).

neo-
▷ is a prefix meaning 'new, revised, revived' (eg *neo-classicism*, *neofascism*) or 'recently' (eg *neonatal*).

net / nett
▷ the first spelling is more common in all senses.

neurosis
▷ has a plural ***neuroses***.

neuter
➤ See **gender**.

neutrino
▷ has a plural ***neutrinos***.

news
▷ is nowadays always treated as a singular noun (eg *the news is bad*).

nexus
▷ has plurals ***nexuses*** (now in general use) and ***nexus***.

nicety
▷ is pronounced *niy-sut-i*.

niello

niello
▷ has a plural **nielli**.

nimbus
▷ has plurals **nimbuses** (now in general use) and **nimbi**.

ninja
▷ has plurals **ninja** and **ninjas**.

no
➤ See **negatives**.

nominative case
▷ is another name for the **subjective case**, which denotes the form taken by pronouns which are the subject of a verb (eg *I* in *I hit him*).

non-defining relative clause
➤ See **clauses and phrases**.

none
▷ when **none** refers back to a plural noun (eg *none of the boys*) it is followed by a singular verb when the sense is 'not one does' and by a plural verb when the sense is 'all do not' (eg *none of us is the least bit interested* / *none of us speak French*).

non-finite clause
▷ denotes in Grammar a clause that has a non-finite verb in it.

non-finite verb
▷ denotes a verb that is in one of the forms (infinitive, participle or gerund) which are not governed by their subject (eg *she likes him to write to her every day* / *I don't like swimming*).
➤ See also **finite verb**, **clauses and phrases**.

non-restrictive relative clause
➤ See **clauses and phrases**.

nouns

Northants
▷ is an abbreviation for Northamptonshire, the English county, and has no full stop after it (except when it ends a sentence).

Norwich
▷ is pronounced **no**-rij.

not
➤ See **negatives**.

noticeable
▷ is spelt -eable.

notifiable
▷ is spelt -iable.

nought / naught
▷ **nought** means 'the figure zero' (eg *knock a couple of noughts off the price and I might consider it*); **naught** means 'nothing' (eg *naught for your comfort*).

noun clause or phrase
➤ See **clauses and phrases**.

---

nouns

A **noun** is a word that is used as the name of a person (eg *John*), animal (eg *sheep*), thing (eg *table*), place (eg *Manchester*), quality (eg *loudness*) or action (eg *dancing*).

• **Classifications of nouns**

There are three main systems for classifying different types of nouns:

○ ***concrete nouns* / *abstract nouns***.
○ ***proper nouns* / *common nouns***.
○ ***count nouns* / *mass nouns* / *collective nouns***.

➤ See separate entries for more information on these noun types.

nova

• Plurals of nouns

Most nouns form their plural by adding -s to their singular form. Exceptions are:

- Nouns that end in -y form their plural in -ies (eg quality, qualities), unless the -y is preceded by a vowel (eg day, days / journey, journeys).
- Nouns that end in s, z, x, or sh form their plural by adding -es to their singular form (eg buzz, buzzes).
- Nouns that end in a -ch that is pronounced as in church form their plural by adding -es to their singular form (eg church, churches); the others simply add -s (eg monarch, monarchs).
- Most (but not all) nouns whose singular ends in -a, -f, -fe, -ful, -ies, -is, -o, -on, -um, -us: their plurals are given at their alphabetical place.
- A small group of nouns that form their plural by changing the root vowel (eg mouse, mice / tooth, teeth) or by adding -en to their singular form or some modification of it (eg child, children / ox, oxen): their plurals are given at their alphabetical place.

➤ There are many exceptions to the above rules: all common words whose plurals are unusual in some way are listed (and their plural form given) at their alphabetical place.

nova
▷ has a plural **novae**.

nucleus
▷ has a plural **nucleae**.

nuisance
▷ is spelt *nuis-* and *-ance*.

number
▷ denotes the grammatical classification of word forms into singular and plural.

number of
▷ **a number of** is followed by a plural verb (eg *a number of cats were sunning themselves on the wall*); **the number of** is followed by a singular verb (eg *the number of accidents is bound to rise*).

numbskull / numskull
▷ the second spelling is more common.

nuncio
▷ has a plural ***nuncios***.

nympho
▷ has a plural ***nymphos***.

O

O / oh
▷ in modern English **O** is only used when calling upon a person or thing whose name, etc immediately follows (eg *O God!*); in all other contexts **oh** is used (eg *oh for a cup of tea!* / *oh, you silly boy!* / *oh no!*).

oasis
▷ has a plural **oases**.

obbligato
▷ has plurals **obbligatos** and **obbligati**.

obedience
▷ is spelt *-ence*.

obeisance
▷ is pronounced *oh-**bay**-sns*.

object
▷ is the grammatical name for

○ the word or phrase that denotes the person or thing that receives the action of the verb, either directly (as *ball* in *Fred kicked the ball*) or indirectly (as in *give me the book*, where *me* is the **indirect object** and *the book* is the **direct object** of the verb *give*).

○ a word or phrase that is governed by a preposition (eg in *they sat under the big tree* the phrase *the big tree* is the **object** of the preposition *under*).

obtrusive

objective case
▷ denotes the form taken by English pronouns when governed by a transitive verb or preposition (eg *him* in *she saw him* and *a policeman stood beside him*). In informal speech the objective case is also often used after the verb *to be* (eg *it's him again*) and when standing alone (eg *'Who did that?' 'Me.'*).

obligatory
▷ is stressed on the second syllable.

oblique
➤ See **punctuation**.

oblivious
▷ means
  ○ 'forgetful' and is followed by *of* (eg *oblivious of his promise to his parents, he drank too much and stayed out all night*).
  ○ 'unaware of' and is followed by *of* or (less correctly) *to* (eg *she seems completely oblivious of/to the disturbance caused by her son's radio*).

obloquy
▷ has a plural ***obloquies***.

observance / observation
▷ although both derived from the verb *to observe*, these nouns have different meanings
  ○ ***observance*** (which is spelt *-ance*) means 'obeying a rule, keeping a custom' (*observance of the speed limit will be strictly enforced / Lord's Day Observance Society*).
  ○ ***observation*** means 'watching or noticing' or 'remark' (eg *kept in hospital for observation / her mother made some tart observations on the new dress*).

obtrusive / intrusive
▷ ***obtrusive*** means 'sticking out, catching the eye when

225

occur

not wanted' (eg *painting the garden shed dark brown will make it less obtrusive*); ***intrusive*** means 'pushing in where not wanted, prying' (eg *I am fed up with his intrusive questions about my private life*).

occur
▷ has a past tense and past participle ***occurred*** and a present participle ***occurring***.

occurrence
▷ is spelt *-ence*.

octavo
▷ has a plural ***octavos***.

octet
▷ is spelt *tet*.

octopus
▷ has a plural ***octopuses***.

odds
▷ is plural.

Odysseus
▷ is pronounced *o-**dis**-yoos*.

Oedipus
▷ is pronounced ***ee**-di-pus*.

-oes / -os / -i
▷ certain words of Italian origin whose singular ends in *-o* have a plural in *-i*; most other words whose singular ends in *-o* have plurals in *-os* or *-oes*. There are no simple universal rules for deciding the plural of a particular *-o* word and the commonest ones are listed at their alphabetical place in this book.

official / officious
▷ ***official*** means 'of or about or for persons in authority' (eg *official dress*) or 'having authority' (eg *the official re-*

sults are not available yet); **officious** means 'eager to interfere' and 'over-strict in enforcing rules' (eg *by the time I had noticed Steve was missing some officious bystander was already marching him off to the Lost Children tent*).

offspring
▷ has a plural **offspring**.

ogreish / ogrish
▷ the first spelling is marginally better.

oh / O
▷ in modern English **O** is only used when calling upon a person or thing whose name, etc immediately follows (eg *O God!*); in all other contexts **oh** is used (eg *oh for a cup of tea! / oh, you silly boy! / oh no!*).

older, oldest / elder, eldest
▷ **older, oldest** are always correct; they may be replaced by **elder, eldest** only when
- ○ the topic is relative age within a family and
- ○ the adjective is immediately followed by its noun (eg *Fred's elder brother came in*) or immediately preceded by a limiting adjective such as *the, my, his* (eg *she is my elder by three years*).

Olympics
▷ may be treated as a singular or a plural eg
- ✓ the Olympics is about doing your best
- ✓ the Olympics are to be held in Sydney in 2000

omelette
▷ has two *t*s (AmE **omlet**).

on behalf of / on the part of
▷ **on behalf of** means 'for, as a representative of' (eg *I make this application on behalf of the National Trust*); **on the part of** means 'by, of' (eg *this is surely an error on the part of your accountants*).

one

▷ when **one** is used

○ as a personal pronoun meaning 'I/me' or 'anybody', the only pronouns that may be used to refer back to it are **one**, **one's**, etc eg

    ✓ *one must look after <u>oneself</u> and <u>one's</u> own property*

not

    ✗ *one must look after himself / yourself*, etc

○ as a numeral, any verb that it governs will be in the singular (eg *one in two of the citizens <u>owns</u> a car*).

NOTE Watch out for sentences where **one** in fact does not govern the verb (eg *I am one of those people who hate gardening*, where *hate* is correctly in the plural because its subject is not *one* but the plural noun-phrase *those people*).

one another / each other

▷ the traditional rule is that **each other** is used to refer to two persons and **one another** to larger numbers; but nowadays the phrases are interchangeable.

on to / onto

▷ **on to** means 'further towards' (eg *they walked on to Bognor, arriving there about 6 pm*); **onto** means 'into contact with' (eg *the saucepans fell onto the floor*).

onus

▷ is pronounced **oh**-*nus* and has a plural **onuses**.

open

▷ has a present participle **opening** and a past tense and past participle **opened**.

operator

▷ is spelt *-or*.

optics
▷ is singular.

optimum
▷ the noun has plurals **optimums** and **optima**.

opus
▷ is pronounced **oh**-*pus* or **op**-*us* and has plurals **opuses** and **opera**.

-or / -ar / -er
▷ these suffixes denote 'doers' (eg *runner, actor, beggar*); the *-er* form is by far the most common and is used on all new coinings. All words ending in *-ar* and *-or* are listed at their alphabetical place in this book.

oral / aural
▷ **oral** means 'of the mouth or by speaking'; **aural** means 'of the ears or sense of hearing'.

orang-outang / orang-utan
▷ the second spelling is more common.

oratorio
▷ has a plural **oratorios**.

ordinal number
▷ denotes a number that expresses sequence (eg *second*) rather than quantity (eg *two*).
➤ See also **cardinal number**.

ordinance / ordnance
▷ **ordinance** means 'law, rule, order' (eg *officers were sent round to see that the king's ordinances were obeyed*); **ordnance** means 'heavy artillery' or 'military supplies'.

orthographic word
▷ denotes a word considered simply as a group of written letters that have no spaces between them, regardless of meaning; so the sentence *he'll go* contains only two

orthographic words, though it has three **lexemes** (*he, will* and *go*) and in the sentence *she lies in bed reading books full of lies* the second and last words are the same orthographic word, though two different lexemes.
➤ See also **grammatical word**, **phonological word**.

-ory / -ary / -ery
▷ there are no simple rules for deciding which of these endings (which tend to sound the same in speech) a given word has. The vowel ending of the related noun is usually kept (eg *director, directory* / *baker, bakery*), but there are many exceptions and it is wise to consult a dictionary when in doubt.

-os / -oes / -i
▷ certain words of Italian origin whose singular ends in *-o* have a plural in *-i*; most other words whose singular ends in *-o* have plurals in *-os* or *-oes*. There are no simple universal rules for deciding the plural of a particular *-o* word and the commonest ones are listed at their alphabetical place in this book.

ostensible
▷ is spelt *-ible*.

ought / aught
▷ *ought* means 'should'; *aught* means 'anything'.

out-
▷ for the inflections of words beginning with this prefix (eg *outbid, outdo*), refer to the simple verb (eg *bid, do*).

ouzo
▷ has a plural ***ouzos***.

over-
▷ for the inflections of words beginning with this prefix (eg *overcome, overdo*), refer to the base form of the verb (eg *come, do*).

overly
▷ this word is regarded by some as a cliché and by others as an Americanism and is best avoided.

owing to / because of / due to
▷ may nowadays be used interchangeably.

ox
▷ has a plural *oxen*.

p

pajamas / pyjamas
▷ is plural; the second spelling is used in British English, the first in American.

palate / palette / pallet
▷ the first is the roof of the mouth; the second is a board on which paints are mixed; the third is a mattress or wooden platform for loads.

palomino
▷ has a plural *palominos*.

palpable
▷ is spelt *-able*.

panic
▷ the verb has a present participle *panicking* and a past tense and past participle *panicked*.

paparazzo
▷ is spelt with two *p*s, one *r* and two *z*s and has a plural *paparazzi*.

papier-mâché
▷ is spelt *-mâché* and pronounced **pap**-*yay* **mah**-*shay*.

papyrus
▷ is pronounced *pu*-**piy**-*rus* and has plurals *papyri* and *papyruses*.

paradigm
▷ is spelt *-digm* but pronounced **pa**-*ru*-*diym*.

paradigmatic
▷ is spelt *-digm-* and pronounced *pa-ru-dig-**mat**-ik*.

paraffin
▷ has two *f*s.

paragraph
▷ denotes a section of a written or printed text which begins with a new sentence that is separated from what precedes it by being set on a new line, often with its first word indented.

parallel
▷ the verb has a present participle ***paralleling*** and a past tense and past participle ***paralleled***.

parentheses
➤ See **punctuation**.

parenthesis
▷ has a plural ***parentheses***.

pariah
▷ may be pronounced *pu-**riy**-u* or (less commonly) ***pa***-*ri-yu*.

partake
▷ has a past tense ***partook*** and a past participle ***partaken***.

partially / partly
▷ both mean 'in part', but
  o ***partially*** means 'not yet completely' (eg *the house was only partially built when we saw it*).
  o ***partly*** means 'this (but also something else)'; for example, to say *X is partly to blame* is to suggest there is a *Y* who is partly to blame too.

participle
▷ denotes a word formed from a verb (eg *paying*, *paid*) and used as an adjective or to form tenses. English verbs have a present and a past participle; for their forms see **verbs**.

part of speech

▷ denotes any of the grammatical classes to which words are assigned: in English they are *nouns*, *verbs*, *adjectives*, *adverbs*, *pronouns*, *prepositions*, *conjunctions* and *interjections*, all of which are explained at their alphabetical place in this book.

pas de deux

▷ is pronounced ***pah**-duh-**duh*** and has a plural **pas de deux**.

passive voice

▷ denotes those forms of the verb that are used when its subject suffers (instead of performing) the action it describes (eg *Fred was kicked by the donkey* instead of *Fred kicked the donkey*); it is formed from the appropriate part of the verb *to be* plus the past participle of the verb.
➤ Compare **active voice**.

past participle

➤ See **participle**.

past perfect tense

▷ denotes that tense of verbs that is used to describe an action that had already taken place before the time of some other mentioned past event (eg *he had left before the others arrived*); it is formed from the past tense of *to have* plus the past participle of the verb.

past progressive tense

▷ denotes that tense of verbs that is used to describe an action or event that was in progress at the same time as some other specified past event (eg *he was eating his dinner when the dog ran in*); it is formed from the appropriate part of the past tense of the verb *to be* plus the present participle of the verb. The progressive tense is also known as the ***continuous tense***.

past tense
▷ denotes that tense of verbs that is used to describe an action that took place, or a situation that existed, before the time of speaking or writing; it is sometimes called the *simple past tense*. For the forms taken by English past tenses see **verbs**.

pasty
▷ the noun is pronounced *pas*-ti and the adjective *pay*-sti.

pâté
▷ is spelt with *â* and *é* and pronounced *pat*-ay.

pathos / bathos
▷ are both pronounced -*ay*-; **pathos** denotes a quality in a story, etc that makes the reader feel pity (eg *orphans abandoned on a stormy night—what could have more pathos than that?*); **bathos** denotes a sudden change from lofty ideas to trivial ones (eg *he felt deserted, betrayed and unloved—and he had forgotten to put out the cat*).

patio
▷ has a plural *patios*.

patois
▷ is pronounced *pat*-wah and has a plural *patois*.

pay
▷ the verb has a past tense and past participle *paid*.

peaceable / peaceful
▷ **peaceable** is spelt -*eable*, means 'wanting peace' or 'quiet-natured' and is mostly used of people (eg *Harry was a peaceable man, always willing to listen to other points of view*); **peaceful** means 'calm' or 'done in peace' and is mostly used of things (eg *extremists bent on turning a peaceful demonstration into a riot / a peaceful snooze in the orchard*).

peccadillo

peccadillo
▷ has two *c*s, one *d* and two *l*s and has plurals **peccadillos** and **peccadilloes**.

pedlar
▷ is spelt *-ar*.

pejorative
▷ is nowadays pronounced *pi-jo-ru-tiv*.

pelican
▷ has two plurals
  ○ **pelican**, when the group is thought of as a whole (eg *a flock of pelican had settled by the pool*).
  ○ **pelicans**, when the group is thought of as a set of individuals (eg *only a couple of pelicans in the enclosure, one of which looked pretty sickly*).

pendant / pendent
▷ **pendant** is the noun, **pendent** the adjective.

penny
▷ has two plurals
  ○ **pence**, when used of a sum of money (eg *the fare will be fifty pence / only 23p left in the petty cash*).
  ○ **pennies**, when used of the coins themselves (eg *constructed a pyramid out of the pennies she had found in the tin*).

penumbra
▷ has plurals **penumbras** (in general use) and **penumbrae** (in scientific and technical use).

perceptible
▷ is spelt *-ible*.

perch
▷ when meaning 'sort of fish' the noun has two plurals

- **perch**, when the group is thought of as a whole (eg *saw a large shoal of perch in a shady pool*).
- **perches**, when the group is thought of as a set of individuals (eg *only two perches in the pool, one of which looked pretty sickly*).

peremptory
▷ may be stressed on the second or (less commonly) first syllable.

perennial / annual
▷ when used of plants **annual** means 'lasting for one year only' and **perennial** means 'lasting for more than two years'; otherwise **annual** means 'happening once every year' (eg *the annual dinner will be held on 23 March*) or 'of one year' (eg *what is his annual income?*) and **perennial** means 'lasting a whole year' or 'continual' (eg *can't stand her perennial whining*).

perfectible
▷ is spelt *-ible*.

perfect tense
▷ denotes in Grammar any one of the three tenses **present perfect** (eg *I have come*), **past perfect** (eg *I had come*) and **future perfect** (eg *I will have come*); see separate entries.

performance
▷ is spelt *-ance*.

perihelion
▷ has a plural **perihelia**.

perimeter / periphery
▷ **perimeter** denotes the precise boundary of any two-dimensional geometrical or actual figure (eg triangle, circle, cricket pitch); **periphery** denotes the outer surface of a three-dimensional object and is also used

periphrasis

metaphorically of the margin of a social group, etc (eg *she went to club meetings every week, but her shyness always kept her on the periphery of things*) or the outer area of a physical space (eg *his voice was not stong enough to reach the periphery of the crowd*).

periphrasis
▷ is stressed on the second syllable and has a plural ***periphrases***.

permanence
▷ is spelt *-ence*.

permissible
▷ is spelt *-ible*.

perseverance
▷ is spelt *-ance*.

persistence, persistent
▷ are spelt *-ten-*.

person
▷ denotes any of the three classes into which the forms of verbs, personal pronouns and possessive adjectives and pronouns fall

○ the ***first person*** is used in the singular by the speaker or writer to refer to himself or herself (eg *I am, I/me, my, mine*) and in the plural to refer to himself/herself and others (eg *we are, we/us, our, ours*).

○ the ***second person*** is used in the singular by the speaker or writer to refer to a single person addressed (eg *you are/thou art, you/thou/thee, your/thy, yours/thine*) and in the plural to refer to several persons addressed (eg *you are, you, your, yours*); *thou, thy* and *thine* are used as archaic or dialectal forms.

○ the **third person** is used in the singular by the speaker or writer to refer to a single person or thing that is spoken of (eg *he/she/it is, he/him/she/her/it, his/hers/its, his/hers*) and in the plural to refer to several persons or things that are spoken of (eg *they are, they/them, their, theirs*).
➤ See also **pronouns**, **verbs**.

personal pronoun
➤ See **pronouns**.

personnel
▷ is spelt *-nnel*.

persuadable, persuasible
▷ both mean 'able to be persuaded'; the first is spelt *-dable*, the second *-sible*.

peso
▷ has a plural ***pesos***.

petit four
▷ has a plural ***petits fours***.

phallus
▷ has plurals ***phalluses*** (in general use) and ***phalli***.

Pharaoh
▷ is spelt *-aoh*.

pharynx
▷ has a plurals ***pharynxes*** (in general use) and ***pharynges*** (in medical use).

pheasant
▷ has two plurals

○ ***pheasant***, when the group is thought of as a whole (eg *a flock of pheasant whirred up from the wood*).

phenomenon

○ *pheasants*, when the group is thought of as a set of individuals (eg *bought a brace of pheasants at the market*).

phenomenon
▷ has a plural *phenomena*.

phlegm, phlegmatic
▷ the *g* is silent in the first of these words, but not in the second.

phonological word
▷ denotes a word considered simply as a continuous group of sounds, regardless of their meaning; so the sound pattern /heel goh/ contains only two phonological words, though it has three **lexemes** (*he*, *will* and *go*) and in the sentence *he'll hurt his heel* the first and last sound groups make the same phonological word, though they are three different lexemes.

➤ See also **grammatical word**, **orthographic word**.

photo
▷ has a plural *photos*.

photodegradable
▷ is spelt *-dable*.

phrase
➤ See **clauses and phrases**.

phrasal verb
▷ denotes a phrase that consists of a verb followed by an adverb, a preposition or both, eg *come in*, *call for (someone)*, *talk (something) over*, *put up with (someone or something)*; phrasal verbs are usually idioms (ie their meaning cannot be worked out exactly from the meanings of the words they contain).

physiognomy
▷ is spelt *-gn-* but pronounced *fi-zi-**o**-nu-mi*.

pistachio

phthisis
> has a plural **phthises**.

phylum
> has a plural **phyla**.

physio
> has a plural **physios**.

piccolo
> has a plural **piccolos**.

picnic
> the verb has a present participle **picnicking** and a past tense **picnicked**.

pied-à-terre
> is spelt *-à-* and has a plural *pieds-à-terre*.

pietà
> is spelt *-à* and has a plural **pietàs**.

pigmy / pygmy
> the second spelling is more common.

pike
> when meaning 'sort of fish' the noun has two plurals
> - **pike**, when the group is thought of as a whole (eg *saw a large shoal of pike in a shady pool*).
> - **pikes**, when the group is thought of as a set of individuals (eg *only two pikes in the pool, one of which looked pretty sickly*).

pimento / pimiento
> both mean the same and both have a plural in **-os**.

pincers
> is plural.

pistachio
> is pronounced *pis-**tash**-yoh* and has a plural **pistachios**.

piteous / pitiable / pitiful
▷ there are three basic meanings
  ○ arousing or deserving pity.
  ○ very sad.
  ○ contemptibly incompetent or half-hearted.
  Pitiable and **pitiful** have all three senses, but **pitiable** is the less common; **piteous** has the first sense only and is now thought to be a rather pretentious word.

placebo
▷ is pronounced *plu-**see**-boh* and has a plural **placebos**.

placenta
▷ has plurals **placentas** (in general use) and **placentae** (in medical use).

plaice
▷ has a plural **plaice**.

Plaid Cymru
▷ is pronounced *pliyd **kum**-ri*.

plateau
▷ has plurals **plateaux** and **plateaus**.

plateful
▷ is spelt *-ful* and has a plural **platefuls**.

platypus
▷ has a plural **platypuses**.

plausible
▷ is spelt *-ible*.

playable
▷ is spelt *-able*.

pluperfect tense
▷ is sometimes called the ***past perfect*** and denotes that tense of verbs that is used to describe an action or event that had already taken place before the time of

another mentioned past event (eg *he had eaten his dinner by the time Tom got back*); it is formed from the appropriate part of the past tense of the verb *to have* plus the past participle of the verb.

plural

▷ denotes that form of a noun, verb, adjective or pronoun that is used to refer to two or more persons, things, etc; for the plural forms used in the English language see **inflection**.

pocketful

▷ is spelt *-ful* and has a plural **pocketfuls**.

podium

▷ has plurals **podiums** (now in general use) and **podia**.

poet laureate

▷ has plurals **poets laureate** and **poet laureates**.

politic / political

▷ **politic** means 'wise, prudent' (eg *thought it politic to leave before someone called the police*) and has an adverb **politicly**; **political** means 'to do with politics' (eg *political science / political party*) and has an adverb **politically**.

political correctness

This terms refers to the avoidance of expressions or actions that may be understood to exclude or denigrate certain groups or minorities traditionally perceived as disadvantaged by eg sex, race, religion, physical and mental disability, etc. Those who wish to avoid giving offence should use recommended alternative expressions intended to be non-discriminatory.

NOTE The nature of political correctness is explained here and an indication is given as to how some of its current requirements may be met. Alternative expressions that are considered to be politically correct are given; however it is up to the indivi-

political correctness ...

dual reader to decide for themselves whether, and to what extent, they wish to use them.

- **Sexism**

  - Try to avoid unnecessary references to a person's sex: so use *firefighter*, *chairperson* (or *chair*), *actor*, *police officers* instead of *fireman*, *chairman*, *actress*, *policemen* unless sexual differentiation is the purpose of the sentence, as in *there are 15 policemen and 12 policewomen on the Foxbury Force*; rather than using, eg, *spokesperson* or *chairperson* throughout a piece of writing, the use (respectively for a man or a woman) of *spokesman* and *spokeswoman* or *chairman* and *chairwoman* is also common.

  - Words ending in *-ess* should be used with caution. Many, such as *authoress* and *manageress*, are no longer used and *author* or *manager* are preferred for both sexes; a few, such as *Jewess* and *Negress*, are considered offensive.

  - Avoid the use of *man* or *men* when the reference is really to people in general (eg *may the best man win*), replacing them by *person*, *people* or *humans*; similarly *manhours* and *man-made* should be replaced by *hours' work* and *artificial* (or *synthetic*), and the verb *to man* replaced by *to staff* or *to attend*.

  - Avoid the use of *he* or *him* when the reference is to persons of either sex by using *he or she*, *he/she*, *s/he*; some writers and speakers avoid the awkwardness of these terms by turning such sentences into the plural whenever possible, and by doing this often break the rules of grammar by using *they*, *them* even after a singular subject (eg *has someone lost their wallet?*); another technique is to use a passive sentence.

political correctness ...

NOTE Make sure that the word you wish to change or avoid really is sexually biased; such words as *menu* (ultimately from Latin *minutus* 'detailed') and *history* (ultimately from Greek *historia* 'narrative') are unacceptable only amongst committed activists.

- **Racism**
  - Avoid slang terms which are often used offensively for nations (eg *Chink, Pak, Eyetie*) and races (eg *wog, nigger, coon*).
  - Avoid using the standard terms for a nationality in a way that suggests that all its members are stupid, dishonest, etc (eg *been jewed by that door-to-door salesman—not one of his seeds grew / the notice read NO LAST TRAIN TO SLOUGH TONIGHT—obviously the station master had Irish blood in him*).
  - Avoid using traditional terms for racial groups that are now unacceptable to the members of those groups (eg *Red Indian, Eskimo* for *Native American, Inuit*).

- **Religion**
  - Avoid using slang terms for Christian denominations (eg *Prod, Pape*).
  - Avoid using traditional terms for other religions that are no longer acceptable to the members of that religion (eg *Mohammedan*).

- **Physical and mental disability**
  - The term *handicapped* is considered undesirable by some people, who propose its replacement by *challenged* (eg *visually challenged*).
  - Although the word *challenged* is common in North America, in compounds that refer to particular disabilities (such as *visually challenged* to mean *blind* or *partially sighted*), it tends to be avoided in the UK,

where it has become the supreme satirical tool of those who lampoon the whole concept of political correctness.

politico
▷ has plurals *politicos* and *politicoes*.

politics
▷ is treated as a singular when it denotes an area of study or a career (eg *politics is taught next term / politics doesn't pay—you need a private income or trade union sponsorship*), but plural when it denotes political principles (eg *Labour's politics were much more left-wing in those days*).

polka
▷ the verb has a present participle *polkaing* and a past tense *polkaed*.

poly
▷ has a plural *polys*.

polyanthus
▷ has a plural *polyanthuses*.

polyhedron
▷ has plurals *polyhedrons* and *polyhedra*.

poltergeist
▷ is spelt *-geist* and pronounced **pol**-tur-giyst.

pomelo
▷ has a plural *pomelos*.

poncho
▷ has a plural *ponchos*.

portentous / pretentious
▷ both words mean 'pompous, self-important' or 'inappropriately grandiose', but **pretentious** (eg *a bit pretentious of her to stick that coat of arms on her notepaper*) is the

more common; **portentous** also means 'threatening, ominous' (eg *a portentous dream made him cancel the booking*).

portfolio
▷ has a plural **portfolios**.

portico
▷ has plurals **porticos** and **porticoes**.

portmanteau
▷ has plurals **portmanteaus** and **portmanteaux**.

Portuguese
▷ is spelt *-guese*.

posit
▷ has a present participle **positing** and a past tense and past participle **posited**.

possess, possession, possessive
▷ are all spelt *-ssess-*.

possessive
▷ denotes that form of an adjective, noun or pronoun which indicates ownership, as in *these are my books / Bert's hat / that coat must be hers*.

possessor
▷ is spelt *-ssess-* and *-or*.

possible
▷ is spelt *-ible*.

posthumous
▷ is spelt *-th-*, *-ous* and pronounced **pos**-*tyuu-mus*.

practicable / practical
▷ **practicable** is spelt *-able* and means 'able to be done, used, etc' (eg *there's a practicable short-cut through the woods, but you'll need good boots*); **practical** also means 'able to be done', but often also has the sense 'with the

practice

least effort, expense, etc' (eg *I grant that the route through the woods is practicable, but it's more practical to stick to the road and avoid having to carry clean shoes with us*). When applied to persons ***practical*** means 'able to do things efficiently' (eg *Wilkins was a practical chap: he serviced his own car and had recently replumbed the bathroom*).

practice / practise
▷ the noun is spelt with a *c* and the verb with an *s*.

precede
▷ is spelt with a *c*.

precedence
▷ is spelt *-ence*; the more common pronunciation is ***pres**-i-duns* although ***prees**-i-duns* is also heard.

precipitate, precipitately / precipitous, precipitously
▷ as an adjective ***precipitate*** means 'hasty' or 'over-hasty'; ***precipitous*** means 'very steep': so the two *adjectives* are not interchangeable. The adverb ***precipitously*** can have two meanings; it can mean 'very steeply, like a precipice' (eg *the cliff veered precipitously down to the sea*) and 'as if running down a steep hill'; derived from the latter is the additional meaning 'too fast, out of control' (eg *upon hearing the shot they rushed precipitously out of the room*); in this sense it is close in meaning to ***precipitately***.

précis
▷ is spelt *-éc-* and pronounced ***pray**-see*.

predecessor
▷ is spelt *-or*.

predicate
▷ denotes in Grammar the word or words in a sentence (usually a verb and its complement) that make a statement

premise

about the sentence's subject (eg *is happy* in *Mary is happy* and *has made a great name for herself* in *the new cook has made a great name for herself*).

predicative adjective
➤ See **adjectives**.

predictable
▷ is spelt *-able*.

pre-eminence
▷ is hyphenated and ends *-ence*.

prefer, preferable
▷ ***prefer*** has a present participle ***preferring*** and a past tense and past participle ***preferred***; ***preferable*** is spelt *-able* and is stressed on the first syllable. They are both followed by *to*, not *than* eg

    ✓   *I prefer tea to coffee*
    ✓   *tea is preferable to coffee*

not

    ✗   *I prefer tea than coffee*
    ✗   *tea is preferable than coffee*

preference
▷ is spelt *-ence* and stressed on its first syllable.

prefix
▷ denotes a word-forming element (eg *non-*, *re-*) that is added to the front of an existing word to give it a different meaning (eg *non-* + *swimmer* = *non-swimmer*; *re-* + *consider* = *reconsider*).

première
▷ is spelt *-ère*.

premise
▷ is pronounced ***prem***-*is* and has a plural ***premises*** (pronounced ***prem***-*is-iz*); it has two meanings

preponderance

- presupposition in an argument (eg *if you start with the premise that all men are mortal, of course Socrates must be mortal too*) which can have a plural as well as a singular form.
- a building and its land, regarded as a unit of property (eg *ordered her off the premises*) which exists in the plural (***premises***) only.

preponderance
▷ is spelt *-ance*.

preposition
▷ denotes a class of words or short phrases such as *with, on, to, about, with regard to, in spite of* which link words or phrases (eg *a man with a gun / she sat on the floor / a book about fish / sent him a cake in return for his help*).

prepositional phrase
➤ See **clauses and phrases**.

prescience
▷ is pronounced *pre-si-uns*.

prescribe / proscribe
▷ the first means 'advise, order' (eg *the doctor has prescribed complete rest*); the second means 'ban, outlaw, forbid' (eg *many of the books prescribed for this course were formerly proscribed by the Church*).

present participle
➤ See **participle**.

present perfect tense
▷ denotes that tense of verbs that is used to describe an action or event that is already completed at the time of speaking or writing (eg *I'm afraid my husband has gone out*); it is formed from the appropriate part of the present tense of the verb *to have* plus the past participle of the verb.

present progressive tense

▷ denotes that tense of verbs that is used to describe an action or event that is in progress at the time of speaking or writing (eg *he is eating his dinner*); it is formed from the appropriate part of the present tense of the verb *to be* plus the present participle of the verb. The progressive tense is also known as the **continuous tense**.

present tense

▷ denotes that tense of verbs that is used to describe a situation that exists at the time of speaking or writing (eg *he loves his dog / she knows the answer*), or that is a habitual or ongoing action (eg *he writes home every week*).

presidium

▷ has plurals ***presidiums*** and ***presidia***.

prestige

▷ is spelt *-tige* and pronounced *pre-**steezh***.

pretentious / portentous

▷ both words mean 'pompous, self-important' or 'inappropriately grandiose', but ***pretentious*** (eg *a bit pretentious of her to stick that coat of arms on her notepaper*) is the more common; ***portentous*** also means 'threatening, ominous' (eg *a portentous dream made him cancel the booking*).

prevalence

▷ is spelt *-ence*.

preventable / preventible

▷ both spellings are correct; both words mean the same.

primary auxiliary verb

▷ denotes the verbs *be, have* and *do* when they are used with the participles or infinitives of other verbs in order

primula

to form compound tenses (eg *it is raining* / *we have finished* / *they did go*).
➤ See also **modal**.

primula
▷ has plurals **primulas** (in general use) and **primulae**.

principal / principle
▷ the first means 'chief', the second 'rule'.

principal clause
➤ See **clauses and phrases**.

printable
▷ is spelt *-able*.

prise / prize
▷ the first means 'force open', the second 'reward' or 'value'.

privacy
▷ is pronounced **pri**-vu-si or **pry**-vu-si.

privilege
▷ is spelt *-lege*.

pro
▷ the noun has a plural **pros**.

procedure
▷ is spelt *-ced-*.

proceed
▷ is spelt *-ceed*.

proceedings
▷ is plural.

proceeds
▷ is plural.

professor
▷ is spelt *-or*.

profit
▷ the verb has a present participle **profiting** and a past tense **profited**.

profitable
▷ is spelt *-able*.

prognosis
▷ has a plural **prognoses**.

program / programme
▷ use the first spelling for the computing senses of the noun and verb (which has a present participle **programming** and a past tense and past participle **programmed**) and the second for all the other senses. AmE uses **program** throughout.

programmable
▷ is spelt *-mmable*.

progressive tense
▷ denotes in Grammar one of those tenses of a verb that are formed by the appropriate part of the verb *to be* plus the verb's present participle, as in *we were going, they are sitting*. Progressive tenses are used to indicate an action that is incomplete. The progressive tense is also known as the **continuous tense**.

projector
▷ is spelt *-or*.

promissory
▷ is spelt *-miss-*, *-ory* and pronounced **prom**-*is-aw-ri*.

prone / apt / liable / likely
▷ *apt* means 'tending to, in the habit of' (eg *grandma is apt to nod off after supper*); **prone** is similar in meaning, but should only be used of persons or of things composed of persons (eg *the motor industry is prone to wildcat strikes*) and usually refers to what is considered to be

bad actions. **Likely** means 'will probably' (eg *since he's a keen music-lover you're likely to see him at the concert*). **Liable** means 'runs the risk of, will probably' and usually refers to an unpleasant consequence of the subject of the sentence's previous action (eg *children who play in the road are liable to end up in hospital*).

pronounceable
▷ is spelt *-ceable*.

pronouns

A **pronoun** is a word such as *it, him, whose* that is used to refer back to a noun or noun phrase used earlier, as in *John came in; he poured himself a drink and sat down*. Sometimes the original noun or noun phrase has to be understood, as in *it* (ie the weather) *is windy*, or when someone starts a conversation with *I* or *you* (when, whether we can name them or not, we can *see* that *I* refers to the person who is speaking and *you* to the person addressed by the speaker).

• Types of pronouns
There are nine types of pronouns:

- **Personal pronouns** (eg *I, you, them*).
- **Possessive pronouns** (eg *mine, yours, theirs*).
- **Reflexive pronouns** (eg *myself, yourself, themselves*).
- **Interrogative pronouns** (eg *whose is that?* / *what do you want?* / *which is hers?*).
- **Relative pronouns** (eg *the man who came in next* / *the book that I want* / *the cat which I saw*).
- **Demonstrative pronouns** (eg *that is the one I want*).
- **Indefinite pronouns** (eg *someone, everybody, some, none*).
- **Distributive pronouns** (eg *each, neither*).
- **Reciprocal pronouns** (eg *each other, one another*).

• Inflection of personal pronouns

Each personal pronoun has two forms (subjective and objective respectively) in the following persons and genders:

- First person singular: *I, me*.
- Third person singular masculine: *he, him*.
- Third person singular feminine: *she, her*.
- First person plural: *we, us*.
- Third person plural: *they, them*.

Use the objective form when the pronoun is governed by a transitive verb or preposition (eg *him* in *she saw him* and *a policeman stood beside him*). In informal speech the objective form is also often used after the verb *to be* (eg *it's him again*) and when standing alone (eg *'Who did that?' 'Me.'*; compare *'Who did that?' 'I did.'*).

propellant / propellent
▷ the noun is spelt *-ant* and the adjective *-ent*.

proper noun
▷ denotes any noun which is the name of a particular person or place (eg *George, Paris, the Himalayas*).
➤ See also **common noun, nouns**.

prophecy / prophesy
▷ the first is the noun and the second the verb.

propitious / auspicious
▷ both mean 'promising or favourable to future success', but ***propitious*** usually implies immediate results (eg *the gods seemed propitious to England, who scored 100 in the first hour*) and ***auspicious*** long-term expectations (eg *Lord Megabuck's handsome donation gives an auspicious start to the Building Fund*).

proscenium

proscenium
▷ is spelt -*sceni*-, pronounced *pro-**seen**-i-um* and has plurals **prosceniums** (in general use) and **proscenia**.

proscribe / prescribe
▷ **proscribe** means 'ban, outlaw, forbid' (eg *Galileo's writings on the movement of the earth were proscribed by the Church / the doctor was found guilty of misconduct and proscribed from practising*); **prescribe** means 'advise, order' (eg *the doctor has prescribed complete rest*).

protector
▷ is spelt -*or*.

protégé, protégée
▷ are both spelt with two *é*s; the first form is used of a man or boy, the second of a woman or girl; both are pronounced ***pro**-te-jay*.

protein
▷ is spelt -*tein*.

protuberance
▷ is spelt -*ance*.

provable
▷ is spelt -*vable* but pronounced ***pruuv**-ubl*.

prove
▷ has past participles **proved** (British English) and **proven** (Scots and AmE); **proven** is also used in British English as an adjective, eg *a proven liar*.

proviso
▷ has a plural **provisos**.

psychosis
▷ has a plural **psychoses**.

pubes / pubis
▷ **pubis** has a plural **pubes** and denotes either of the two

punctuation

bones forming the lower front part of each side of the pelvis, known as the pubic region; **pubes** has a plural **pubes** and denotes the pubic region and the hair that grows on it.

punctilio
▷ has one / and a plural **punctilios**.

punctuation

Punctuation denotes the system of written signs that give the reader some indication of the pauses, changes of pitch, etc that would have been heard had someone spoken the sentence that has been written. The principal signs are explained below in alphabetical order.

- **Apostrophe**
➤ See separate entry at **apostrophes**.

- **Brackets**

There are two main types: **parentheses**, written '(' and ')', and **square brackets**, written '[' and ']'.

   ○ *Parentheses*, sometimes called *round brackets*, are used to separate off an extra piece of information from the sentence into which it has been inserted, as in *the final result (a goalless draw) did little credit to either side* and *Bloggs (I hate his guts!) came first yet again*. They may also be used to avoid repetition when indicating an alternative, as in *the candidate(s) will be required to undergo a medical examination* (instead of *the candidate* or *candidates*), or to separate off enumerators, eg *(1)..., (2)...* or *(a)..., (b)...*

   ○ *Square brackets*, sometimes called simply *brackets*, are used to separate off material inserted into a text by a person (eg an editor) who did not write the rest of it, as in *he [John Smith, mayor 1662–3] reports that...*

or *marched towards [2 words illegible] the mayor said*....

• Colon

This sign (:) is used:

- To introduce a part of a sentence that explains or expands on the preceding part (eg *I have something important to tell you: John will be arriving this afternoon* or *you'll need the following: wrapping paper, sticky tape, ribbon, ...*)

- To introduce a part of a sentence that balances or contrasts with the preceding part (eg *To err is human: to forgive, divine*).

- To introduce direct speech (see also *comma* below), as in a narrative (eg *John shouted: 'The wall's coming down!'*) or as in the text of a play (eg *John (shouting): The wall's coming down!*).

- To introduce a long extract (ie 4 lines or more) from another piece of writing, as in:

    On another page Jones writes:
    The previous policies advocated by Wirtsubski and Hareng were not continued, and the economy suffered a steady deterioration from the beginning of the nineteenth century, with the consequent public unrest culminating in the assassination of King Zog (1806–76) during a masked ball in celebration of the approaching millennium of the Kratchovski dynasty.
    He seems here to have overlooked the fact that Zog, being only an uncle by marriage to the Grand Duchess Ludmila Bogarovchitka, was not actually a Kratchovski by blood...

- To separate the main and secondary titles of a book, etc, as in *Margaret Thatcher: A Political Biography*.

punctuation ...

• Comma

This sign (,) is used:

- To separate two main causes in a compound sentence (eg *John laughed, but Mary turned deadly pale*).
- To indicate the end of a subordinate clause that precedes the main clause of a sentence (eg *when he got home, the children ran to greet him*).
- To separate the main clause of a sentence from a following subordinate clause that expresses a result or consequence (eg *she works in the evenings, so her husband looks after the children*).
  NOTE No other type of following subordinate clause (eg *they all stood up when the king came in*) requires a comma.
- To group words together in a sentence to clarify or change their meaning (compare *she felt sick and tired of the modern art* with *she felt sick, and tired of the modern art*).
- In pairs to separate off an extra piece of information that has been put into the middle of another sentence (eg *one theory, not previously made public, was that...*). Non-restrictive relative clauses (see **clauses and phrases**) count as 'extra information', and are treated this way.
- To follow *yes* and *no* and to precede *please* when they are part of a longer sentence (eg *yes, we have no bananas* / *shut the door, please!*).
- To indicate where a slight pause would be made in speaking the sentence (eg *Madam Speaker, may I ask...*).
- To separate the items in a list (eg *bread, baked beans, eggs and potatoes*).
  NOTE A comma may also be used before the *and* that introduces the last item in the list.

○ To introduce direct speech (see also *colon* above) (eg *Peter at once said, 'I want to come too'*).

• Dash
There are two types of dash, the **en-dash** (–) and the **em-dash** (—). They are different from the **hyphen**, but typists and word-processor users often type a hyphen when a dash should be used.

○ The **en-dash** is used in number or letter series (eg *1914–18 / an A–Z guide*) and to link two or more words that do not themselves form a compound but together modify a following word (eg *the space–time continuum / the Paris–Lyon autoroute*).

○ The **em-dash** is slightly longer than the en-dash and is used to introduce a second part of a sentence which explains or counterbalances what has been said in the first part (eg *a spectre is haunting Europe — the spectre of Communism / he can do it — and he will!*) or to indicate that a word, or part of a word, has been omitted (eg *her affair with Lord — was the talk of the town*). In informal writing a pair of em-dashes may be used to separate off an extra piece of information from the sentence into which it has been inserted (eg *his new boss — a nasty piece of work — greets me with a supercilious smile*).

• Exclamation mark
This sign (!) is used:

○ To mark the end of a sentence (replacing the full stop if there is one) that expresses anger, surprise, etc (eg *help! / good Lord! / damn and blast you!*).

○ To indicate the author's annoyance, disbelief, etc, when placed in parentheses immediately after the offending word or phrase (eg *due to operating difficulties(!) the train was now three hours late*).

punctuation ...

• Full stop
This sign (.) is used:

- To show the end of a sentence that does not end with an exclamation mark or question mark.
- To show the end of an abbreviation (see **abbreviations**).
- In a set of three (called **ellipsis**) with spaces between them to show the end of an uncompleted sentence (eg *we waited and waited ... Finally the train arrived*) or to indicate the omission of several words from a quoted passage, for example *it is in the language itself, and not in books, that these facts must be sought* can be shortened to *it is in the language itself... that these facts must be sought*.

• Oblique
This sign (/; also called **slash** and **solidus**) is used:

- To indicate alternatives, as in *tea/coffee will be served at 11am*.
- To indicate a period of time, as in *the financial year 1995/6*.
- To link places on a route, as in *the London/Frankfurt/Salonika flight*.
- To express rates or ratios in measurements (eg *100 km/hr*).
- In certain abbreviations, eg *a/c* (for *account*), *c/o* (meaning *care of*), *i/c* (meaning *in charge* or *in command of*), *o/c* (meaning *over charge*).

• Question mark
This sign (?) is used:

- To mark the end of a sentence (replacing the full stop if there is one) that asks a question (eg *how much is it?* '*What is your name?*' *she asked*).

○ To indicate the author's disbelief or uncertainty (eg *he gave his name as Smith(?) and said that the silverware had fallen off a lorry* / *Thomas Tallis (?1505–1585)*.

• Quotation marks

These marks (also called **inverted commas**) are used:

○ To enclose direct speech (eg *'Do come in', he said* / *'Why not?' she asked* / *'You', he said, 'must help her'.* / *Why did you say 'Who goes there'?*).
NOTE When a piece of direct speech is part of a larger sentence, as in the examples above, there are complex rules for dealing with the punctuation at the end of the direct speech, which are set out in detail in *Chambers Guide to Grammar and Usage*. Basically, the punctuation of the direct speech is retained inside the quotation marks unless it clashes with punctuation needed by the larger sentence.

○ To highlight a word or phrase (eg *the play is full of 'thous' and 'thees', which the author seems to think will give it 'atmosphere'*).
NOTE Both single and double quotation marks are correct, but modern British usage prefers single quotation marks. However, if there is a quotation or highlighted passage within another quotation, both single and double quotes must be used eg

    ✓   *'What do you mean by "an accessary after the fact"?' he asked.*

○ To indicate that the enclosed words are the title of a book, film, etc (eg *going to see 'Hamlet' tonight*).
NOTE This use is only permitted in informal writing. For the complex rules governing the citation of published material when writing books, theses, etc, consult *Chambers Guide to Grammar and Usage*.

Semicolon

This (;) is used:

- To separate two major (often contrasted) parts of a long sentence (eg *he may have seemed a competent prime minister; yet he totally failed to appreciate the changing circumstances of the country*).

- To separate off the main sections of a list whose individual items are separate by commas (eg *the chief industries are shipbuilding, engineering and steel manufacturing; textiles and clothing; coal-mining; and brewing*).

pupa
▷ has plurals **pupae** and **pupas**.

purée
▷ is spelt *-ée*.

purposefully / purposely
▷ ***purposefully*** means 'determinedly, resolutely' (eg *she strode purposefully towards him, clearly intent on settling things once and for all*); ***purposely*** means 'intentionally, on purpose' (eg *she purposely failed her exams so that she could stay at school for another year*).

purulence, purulent
▷ are both spelt *-len-*.

put
▷ has a past tense and past participle ***put*** and a present participle ***putting***.

putrefy
▷ is spelt *-efy*.

Pwllheli
▷ is pronounced *pu-**thel**-i*.

pygmy / pigmy
▷ the first spelling is more common.

pyjamas / pajamas
▷ is plural; the first spelling is used in British English, the second in American.

pyramidal
▷ is pronounced *pi-**ram**-id-ul*.

q

quadraphonic
▷ is spelt *quadra-*.

quadri-, quadru-
▷ are prefixes meaning 'four' (eg a *quadrilateral* has four sides, a *quadruped* has four legs).

qualifier
▷ is in Grammar another name for **modifier**.

quango
▷ has a plural ***quangos***.

quantifier
▷ is a general name used in some grammars for those adjectives and pronouns that answer the question 'how many?' (eg *all*, *every*, *none*, *some*).

quantum
▷ is pronounced **kwon**-*tum* and has a plural ***quanta***.

quartet / quartette
▷ the first spelling is more common.

quarto
▷ has a plural ***quartos***.

quasi-
▷ is a prefix meaning 'almost' or 'as if'; it is best pronounced ***kway***-*siy*.

Queen's English
➤ See under **Standard English**.

question

question
▷ the verb has a present participle **questioning** and a past tense and past participle **questioned**.

questionable
▷ is spelt *-able*.

question mark
➤ See **punctuation**.

questionnaire
▷ is spelt *-nnaire* and pronounced *kwest-shu-**nayr*** or *kest-shu-**nayr***.

quick-freeze
▷ has a past tense **quick-froze** and a past participle **quick-frozen**.

quid
▷ has two meanings
- ○ 'a pound sterling', which has a plural **quid** if it follows a figure or a quantifying adjective (eg *cost me a thousand quid* / *that'll cost him a few quid*) and a plural **quids** in all other cases (eg *she must be quids in on the deal*).
- ○ 'a plug of tobacco', which has a plural **quids**.

quiescent
▷ is spelt *-sc-* and pronounced *kwi-**es**-unt* or *kwiy-**es**-unt*.

quintet / quintette
▷ the first spelling is more common.

quit
▷ has past tenses and past participles **quit** and **quitted**, and a present participle **quitting**.

quite
▷ another speaker or writer's use of this word must be interpreted with caution, since it can mean 'completely' (eg *have*

you quite finished?), 'very' or 'a little', so that *I'm quite pleased with your work* may indicate strong praise or mild criticism; the intonation of a speaker or the context of a written text usually helps to disambiguate.

quittance
▷ is spelt *-ttance*.

Quixote
▷ may be pronounced ***kwik***-*sot* or *ki-**hoh**-ti*.

quixotic
▷ is pronounced *kwik-**sot**-ik*.

quiz
▷ the noun has a plural ***quizzes***.

quotation marks
➤ See **punctuation**.

Qur'an / Koran
▷ the second spelling is more common.

r

rabbet / rabbit
▷ as a noun *rabbet* denotes a type of notched joint in woodworking; the verb has a present participle *rabbeting* and a past tense and past participle *rabbeted*. As a noun *rabbit* denotes a small burrowing mammal that is furry with long ears and is often kept as a pet; the verb (which has a present participle *rabbiting* and a past tense and past participle *rabbited*) means 'hunt rabbits' or 'chatter on ramblingly'.

rabies
▷ is singular (eg *rabies is a dangerous disease*).

raccoon / racoon
▷ the first spelling is more common.

racialism / racism
▷ both mean the same.

racket / racquet
▷ *racket* is the preferred spelling for the sense 'tennis, etc bat' and the only spelling for all other senses.

rackets
▷ is singular when used as the name of the game (eg *rackets is dead boring*), but plural when meaning a bat for tennis, badminton, etc (eg *the rackets are kept in that cupboard*).

radiccio
▷ has a plural *radiccios*.

radio
> the noun has a plural **radios** and the verb a present participle **radioing** and a past tense and past participle **radioed**.

radius
> has plurals **radiuses** (in general use) and **radii**.

raja / rajah
> the first spelling is more common.

Ralph
> the traditional pronunciation *rayf* is now almost completely replaced by *ralf*.

ranee / rani
> the second spelling is more common.

rarefy
> is spelt *-refy*.

rarity
> is spelt *-rity*.

ratio
> has a plural **ratios**.

re-
> is a prefix used to show repetition or reversal of the action described by the word to which it is attached (eg *reread* = read again, *rewrite* = write differently).

reactor
> is spelt *-or*.

read
> has a past tense and past participle **read** (pronounced *red*).

readable
> is spelt *-able*.

reassurance
▷ is spelt *-ance*.

rebound / redound
▷ **rebound** means 'bounce back', both literally and metaphorically (eg *ball rebounded from the wall* / *after a disappointing early performance profits rebounded in the second half*); **redound** has two meanings, both metaphorical

- 'be to the credit or advantage of' (eg *it redounds to her credit that she immediately rejected the bribe*).

- 'recoil upon, come home to' (eg *his bullying tactics redounded upon him in the end, when the whole class made a complaint to the headmaster*).

rebus
▷ has a plural **rebuses**.

recce
▷ is pronounced **rek**-*ee*; the verb has a present participle **recceing** and past tenses and past participles **recced** or **recceed**.

recede
▷ is spelt *-cede*.

recherché
▷ is spelt *-é*.

reciprocal pronoun
➤ See **pronouns**.

recommendable
▷ is spelt *-able*.

reconnaissance
▷ is spelt *-nnaissance*.

reconnoitre
▷ is spelt *-nnoitre*.

recoverable
▷ is spelt *-able*.

recto
▷ has a plural **rectos**.

rector
▷ is spelt *-or*.

rectum
▷ has plurals **rectums** (now in general use) and **recta**.

recurrence, recurrent
▷ are spelt *-rren-*.

redo
▷ has a past tense **redid** and a past participle **redone**.

redound / rebound
▷ **redound** has two meanings, both metaphorical

  ○ 'be to the credit or advantage of' (eg *it redounds to her credit that she immediately rejected the bribe*).

  ○ 'recoil upon, come home to' (eg *his bullying tactics redounded upon him in the end, when the whole class made a complaint to the headmaster*).

  rebound means 'bounce back', both literally and metaphorically (eg *ball rebounded from the wall / after a disappointing early performance profits rebounded in the second half*).

reducible
▷ is spelt *-ible*.

redundant
▷ is spelt *-ant*.

referable / referrable
▷ the first spelling is more common; both are pronounced ri-**fuhr**-ubl.

reference
▷ is spelt *-ence*.

referendum
▷ has plurals **referendums** and **referenda**.

refillable
▷ is spelt *-able*.

reflector
▷ is spelt *-or*.

reflexive pronoun
➤ See **pronouns**.

refrigerator
▷ is spelt *-or*.

refundable
▷ is spelt *-able*.

refute / deny
▷ to **deny** a fact or statement is to *claim* it is not true; to **refute** a statement or theory is to *prove* it is not true. **Refute** should not be used to mean 'deny strongly'.

regal / royal
▷ **regal** means 'like or suitable for a king or queen' (eg *the regal splendour of the Governor's residence / the old lady's regal bearing*); **royal** means 'of the king or queen or their family' (eg *a royal pardon / another royal divorce*).

regalia
▷ is plural.

register

This term denotes the different styles of speech or writing (both in vocabulary and grammar) that are appropriate to various circumstances (for example, a person will use English of one register when writing a business letter and of quite a different register when talking to family or friends). None of these registers is 'wrong'; they are just appropriate to different occasions. The principal registers are:

- ○ **Formal** denotes a type of English that is mostly written and is used in business reports, scholarly publications, official speeches, documents, etc.
- ○ **Colloquial** (or **informal**) denotes the type of informal English that is used by most people when chatting privately or writing personal letters.
- ○ **Slang** denotes a type of very informal English which is seldom written or spoken in formal contexts; it may also refer to words or phrases used only by a certain social or professional group, such as schoolchildren, Cockneys, actors, jockeys or criminals.
- ○ **Archaic** denotes a word or phrase which is now old-fashioned but may remain as a technical term (for example, in legal writing: eg *accessary before the fact*) or be used occasionally for special effect (eg *lo and behold*).
- ○ **Literary** denotes the type of English (eg the words *benighted* and *brown study*) that is found in books that are read principally for the quality of the writing they contain.
- ○ **Poetic** denotes a type of English that is found only in poetry (eg *steed* instead of *horse*).
- ○ **Technical** denotes a type of English that is used and understood only by experts in a particular area of study.

➤ See also **standard/non-standard English**.

regretful / regrettable

▷ **regretful** means 'remorseful, sorry for what one has done' and is used of persons; **regrettable** is spelt *-ttable*,

regular

means 'to be regretted' and is used of facts, actions, etc (eg *it is regrettable that your son slipped in the playground, but these accidents do happen and you cannot expect any of my staff to be particularly regretful about it*).

regular
▷ is used in Grammar to denote a word or construction that follows the standard grammatical rules (eg it is said to be ***regular*** in English to form the plural of a noun by adding s to the singular as in *book, books* because most (but not all) English nouns do form their plurals in this way).

regulator
▷ is spelt *-or*.

reindeer
▷ has two plurals
- ○ ***reindeer***, when the group is thought of as a whole (eg *saw a large herd of reindeer charging across his path*).
- ○ ***reindeers***, when the group is thought of as a set of individuals (eg *a few reindeers came past, some limping badly*).

relation / relative
▷ in the sense 'person to whom one is related' these words are interchangeable.

relative adjective
➤ See **adjectives**.

relative clause
➤ See **clauses and phrases**.

relative pronoun
➤ See **pronouns**.

relevance, relevant
▷ are spelt *-van-*.

reliable
▷ is spelt *-iable*.

reliance, reliant
▷ are spelt *-ian-*.

reluctance, reluctant
▷ is spelt *-tan-*.

remains
▷ is plural.

remake
▷ has a past tense and past participle ***remade***.

remediable
▷ is spelt *-iable* and pronounced *re-**meed**-i-ubl*.

remember
▷ has a present participle ***remembering*** and a past tense and past participle ***remembered***.

reminiscence, reminiscent
▷ are spelt *-scen-*.

remission / remittance
▷ ***remission*** is to do with 'letting off' (eg the reduction of a prison sentence or the easing of the symptoms of a disease); ***remittance*** (spelt *-ance*) refers to sending money, or to the money sent (eg *your remittance has arrived here safely*).

remittent
▷ is spelt *-ttent*.

rend
▷ has a past tense and past participle ***rent***.

render
▷ has a present participle ***rendering*** and a past tense and past participle ***rendered***.

renege
▷ is pronounced *re-**neeg*** or *re-**nayg***.

reopen
▷ has a present participle ***reopening*** and a past tense and past participle ***reopened***.

repairable / reparable
▷ both are spelt *-able*; the first means 'able to be repaired', the second (pronounced ***rep***-*ur-ubl*) 'able to be put right' (eg *is the situation still reparable now that she has disclosed our intentions?*).

repayable
▷ is spelt *-able*.

repealable
▷ is spelt *-able*.

repeatable
▷ is spelt *-able*.

repellence, repellent
▷ are spelt *-llen-*.

repentance, repentant
▷ are spelt *-an-*.

repetitious / repetitive
▷ both mean 'full of repeats'
  ○ ***repetitious*** is mostly used of speech or writing and often suggests that the repetitions are boring and/or unnecessary (eg *fell asleep during yet another of his repetitious monologues*).
  ○ ***repetitive*** is used of tasks as well as of speech and writing and does not always suggest boredom, etc (eg *the work is quite repetitive, so you'll soon pick it up*).

replace / substitute
▷ both mean much the same; but note that we substitute *for* and replace *by* or *with* (eg *Knee was substituted for Pevsner in the 49th minute / replacing the broken TV with a vase of flowers is hardly what the lodger will expect*).

replaceable
▷ is spelt *-eable*.

replicable
▷ is spelt *-able* and pronounced ***rep**-lik-ubl*.

reported speech
▷ denotes the method of recording what someone has said in which their words are altered to fit the point of view of the person repeating them (eg *we will come* becomes *they said they would come*). Also called **indirect speech**.

reprehensible
▷ is spelt *-ible*.

repress / suppress
▷ both mean 'control, put down'; but sometimes **suppress** is used of eradication and **repress** of mere containment (eg *the 1745 rebellion was brutally suppressed and nothing was heard of Scottish nationalism for centuries after / sobbed as she struggled to repress her feelings*).

repressor
▷ is spelt *-or*.

reproducible
▷ is spelt *-cible*.

repugnance, repugnant
▷ are spelt *-nan-*.

reputable
▷ is spelt *-table* and stressed on its first syllable.

reroute
▷ has a present participle *rerouteing*.

rerun
▷ the verb is stressed on its second syllable and has a past tense *reran* and a past participle *rerun*; the noun is stressed on its first syllable.

resemblance, resemblant
▷ are spelt *-lan-*.

resistance, resistant
▷ are spelt *-tan-*.

respectable
▷ is spelt *-able*.

respirator
▷ is spelt *-or*.

respondent
▷ is spelt *-ent*.

responsible
▷ is spelt *-ible*.

restaurateur
▷ is spelt without an *n*.

rest of
▷ when *rest of* is followed by a singular noun, it takes a singular verb; when it is followed by a plural noun it takes a plural verb (eg *the rest of the cake was put into a tin* / *the rest of the passengers were offered seats on the next bus*).

restrictive relative clause
➤ See **clauses and phrases**.

résumé
▷ has two *é*s.

retake
▷ the verb is stressed on its second syllable, has a past tense **retook** and a past participle **retaken**; the noun is stressed on its first syllable.

rethink
▷ the verb is stressed on its second syllable and has a past tense and past participle **rethought**; the noun is stressed on its first syllable.

retread
▷ the verb is stressed on its second syllable, has a past tense **retrod** and past participles **retrod** and **retreaded**; the noun is stressed on its first syllable.

retroussé
▷ is spelt *-ssé*.

reveille
▷ is spelt *-veille* and pronounced *ri-**va**-li* or *ri-**ve**-li*.

revenge / avenge
▷ although these verbs are often used as if they were interchangeable, it is best to follow the rule that we **avenge** the wrongs done to others (eg *he set out to avenge his father's murder*) and **revenge** those done to ourselves (eg *at last she could revenge herself upon those who had publicly humiliated her so many years ago*).

revers
▷ is pronounced *ri-veer*; it has a plural **revers** which is pronounced *ri-veerz*.

reversible
▷ is pronounced *-ible*.

review / revue
▷ a **review** is an inspection or evaluation (eg *the latest review of progress is discouraging*); a **revue** is a variety show (eg *used to appear in revue with Charlie Chester*).

reward

reward / award
▷ a **reward** is a payment, etc given or received for a specific service performed (eg *£10 reward for finding the dog*); an **award** is something symbolic given or received for excellence, merit or bravery, or is a sum of compensation, etc decided by a court (eg *The Queen's Award for Industry* / *the court made her an award of £2,000 in damages*).

rhetorical
▷ is spelt *rhetor-*.

rheumatism
▷ is spelt *rheum-*.

rhino
▷ has a plural **rhinos**.

rhinoceros
▷ has two plurals
- **rhinoceros**, when the group is thought of as a whole (eg *saw a large herd of rhinoceros charging across his path*).
- **rhinoceroses**, when the group is thought of as a set of individuals (eg *a few rhinoceroses came past, some limping badly*).

rhombus
▷ has plurals **rhombuses** (in general use) and **rhombi**.

rhubarb
▷ is spelt *rhu-*.

rhyme / rime
▷ **rhyme** is used of poetry and **rime** of frost; but note the poem-title *Rime of the Ancient Mariner*.

rhythm
▷ is spelt *rhy-*.

ribald
▷ is best pronounced **ri**-*bawld*.

rickets
▷ may be treated as a singular or plural.

rid
▷ has a past tense and past participle **rid** and a present participle **ridding**.

ride
▷ has a past tense **rode** and a past participle **ridden**.

Riesling
▷ is pronounced **reez**-*ling*.

Rievaulx
▷ is pronounced **ree**-*voh*.

rigorous
▷ is spelt -*or*- and -*ous*.

rime / rhyme
▷ **rime** is used of frost and **rhyme** of poetry; but note the poem-title *Rime of the Ancient Mariner*.

ring
▷ the verb has a past tense **rang** and a past participle **rung**.

Rioja
▷ is pronounced *ree-***oh**-*ku*.

rise
▷ the verb has a past tense **rose** and a past participle **risen**.

risible
▷ is spelt -*ible* and rhymes with *visible*.

risotto
▷ has a plural **risottos**.

risqué
▷ is spelt -*qué* and may be stressed on either syllable.

rivet
▷ the verb has a present participle ***riveting*** and a past tense and past participle ***riveted***.

rodeo
▷ has a plural ***rodeos***.

role / rôle
▷ the first spelling is more common although the second is closer to the original French and is preferred by some writers.

romance
▷ is stressed on its second syllable.

Romania / Rumania
▷ the first spelling is more common.

rondeau / rondo
▷ a ***rondeau*** is a sort of poem and has a plural ***rondeaux***; a ***rondo*** is a sort of musical piece and has a plural ***rondos***.

roof
▷ has a plural ***roofs***.

roomful
▷ is spelt *-ful* and has a plural ***roomfuls***.

root
▷ denotes in Grammar the basic part of a word that remains after all prefixes and suffixes have been removed and which may form the basis of a number of related words (eg *love* is the root of *lovable*, *lovely*, *lover* and *unloved*).
➤ See also **stem**.

rosé
▷ ends with an *-é*.

rostrum
▷ has a plural ***rostra***.

rouble / ruble
▷ the first spelling is more common.

rounders
▷ the name of the game is singular (eg *rounders is the ancestor of baseball*).

roux
▷ has a plural *roux*.

rowlock
▷ is pronounced *ro-luk*.

royal / regal
▷ *royal* means 'of the king or queen or their family' (eg *a royal pardon / another royal divorce*); *regal* means 'like or suitable for a king or queen' (eg *the regal splendour of the Governor's residence / the old lady's regal bearing*).

Rumania / Romania
▷ the second spelling is more common.

run
▷ the verb has a past tense *ran* and a past participle *run*.

S

saccharin / saccharine
▷ **saccharin** is a noun (and is sometimes used as an adjective) and **saccharine** is the adjective.

sackful
▷ is spelt *-ful* and has a plural **sackfuls**.

sacrilege, sacrilegious
▷ in both, the third syllable is spelt *-leg-* but pronounced *-lij-*.

sadden
▷ has a present participle **saddening** and a past tense and past participle **saddened**.

sailer / sailor
▷ the first is used of things (eg *this ship is a fast sailer*), the second of persons (eg *he was a sailor all his life*).

salable / saleable
▷ the second spelling is more common.

Salisbury
▷ is pronounced ***solz****-bu-ri*.

salmon
▷ has two plurals
  ○ **salmon**, when the group is thought of as a whole (eg *saw a large shoal of salmon in a shady pool*).
  ○ **salmons**, when the group is thought of as a set of individuals (eg *I've found a couple of salmons in the deep-freeze*).

salvageable
▷ is spelt *-geable*.

salvo
▷ has plurals *salvos* and *salvoes*.

samurai
▷ has a plural *samurai*.

sanctum
▷ has plurals *sanctums* (in general use) and *sancta*.

sarcophagus
▷ has plurals *sarcophagi* and *sarcophaguses*.

satiable
▷ is spelt *-iable* and pronounced **say**-shu-bl.

satyr
▷ is pronounced **sa**-tur.

sauna
▷ is pronounced **saw**-nu; **sow**-nu is also correct.

sauté
▷ is spelt *-té*; the verb has a present participle *sautéing* and a past tense and past participle *sautéd*.

savannah
▷ is spelt *-annah*.

say
▷ has a past tense and past participle *said*.

scales
▷ is plural when meaning 'weighing machine' (eg *the scales <u>are</u> in the top cupboard*).

scarf
▷ has plurals *scarfs* and *scarves*.

scenario
▷ has a plural *scenarios*.

sceptic / septic
▷ a *sceptic* (AmE *skeptic*) is a doubter; *septic* means 'contaminated' (eg a wound may be septic) or 'putrefying'.

schedule
▷ is spelt *sch-* and pronounced **shed**-*yuul* (AmE **sked**-*yool*).

schema
▷ is pronounced **skee**-*mu* and has a plural *schemata*.

scheme
▷ is spelt *sch-*.

scissors
▷ is plural (eg *the scissors <u>are</u> in the drawer*).

Scone
▷ the place-name is pronounced *skuun*.

scone
▷ the noun denoting a type of cake is pronounced *skohn* or *skon*.

Scotch / Scots / Scottish
▷ all these adjectives mean 'of Scotland'
  - *Scottish* is in general use.
  - *Scotch* should be limited to the terms *Scotch egg, Scotch mist, Scotch pine, Scotch terrier, Scotch thistle, Scotch whisky*.
  - *Scots* should be limited to the terms *Scots language, Scots law, Scots pine, Scots Guards*.

scrotum
▷ has plurals *scrota* and *scrotums*.

sculptor
▷ is spelt *-or*.

scurrilous
▷ has two *r*s, one *l* and ends in *-ous*.

séance
▷ is spelt *séa-*.

seasonable
▷ is spelt *-able*.

secateurs
▷ is spelt *-teurs* and is plural.

second
▷ the adjective and noun are stressed on the first syllable; the verb is stressed on the second syllable when it means 'transfer elsewhere' (as is the related noun **secondment**) and on the first when it means 'support a proposal'.

second person
➤ See **person**.

-sede / -cede / -ceed
▷ although these endings sound alike, it is easy to know which spelling to use: the only words that end in *-ceed* are **exceed**, **proceed**, **succeed** and the only word that ends in *-sede* is **supersede**; all the others end in *-cede*.

see
▷ has a past tense **saw** and a past participle **seen**.

seek
▷ has a past tense and past participle **sought**.

seize, seizure
▷ are spelt *seiz-*.

selector
▷ is spelt *-or*.

self
▷ has a plural **selves**.

sell
▷ has a past tense and past participle **sold**.

selvage

selvage
▷ is spelt *-age*.

semblance
▷ is spelt *-ance*.

semi
▷ has a plural **semis**.

semi-
▷ is a prefix that forms words meaning 'half' (eg *semicircle*), 'partly' (eg *semiconscious*) and 'occurring twice in the stated period' (eg *semiannual*).

semicolon
➤ See **punctuation**.

semiotics
▷ is singular (eg *semiotics is a popular subject*).

semi-vowel
▷ denotes any speech sound that is vowel-like in sound but functions as a consonant, as the two letters *w* and *y* in English when used in such words as *will* and *you*.

senator
▷ is spelt *-or*.

send
▷ has a past tense and past participle **sent**.

sensible
▷ is spelt *-ible*.

sensor
▷ is spelt *-or*.

sensual / sensuous
▷ ***sensuous*** means 'pleasing or designed to please the senses' (eg *this silk has a sensuous feel*) and 'very aware of what is perceived by the senses' (eg *when the music began she closed her eyes and stood stock still, rapt in*

sensuous attention); **sensual** means 'pleasing or designed to please the lower senses, or to stimulate sexually' and 'pursuing the lower pleasures (ie food, drink and sex)'.

sentence
▷ is spelt *-ence* and in Grammar denotes a unit of language that can stand alone and which contains at least one clause which has both a subject and a finite verb in it. In written English sentences usually begin with a capital letter and end with a full stop, question mark or exclamation mark.

separable
▷ is spelt *-par-* and *-able*.

sepsis
▷ has a plural **sepses**.

septet / septette
▷ the first spelling is more common.

septic / sceptic
▷ **septic** means 'contaminated' (eg a wound may be septic) or 'putrefying'; a **sceptic** (AmE **skeptic**) is a doubter.

seraglio
▷ is pronounced *se-**rahl**-yoh* and has a plural **seraglios**.

seraph
▷ has plurals **seraphs** and **seraphim**.

sergeant / serjeant
▷ the first denotes a rank in the police or armed forces; the second is now used only in the title of certain parliamentary and court officials (eg *serjeant-at-arms*) who are responsible for discipline.

serum
▷ has a plural **sera**.

serviceable
▷ is spelt *-ceable*.

servo
▷ has a plural ***servos***.

set
▷ the verb has a past tense and past participle ***set*** and a present participle ***setting***.

severance
▷ is spelt *-ance*.

sew
▷ has past participles ***sewn*** and ***sewed***.

sexism
➤ See **political correctness**.

shad
▷ has two plurals
- ***shad***, when the group is thought of as a whole (eg *saw a large shoal of shad on the port bow*).
- ***shads***, when the group is thought of as a set of individuals (eg *only two shads in the pool, one of which looked pretty sickly*).

shake
▷ the verb has a past tense ***shook*** and a past participle ***shaken***.

Shakespearean / Shakespearian
▷ the first spelling is more common.

shako
▷ is spelt *-ako*, pronounced ***shak***-*oh* and has plurals ***shakos*** and ***shakoes***.

shall / will
▷ the basic rules for formal standard speech or writing are

shears

- when simply talking about the future, use **shall** with the first person and **will** with the second and third (eg *I shall be glad to see the last of him / you will be served shortly*).
- when talking about the future and also expressing determination, permission, compulsion, etc, use **will** with the first person and **shall** with the second and third (eg *I will not do it! / you shall go whether you want to or not*).

NOTE Many variations to these two rules will be found in regional or informal speech.

shampoo
▷ the noun has a plural **shampoos**; the verb has a third person singular present **shampoos**, a past tense and past participle **shampooed**, and a present participle **shampooing**.

shanghai
▷ the verb has a third person singular present **shanghais**, a present participle **shanghaiing** and a past tense and past participle **shanghaied**.

shaykh / sheik / sheikh
▷ the last spelling is more common; the word is pronounced *shayk*.

sheaf
▷ has a plural **sheaves**.

shear
▷ the verb has a past tense **sheared** and a past participle **shorn**.

shears
▷ when denoting the two-bladed cutting tool this noun is plural and has no singular.

sheath

sheath / sheathe
▷ the first is the noun, the second the verb.

shed
▷ the verb has a past tense and past participle **shed**.

sheep
▷ has a plural **sheep**.

sheik / shaykh / sheikh
▷ the last spelling is more common; the word is pronounced *shayk*.

shelf
▷ the noun has a plural **shelves**.

shingles
▷ when denoting the disease this noun is plural and has no singular.

shit
▷ the verb has past tenses and past participles **shit**, **shitted** or **shat**.

shoe
▷ the verb has a present participle **shoeing** and a past tense and past participle **shod**.

shoot
▷ has a past tense and past participle **shot**.

show
▷ the verb has past participles **shown** and **showed**.

Shrewsbury
▷ is pronounced **shrohz**-*bu-ri*.

shrink
▷ the verb has a past tense **shrank** and a past participle **shrunk** (**shrunken** when used as an adjective).

shut
▷ the verb has a past tense and past participle **shut**.

shy
▷ the adjective has comparatives **shyer** and **shier** and superlatives **shyest** and **shiest**.

sibilance, sibilant
▷ are spelt *-lan-*.

signet / cygnet
▷ a **cygnet** is a young swan and a **signet** is a sort of seal-stamp for official documents; both are pronounced **sig**-*nit*.

significance, significant
▷ are spelt *-can-*.

silicon / silicone
▷ **silicon** is an element whose crystals are used in the computer industry (eg *silicon chips*); **silicone** is a compound made from silicon, carbon and oxygen and used in water repellants, lubricants, polishes and breast implants.

silo
▷ has a plural ***silos***.

similar / analogous
▷ these words are not interchangeable, since **analogous** means 'similar in certain respects only'.

simile
▷ is a **figure of speech** in which a person or thing is described by being likened to something else (eg *she is as bold as brass / his smile is like a slap round the face with a wet kipper*).

simple past tense
➤ See **past tense**.

simple sentence
▷ denotes a sentence that consists of a single clause, as *the*

cat sat on the mat.
➤ See also **compound sentence, complex sentence, clauses and phrases**.

simulator
▷ is spelt *-or*.

sing
▷ has a past tense ***sang*** and a past participle ***sung***.

singular
▷ denotes that form of a noun, verb, adjective or pronoun that is used to refer to one person, thing, etc.

sink
▷ the verb has a past tense ***sank*** and a past participle ***sunk*** (***sunken*** when used as an adjective).

Sion / Zion
▷ use the *S-* spelling for Old Testament references and the *Z-* for modern political terms, eg *In Jewry is God known: His name is great in Sion* | *Zionist bomb kills 30 on the Gaza Strip.*

sister-in-law
▷ has a plural ***sisters-in-law***.

sit
▷ has a past tense and past participle ***sat*** and a present participle ***sitting***.

Sioux
▷ is pronounced *suu*.

skate
▷ when meaning 'sort of fish' has two plurals
  ○ ***skate***, when the group is thought of as a whole (eg *saw a large shoal of skate on the port bow*).

sleight

○ **skates**, when the group is thought of as a set of individuals (eg *only two skates in the pool, one of which looked pretty sickly*).

ski
▷ the verb has a third person singular present **skis**, a present participle **skiing** and past tenses **skied** or **ski'd**.

skilful
▷ has one *l* before the *f* and one *l* at the end of the word.

skinful
▷ is spelt *-ful* and has a plural **skinfuls**.

skittles
▷ is singular when used of the game (eg *skittles is usually played in pubs*), but is plural (and has a singular *skittle*) when used of several of the missiles (eg *two skittles were lying on the floor*).

slander / libel
▷ in English law, both terms refer to making an untrue statement which damages the reputation of a living person; **libel** is uttered publicly and deliberately (eg in print, on stage or in a broadcast), whereas **slander** occurs casually (eg in conversation). Neither term exists in Scottish law.

slang
➤ See **register**.

slash
➤ See **punctuation**.

slay
▷ has a past tense **slew** and a past participle **slain**.

sleight
▷ is spelt *-ei-* and pronounced *sliyt*.

slide
▷ has a past tense and past participle **slid**.

Slough
▷ the place-name is pronounced *slow*.

slough
▷ has different pronunciations according to its meaning
- *slow* when it means 'bog'.
- *sluf* when it means 'cast off (skin, etc)'.

sly
▷ has comparatives **slyer** or **slier** and superlatives **slyest** and **sliest**.

smell
▷ the verb has past tenses and past participles **smelled** and **smelt**.

smidgen
▷ is spelt *-dg-*.

smite
▷ has a past tense **smote** and a past participle **smitten**.

smooth
▷ **smooth** is never spelt with a final *-e*, ie ✗ *smoothe* is always wrong.

smorgasbord
▷ is now spelt without any accents.

sociable
▷ is spelt *-able*.

soft consonant
▷ the consonants *c* and *g* are said to be **soft** when they are pronounced as in the starts of *centre* and *gentle* (and **hard** when they are pronounced as in the starts of *cat* and *get*).

sole
▷ when meaning 'sort of fish' has two plurals
- ○ **sole**, when the group is thought of as a whole (eg *saw a large shoal of Dover sole on the port bow*).
- ○ **soles**, when the group is thought of as a set of individuals (eg *found a couple of soles in the deep-freeze*).

solicitor
▷ is spelt *-or*.

solidus
➤ See **punctuation**.

solo
▷ has a plural **solos**.

sombrero
▷ has a plural **sombreros**.

somersault
▷ is spelt *som-*.

soprano
▷ has a plural **sopranos**.

Southwark
▷ is pronounced **sudh**-*uk*.

sou'wester
▷ is spelt *sou'w-*.

sovereign, sovereignty
▷ are spelt *-ereig-*.

sow
▷ the verb has a past tense **sowed** and past participles **sown** and **sowed**.

spaghetti
▷ is spelt *-ghetti*.

speak
▷ has a past tense **spoke** and a past participle **spoken**.

speciality / specialty
▷ these words mean the same; use **speciality** in British English and **specialty** in American English.

specially / especially
▷ **specially** means 'solely for' (eg *I made this specially for you*); **especially** means 'particularly' (eg *this sort are expensive, especially the red ones*).

specie / species
▷ **specie** means 'money in coins, not notes' and has no plural; **species** means 'sort' and has a plural **species**.

spectacles
▷ is always plural when it means 'eyeglasses'.

spectator
▷ is spelt *-or*.

spectrum
▷ has plurals **spectra** and **spectrums**.

speedo
▷ has a plural **speedos**.

spell
▷ the verb has past tenses and past participles **spelt** and **spelled**.

spend
▷ has a past tense and past participle **spent**.

sphagnum
▷ has a plural **sphagna**.

spill
▷ the verb has past tenses and past participles **spilt** and **spilled**.

spin
▷ the verb has a past tense and past participle **spun** and a present participle **spinning**.

spit
▷ the verb has a past tense and past participle **spat** and a present participle **spitting**.

split
▷ the verb has a past tense and past participle **split** and a present participle **splitting**.

split infinitive
▷ the word or part of a word that remains when a prefix or suffix is removed. For example, the stem of *unloved* is *loved* and the stem of *loveliness* is *lovely*.
➤ See also **root**.

spoil
▷ the verb has past tenses and past participles **spoilt** and **spoiled**.

sponsor
▷ is spelt *-or*.

spoonful
▷ is spelt *-ful* and has a plural **spoonfuls**.

spotlight
▷ the verb has past tenses and past participles **spotlit** and **spotlighted**.

spread
▷ the verb has a past tense and past participle **spread**.

spring
▷ the verb has a past tense **sprang** and a past participle **sprung**.

sputum
▷ has a plural **sputa**.

squid

squid
▷ has two plurals
- ○ ***squid***, when the group is thought of as a whole (eg *net contained upwards of a dozen squid when we drew it in*).
- ○ ***squids***, when the group is thought of as a set of individuals (eg *bought a couple of squids in the market*).

stadium
▷ has plurals ***stadiums*** (in general use) and ***stadia***.

staff
▷ the noun has three senses
- ○ 'employees'; in this sense it may be treated as a singular noun when the staff is thought of as a unified group of people (eg *the staff is half the size it used to be*) and have a plural ***staffs*** (eg *the staffs of both companies are on strike*), or it may be treated as a plural when the staff is thought of as a set of individuals (eg *the staff were taking their tea break*).
- ○ 'stick' and 'set of lines in a music score'; in both these senses ***staff*** is singular and has plurals ***staffs*** and ***staves***.

stalactite / stalagmite
▷ both denote limestone spikes formed in caverns by dripping water; the ***stalagmites*** grow up from the floor and the ***stalactites*** grow down from the roof.

stanch / staunch
▷ both words mean 'stop the flow', but only ***staunch*** means 'trusty, steadfast'.

stand
▷ has a past tense and past participle ***stood***.

Standard/non-standard English

Standard English is the variety of formal English (see **register**) that is found throughout the English-speaking world. Standard English has a broad overlap in grammar, spelling, pronunciation and vocabulary, and is widely used in written form in newspapers or in spoken form by newsreaders. Each nation's Standard English as taught in its schools and spoken by its educated citizens will be found to contain a few local variants, but any speaker of Standard English will have little difficulty in understanding (and making himself or herself understood by) any other Standard-English speaker, regardless of their national origins. Unlike some languages, English has never been standardized by any authority or committee and so, apart from a central core, it is not possible to give an absolute ruling on what is or is not 'standard'. Two main forms of Standard English can be identified: *Standard British English* (often called **BBC English** or **the Queen's English**) and *Standard American English* which are very similar to each other but differ slightly in grammar and vocabulary.

Non-standard English denotes all those varieties of English whose vocabulary and grammar differ markedly from Standard English. These differences do not make non-standard English 'wrong', but they do make its use inappropriate in contexts where formal English is expected.

stationary / stationery
▷ the first means 'not moving', the second means 'writing materials'.

status
▷ is pronounced **stay**-*tus* (AmE **stat**-*us*).

stave
▷ the verb has past tenses and past participles **stove** and **staved**.

steal

steal
▷ the verb has a past tense **stole** and a past participle **stolen** and a present participle **stealing**.

stem
▷ the word or part of a work that remains when a prefix or suffix is removed. For example, the stem of *unloved* is *loved* and the stem of *loveliness* is *lovely*.
➤ See also **root**.

sternum
▷ has plurals **sternums** (in general use) and **sterna**.

stick
▷ the verb has a past tense and past participle **stuck**.

stigma
▷ has two plurals
- **stigmata** (stressed on the second syllable) when it means 'wounds of Christ'.
- **stigmas** for all other senses.

stiletto
▷ is spelt with one *l* and three *t*s and has a plural **stilettos**.

still life
▷ has a plural **still lifes**.

stimulant / stimulus
▷ **stimulant** is used of medicines, etc that give people energy or keep them awake (eg *drank strong coffee as a stimulant when working through the night*); **stimulus** (which has a plural **stimuli**) is used of anything that causes a reaction in a living organism (eg *light is the stimulus that makes this flower open each morning*); either word may be used metaphorically to mean 'encouragement, enlivening' (eg *the new profit-sharing scheme proved an excellent stimulus to/stimulant of productivity*).

sting
▷ the verb has a past tense and past participle **stung**.

stink
▷ the verb has past tenses **stank** and **stunk** and a past participle **stunk**.

stone / stones
▷ when used of a weight and preceded by a numeral that is greater than one, either form is correct eg
- ✓ *one stone of potatoes*
- ✗ *one stones of potatoes*
- ✓ *she weighs eight stone*
- ✓ *I'll take three stones of potatoes*

although some (eg *she weighs eight stones*) may be ambiguous.

stratum / stratus
▷ **stratum** means 'layer' or 'social grade' and has a plural **strata**; **stratus** is a sort of cloud and has a plural **strati**.

stress
▷ denotes the emphasis placed upon a particular word or syllable by speaking it more loudly or at a different pitch. Except for monosyllables every English word has at least one stressed syllable, but there are no simple rules for working out which it will be, nor any system of accents to indicate it: where pronunciations are given in this book the stressed syllable is printed in ***bold italic*** type. Whole words may also be stressed to show their importance and this may be shown in writing by using a different or larger script (eg *didn't I tell you NEVER to do that?*).

strew
▷ has a past tense **strewed** and past participles **strewn** and **strewed**.

stride
▷ the verb has a past tense **strode** and a past participle **stridden**.

strike
▷ the verb has a past tense and past participle **struck**.

string
▷ the verb has a past tense and past participle **strung**.

strive
▷ the verb has a past tense **strove** and a past participle **striven**.

strong verb
▷ denotes any one of that class of verbs which are irregular in that they form their past tense and past participle by changing one or more vowels of the form used in their present tense (eg *begin, began, begun*). All the strong verbs are listed at their alphabetical place in this book, together with their past-tense and past-participle forms.

stucco
▷ has plurals **stuccos** and **stuccoes**.

studio
▷ has a plural **studios**.

stupefy
▷ is spelt *-efy*.

stylus
▷ has plurals **styluses** and **styli**.

stymie
▷ the verb has present participles **stymieing** and **stymying**.

subcontractor
▷ is spelt *-or*.

subject
▷ is the grammatical name for the word or phrase tha

substitute

determines the number and person of a verb (eg *Fred kicks the ball / cabbage and lettuce are in short supply / whether you like it or not is irrelevant*).

subjective case
▷ denotes the form taken by English pronouns when they govern a verb eg *she* in *she met her at the door*.

subjunctive
▷ denotes a set of verb forms (see **mood**) used to express condition, wish or uncertainty (eg *if I were you / I suggest he leave now*). Most of the forms taken by subjunctive verbs in English are the same as in the indicative, but

○ the third person singular present loses its -s (eg *I suggest he learn it thoroughly*).

○ in the verb *to be* the third person singular present is *be* and the third person singular past is *were* (eg *I suggest he be told immediately / if I were to do it, there'd be an awful row*).

subordinate clause
➤ See **clauses and phrases**.

subsidence
▷ is spelt *-ence* and stressed on the second syllable (*sub-**siy**-duns*).

substance
▷ is spelt *-ance*.

substantive
▷ in Grammar means the same as 'noun'.

substitute / replace
▷ both mean much the same; but note that we substitute *for* and replace *by* or *with* (eg *Knee was substituted for Pevsner in the 49th minute / replacing the broken TV with a vase of flowers is hardly what the lodger will expect*).

substratum
▷ has a plural **substrata**.

subtly
▷ is spelt *-btly-* and pronounced **sut**-*li*.

succeed
▷ is spelt *-cceed*.

successor
▷ has three *s*s, two *c*s and ends in *-or*.

succubus
▷ has a plural **succubi**.

suddenness
▷ is spelt with two *d*s and two *n*s.

sufferance
▷ ends in *-ance*.

suffix
▷ denotes a word element added to the end of a word or word stem to mark a grammatical inflection (eg *gives*) or to form a derivative (eg *stupidity*).

suitable
▷ is spelt *-able*.

summertime / summer time
▷ the first means 'the season of summer'; the second means 'time one hour ahead of Greenwich Mean Time' and is officially known as **British Summer Time** (**BST**).

summons
▷ has a plural **summonses**.

superintendence
▷ is spelt *-ence*.

superlative
▷ denotes that form of adverbs and adjectives that indicates

the highest degree of the quality or manner described (eg *biggest, fastest, most stupidly*).

➤ See also **comparative**.

supernova
▷ has plurals *supernovae* and *supernovas*.

supersede
▷ is spelt *-sede*.

supervise
▷ is spelt *-ise*.

supervisor
▷ is spelt *-or*.

supplely
▷ is spelt *-pplely* and pronounced **sup**-*ul-li*.

supposedly
▷ has four syllables.

suppress / repress
▷ both mean 'control, put down'; but sometimes **suppress** is used of eradication and **repress** of mere containment (eg *the 1745 rebellion was brutally suppressed and nothing was heard of Scottish nationalism for centuries after* / *sobbed as she struggled to repress her feelings*).

supremo
▷ has a plural *supremos*.

surmise
▷ is spelt *-ise*.

surprise
▷ is spelt *-ise*.

surveillance
▷ is spelt *-veil-* and *-lance* and pronounced *sur-***veil***-uns*.

surveyor
▷ is spelt *-or*.

susceptible
▷ is spelt -sc- and -ible.

sustenance
▷ is spelt -ance.

swap / swop
▷ the first spelling is more common.

swat / swot
▷ the first means 'hit sharply', the second 'study hard'; they are both pronounced *swot*.

swath / swathe
▷ either spelling may be used to mean 'strip of land, or of a harvested crop'; **swathe** also means 'bandage or wrapping' or 'to wrap'.

swear
▷ has a past tense **swore** and a past participle **sworn**.

sweep
▷ the verb has a past tense and past participle **swept**.

swell
▷ the verb has a past tense **swelled** and past participles **swollen** and **swelled**.

swim
▷ the verb has a past tense **swam**, a past participle **swum** and a present participle **swimming**.

swine
▷ has two plurals
  ○ **swine** when it means 'pig'.
  ○ **swines** when it means 'nasty person'.

swing
▷ the verb has a past tense and past participle **swung**.

syllable
▷ denotes any one of the sound units of which a word is composed; each unit usually consists of a vowel together with any consonants that are pronounced with it. For example, *telephone* has three syllables (*te-le-phone*).

syllabus
▷ has plurals **syllabuses** and **syllabi**.

symbiosis
▷ has a plural **symbioses**.

symbol
▷ denotes a letter or group of letters or a sign used to represent some item, amount, idea or mathematical operation, eg *Cu* (meaning 'copper'), £ (meaning 'pounds' in money), $ (meaning 'dollars'), *lb* (meaning 'pound' in weight), @ (meaning 'at'), + (meaning 'plus'), © (meaning 'copyright'), ® (meaning 'registered trademark'), ¶ (meaning 'paragraph'). *Cu* is the scientific symbol for *copper* and is an abbreviation of the Latin *cuprum*; it is considered to be a symbol rather than an abbreviation because the letters of the symbol do not correspond with the English full form but are taken from a foreign term, in this case a Latin term; there are many symbols of this type.

symposium
▷ has plurals **symposia** and **symposiums**.

synecdoche
▷ is pronounced *si-**nek**-du-ki* and denotes a **figure of speech** in which a part is used to refer to the whole, eg *wiser <u>heads</u>* (meaning 'people') *might have been more cautious*.

synonym
▷ denotes a word that has the same (or very nearly the

synopsis

same) meaning as another (eg *big* and *large*).
➤ Compare **antonym**.

synopsis
▷ has a plural ***synopses***.

synthesis
▷ has a plural ***syntheses***.

t

tableau
▷ is spelt *-leau* and has a plural ***tableaux***.

table d'hôte
▷ is spelt with an *ô*, is pronounced *tah-bul-**doht*** and has a plural ***tables d'hôte***.

tablespoonful
▷ is spelt *-ful* and has a plural ***tablespoonfuls***.

taboo / tabu
▷ the first spelling is more common.

tagliatelle
▷ is spelt *-gli-* and *-elle* and pronounced *tal-ya-**tel**-i*.

tag question
▷ denotes a question that is 'tagged' on to the end of a statement turning it into a question (eg *you are coming, aren't you?* / *I just thought you'd help yourself, did you?*).

t'ai chi / t'ai chi ch'uan
▷ the first form is more common and is a shortened form of the second; note the apostrophe in *t'ai*, which is pronounced *tiy*; when used, the third word is pronounced *chwahn*.

take
▷ the verb has a past tense ***took*** and a past participle ***taken***.

takings
▷ when referring to money received (eg *the shop's takings have doubled over the past six months*) this noun is plural and has no singular.

talisman
▷ has a plural **talismans**.

tamable / tameable
▷ the first spelling is more common; both end in *-able*.

tango
▷ has a plural **tangos**.

tankful
▷ is spelt *-ful* and has a plural **tankfuls**.

taoiseach
▷ is spelt *taoise-* and pronounced **tee**-*shak*.

tapir
▷ is pronounced **tay**-*pur* and has plurals **tapir** and **tapirs**.

tastable
▷ is spelt *-table*.

tattoo
▷ the nouns have a plural **tattoos**; the verb has a third person singular present **tattoos** and a past tense and past participle **tattooed**.

tautology
▷ denotes the use in a sentence of two or more words or phrases that mean the same thing (eg *I myself personally…*).

taxable
▷ is spelt *-able*.

taxi
▷ the noun has a plural **taxis**; the verb has a third perso

singular present **taxis**, present participles **taxiing** and **taxying** and a past tense and past participle **taxied**.

teach
▷ has a past tense and past participle **taught**.

teachable
▷ is spelt *-able*.

teacupful
▷ is spelt *-ful* and has a plural **teacupfuls**.

team
▷ is singular when its membership is thought of as a unified group (eg *a team of experts has been flown in*) but plural when the members are thought of as individuals (eg *the team were all asleep in their rooms when the bomb went off*).

tear
▷ the verb has a past tense **tore** and a past participle **torn**.

teaspoonful
▷ is spelt *-ful* and has a plural **teaspoonfuls**.

teeth / teethe
▷ **teeth** is the plural of *tooth*; **teethe** is the verb 'grow teeth'.

tele-
▷ is a prefix that forms words meaning 'at, to or over a distance' (eg *telegram*), 'television' (eg *teletext*), or 'telephone' (eg *telesales*).

telecast
▷ the verb has past tenses and past participles **telecast** and **telecasted**.

televise
▷ is spelt *-ise*.

tell

tell
▷ the verb has a past tense and past participle ***told***.

temperance
▷ is spelt *-ance*.

tempo
▷ has plurals ***tempos*** and ***tempi***.

tench
▷ has a plural ***tench***.

tendency
▷ is spelt *-ency*.

tense
▷ denotes in Grammar a form of a verb that shows
  ○ the time of its action in relation to the time of speaking or writing.
  ○ whether the action it describes was completed or not.
  ➤ See **past tense, perfect tense, progressive tense, future tense**.

terminus
▷ has plurals ***termini*** and ***terminuses***.

terrarium
▷ has plurals ***terraria*** and ***terrariums***.

testable
▷ is spelt *-able*.

testis
▷ has a plural ***testes***.

tête-à-tête
▷ is spelt with two *-ês* and one *à* and has a plural *tête-à-têtes*.

than
▷ when the ***than*** in a comparison is followed by a persona

314

pronoun:
- ○ **whom** must always be in the objective case (eg *Dr Edmonds, than whom there is no finer living lexicographer*).
- ○ in formal English the other pronouns should be in the subjective case (eg *there is no finer pastrycook than she*), but in less formal speech and writing the objective case is used (eg *I'm a better bowler than him*).

themself
▷ the use of this 'singular' form instead of *themselves* (eg *each one would have had an attendant to stop them doing themself harm*) is only acceptable in informal contexts.

thesaurus
▷ has plurals **thesauruses** (in general use) and **thesauri**.

thesis
▷ has a plural **theses**.

they / he or she
➤ See **political correctness**.

thief
▷ has a plural **thieves**.

thimbleful
▷ is spelt *-ful* and has a plural **thimblefuls**.

think
▷ the verb has a past tense and past participle **thought**.

third person
➤ See **person**.

thorax
▷ has plurals **thoraxes** (in general use) and **thoraces**.

thousand / thousands
➤ when preceded by a numeral use **thousand** (eg *it cost me three thousand pounds*); when just meaning 'a lot' use

thrash

thousands (eg *I've told you thousands of times I don't like toffees*).

thrash / thresh
▷ although these terms can be used interchangeably it is best to reserve **thrash** for the senses 'beat a person' and 'wave arms around' and **thresh** for 'beat out grain'.

thrive
▷ has past tenses ***throve*** and ***thrived*** and past participles ***thriven*** and ***thrived***.

throw
▷ the verb has a past tense ***threw*** and a past participle ***thrown***.

thrust
▷ the verb has a past tense and past participle ***thrust***.

tic / tick
▷ **tic** refers to a habitual nervous movement (eg *has the annoying tic of constantly rubbing his hands together while talking to strangers*); **tick** refers to the sound of a clock, a moment of time (eg *just a tick while I lock up*) and the mark used by teachers, etc to show that a written answer is correct.

tilde
▷ denotes the mark or diacritic ~ placed over certain letters in Spanish and Portuguese to indicate their pronunciation.

tillable
▷ is spelt *-able*.

tiro / tyro
▷ the second spelling is more common; their plurals are ***tiros*** and ***tyros***.

titillate / titivate
▷ the first means 'excite' or 'tickle', the second 'smarten up by making small improvements'.

tobacco
▷ has plurals **tobaccos** and **tobaccoes**.

'to'-infinitive
▷ denotes the form of the infinitive that uses 'to', as in *to err is human | they asked him to leave*.
➤ See also **bare infinitive**.

tolerable, tolerance, tolerant
▷ are spelt with an *a*.

tolerance, tolerant
▷ are spelt *-an-*.

ton / tonne / tun
▷ the first denotes the imperial weight (20cwt), the second the metric (1,000kg); the third denotes a large cask.

tongs
▷ is plural and has no singular.

tonsillitis
▷ is spelt *-ll-*.

tooth
▷ has a plural **teeth**.

torso
▷ has a plural **torsos**.

total
▷ is usually followed by a singular verb (eg *a total of £5,000 has been collected*), although when attention is drawn to the total's individual constituents a plural is also correct (eg *a total of five research fellowships, three tenable abroad, have/has been endowed*).

tournedos

tournedos
▷ is spelt *tourne-*, pronounced **toor**-*nu-doh* and has a plural ***tournedos*** (pronounced **toor**-*nu-dohz*).

trachea
▷ has a plural ***tracheae***.

tractable
▷ is spelt *-able*.

trade union / trades union
▷ the first form (which has a plural **trade unions**) is now in general use; but the second is still used in ***Trades Union Congress*** (which is what *TUC* stands for).

traffic
▷ the verb has a present participle ***trafficking*** and a past tense and past participle ***trafficked***.

traipse / trapes
▷ the first spelling is more common.

tranquillize, tranquillity
▷ are spelt *-ll-*.

transcendence
▷ is spelt *-ence*.

transferable / transferrable
▷ the first spelling is more common; both may be stressed on the first or second syllable.

transfixion
▷ is spelt *-x-*.

transitive
▷ denotes those verbs that govern a direct object, as in *Jane kicked the cat* (where *kick* is the verb that governs the direct object *cat*) and not as in *this meat stinks* or *Fred is very stupid*.

trillion

translator
▷ is spelt *-or*.

translucence, translucent
▷ are spelt *-cen-*.

transportable
▷ is spelt *-able*.

transposable
▷ is spelt *-able*.

transsexual
▷ is spelt *-ss-*.

transship
▷ is spelt *-ss-*.

trapezium
▷ has plurals ***trapeziums*** and ***trapezia***.

tread
▷ the verb has a past tense ***trod*** and past participles ***trodden*** and ***trod***.

trellis
▷ the verb has a present participle ***trellising*** and a past tense and past participle ***trellised***.

tri-
▷ is a prefix that forms words meaning 'three' or 'threefold' (eg *triangle, triathlon*).

trillion
▷ in informal speech ***trillion*** simply means 'a lot' (eg *I've told you a trillion times not to talk when I'm reading*). When used as a statistic (and always in American English) a ***trillion*** means a thousand billion (ie, the unit and 12 zeros, or 10^{12}). However, always check what the speaker or writer means since, in the UK, ***trillion*** was formerly

trio

used to represent a billion billion (ie, the unit and 18 zeros, or 10^{18}).

trio
▷ has a plural **trios**.

troop / troupe
▷ use the first of a group of soldiers, the second for a group of entertainers.

trousseau
▷ is spelt *-sseau* and has plurals **trousseaux** and **trousseaus**.

trout
▷ when referring to fish, has two plurals

  ○ **trout**, when the group is thought of as a whole (eg *saw a large shoal of trout on the port bow*).

  ○ **trouts**, when the group is thought of as a set of individuals (eg *only two trouts in the pool, one of which looked pretty sickly*).

try and / try to
▷ **try to** is always correct; **try and** may not be used in

  ○ formal speech or writing.

  ○ in sentences where *try* is inflected, eg

  ✓ *she tried to come to the meeting*
  ✓ *she was trying to come to the meeting*
not
  ✗ *she tried and came to the meeting*
(which would mean that she made an effort and actually got there) or
  ✗ *she was trying and coming to the meeting*
(which would mean that she was making a general effort and was also on her way to the meeting).

tsar / czar
▷ the spelling **tsar** is now standard and correctly reflects

the Russian spelling and pronunciation of this word, which was first anglicized as **czar**; in English, both spellings are pronounced *zahr*.

tubful
▷ is spelt *-ful* and has a plural **tubfuls**.

tumblerful
▷ is spelt *-ful* and has a plural **tumblerfuls**.

tumulus
▷ has a plural **tumuli**.

tun / ton / tonne
▷ the first denotes a large cask (eg *the Duke of Clarence was drowned in a tun of Malmsey*); the second denotes an imperial weight (20cwt) and the last a metric weight (1000kg).

tunable
▷ is spelt *-nable*.

turbot
▷ has two plurals
  ○ **turbot**, when the group is thought of as a whole (eg *saw a large shoal of turbot on the port bow*).
  ○ **turbots**, when the group is thought of as a set of individuals (eg *only two turbots in the pool, one of which looked pretty sickly*).

turf
▷ has plurals **turfs** and **turves**.

tuxedo
▷ has a plural **tuxedos**.

twelfth
▷ is spelt *-lfth*.

typecast
▷ the verb has a past tense and past participle ***typecast*** and a present participle ***typecasting***.

typeset
▷ the verb has a past tense and past participle ***typeset*** and a present participle ***typesetting***.

typewrite
▷ has a past tense ***typewrote*** and a past participle ***typewritten***.

tyro / tiro
▷ the first spelling is more common; their plurals are ***tyros*** and ***tiros***.

u

ugli
▷ has plurals **uglis** and **uglies**.

ukulele
▷ has two *u*s and two *l*s.

ultimatum
▷ has plurals **ultimatums** and **ultimata**.

umlaut
▷ denotes a pair of dots placed over certain vowels in Germanic languages to indicate a modification in the pronunciation of the vowel; eg *ä* in German *Mädchen* or *ü* in *Übermensch*.
➤ See also **diaeresis**.

-ums / -a
▷ most words ending in *-um* form plurals by adding an *s* in the usual way, but a few (eg *addendum, desideratum*) still reflect their Latin origin by replacing the *-um* by *-a* and are listed at their alphabetical place in this book.

unaware / unawares
▷ the first is the adjective, the second the adverb.

uncountable noun
➤ See **mass noun**.

undercut
▷ the verb has a past tense and past participle **undercut** and a present participle **undercutting**.

undergo

undergo
▷ has a third person singular present **undergoes**, a past tense **underwent** and a past participle **undergone**.

underlay
▷ the verb has a past tense and past participle **underlaid**.

underlie
▷ has a present participle **underlying**, a past tense **underlay** and a past participle **underlaid**.

underrate
▷ is spelt *-rr-*.

undersell
▷ has a past tense and past participle **undersold**.

undershoot
▷ has a past tense and past participle **undershot**.

understand
▷ has a past tense and past participle **understood**.

understandable
▷ is spelt *-able*.

undertake
▷ has a past tense **undertook** and a past participle **undertaken**.

underwrite
▷ has a past tense **underwrote** and a past participle **underwritten**.

unexceptionable / unexceptional
▷ the first means 'unobjectionable'; the second means 'ordinary'.

unforgettable
▷ is spelt *-ttable*.

uninterested / disinterested
▷ *uninterested* means 'not interested, bored'; *disinterested* means 'fair, unbiased'.

unique
▷ strictly speaking, *unique* means 'the only one of its kind'; so either a thing *is* unique or it *isn't*. In informal speech and writing, however, *unique* has come to have a weaker meaning 'rare, special, unusual', which can be modified (eg *his collection of newts is quite unique*) or be subject to comparison (eg *her car may be customized, but it's not so unique as the one in the Beaulieu collection*).

United Kingdom
▷ denotes the political unit Great Britain and Northern Ireland.
➤ See also **Great Britain**, **British Isles**.

unmistakable / unmistakeable
▷ the first spelling is more common.

unnatural
▷ has two *n*s and one *t*.

unnecessary
▷ has two *n*s, one *c* and two *s*s.

unreadable
▷ is spelt *-able*.

unreservedly
▷ has five syllables.

unsociable / unsocial
▷ *unsociable* means 'not liking company' (eg *you'll never see Joe at an office party—he's an unsociable type*); *unsocial* means 'causing annoyance to others' (eg *it's pretty unsocial of her to park her car across the neighbours' drive*) or, when said of working hours, etc, 'preventing social activity' (eg *shift work involves plenty of unsocial hours*).

unspeakable
▷ is spelt *-able*.

unstoppable
▷ is spelt *-able*.

untouchable
▷ is spelt *-able*.

unutterable
▷ is spelt *-able*.

uphold
▷ has a past tense and past participle ***upheld***.

upset
▷ has a past tense and past participle ***upset*** and a present participle ***upsetting***.

upside / upsides
▷ ***upside*** is a noun meaning 'the top side' (eg *the address was on the upside of the box*); ***upsides*** is an adjective meaning 'even with someone (eg, through revenge, etc)' as in *I'll be upsides with you yet!*.

Uranus
▷ is pronounced **yoo-ray**-*nus* or **yoor**-*u-nus*.

urban / urbane
▷ ***urban*** means 'of or in a town or city' (eg *urban violence is on the increase*); ***urbane*** means 'sophisticated, elegant' (eg *the urbane wit of Wilde's play fell flat in last night's performance by the Upton Snodsbury Thespians*).

urethra
▷ has plurals ***urethras*** (in general use) and ***urethrae***.

urinal
▷ is pronounced *yoo-***riy**-*nul* or ***yuu***-*ri-nul*.

urine
▷ is pronounced ***yuu***-*rin*.

use / usage
▷ **use** refers to the act of using (eg *that is an incorrect use of the word*) or the purpose for which something can be used (eg *this gadget has a thousand uses, from getting stones out of horses' hooves to slicing bread*); **usage** refers to the way a thing has been used (eg *these tools have been subjected to rough usage*) or to customs, especially those followed in speaking or writing a language (eg *this book is a guide to English usage*).

usual
▷ may be pronounced as three syllables or two.

Utah
▷ is pronounced **yuu**-*tah* (AmE **yuu**-*taw*).

uterus
▷ has a plural ***uteri***.

utterance
▷ denotes in Grammar a word or words that do not make a complete sentence (eg because they lack a subject and/or a finite verb), but are spoken and written as if they were sentences. Ordinary conversation (eg *'Where are you going?' 'Into town.' 'Why?' 'To buy some shoes.'*) is full of utterances, which avoid tiresome repetitions (eg *'Where are you going?' 'I am going into town.' 'Why are you going into town?' 'I am going into town to buy some shoes.'*).

V

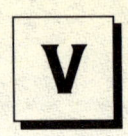

vacuum
▷ has plurals **vacuums** (in general use) and **vacua** (in scientific and technical use).

valance / valence
▷ **valance** means 'strip of fabric', is spelt *-ance* and pronounced **val**-*uns*; **valence** means 'combining power of an atom', is spelt *-ence* and pronounced **vay**-*luns*.

valet
▷ is pronounced *va-lay* or **va**-*lit*; the verb has a present participle **valeting** and a past tense and past participle **valeted**.

valuable
▷ is spelt *-uable*.

Van Gogh
▷ is pronounced *van* **gokh** or *van* **gof** (AmE also *van* **goh**).

vas
▷ has a plural **vasa**.

vas deferens
▷ has a plural **vasa deferentia**.

vasoconstrictor
▷ is spelt *-or*.

vasodilator
▷ is spelt *-or*.

vehement
▷ is spelt *vehe-* and pronounced **vee**-*u-munt*.

vehicle
▷ is spelt *vehi-* and pronounced ***vee**-kl*.

vehicular
▷ is spelt *vehi-* and pronounced *ve-**hik**-yuu-luh*.

veld / veldt
▷ the first spelling is more common; both are pronounced *felt* or *velt*.

vena cava
▷ has a plural ***venae cavae***.

venal / venial
▷ ***venal*** means 'bribable'; ***venial*** means 'forgivable'.

vender / vendor
▷ both mean 'seller'
  ○ the *-er* form is in general use.
  ○ the *-or* form is used in legal documents relating to house sales.

vengeance
▷ is spelt *-geance*.

veranda / verandah
▷ the first spelling is more common.

verbal noun
▷ denotes a form of a verb ending in *-ing* that functions as a noun. It is also called ***gerund***.
  ○ It can be the subject or object of a verb, as in *walking is good for you* and *I don't like dancing*, can be qualified by an adjective or governed by a preposition, as in *his tuneless singing emptied the hall* and *the weather looks good for walking*.
  ○ Like a verb it can also govern an object or be qualified by an adverb, as in *giving him the money was a mistake* and *singing tunelessly is a sign of deafness*.

verb clause

verb clause or **phrase**
➤ See **clauses and phrases**.

verbless clause

▷ denotes in Grammar a clause whose verb and subject have to be understood from the context (eg *if possible, I will get it done tomorrow*).
➤ See also **clauses and phrases**.

verbs

A *verb* is a word that describes an action or a state, as *came, helps, will go*. English verbs generally change form in order to agree with their subject in person and number (eg *he comes, they come*) or to indicate tense (eg *come, came*). English also has a number of compound tenses; see **perfect tense, progressive tense, future tense**.

• Inflection

The following rules will enable you to construct the simple tenses and participles of most verbs. Formation of the compound tenses is explained at their alphabetical entries in this book. Strong and irregular verbs each have their own entry in this book, where their inflections are explained.

○ The *third person singular present* is formed by adding *-s* (eg *I come, she comes*), except for verbs ending in *-s, -x, -z, -sh* (or *-ch when pronounced as in crunch*), which add *-es* (eg *I bless, she blesses*).

○ The *past tense* and *past participle* are formed by adding *-ed* (eg *I pass, she passed, they were passed*), dropping any final *-e* (eg *interfere, interfered*).

○ The *present participle* is formed by adding *-ing* (eg *pass, passing*), dropping any final *-e* (eg *interfere, interfering*).

- Verbs ending in *-y* preceded by a consonant form endings in *-ies*, *-ied* and *-ying* (eg *I cop__y__, she cop__ies__, they cop__ied__, cop__ying__*).
- Verbs ending in *-ie* form present participles in *-ying* (eg *I d__ie__, d__ying__*).
- Verbs ending in *-c* preceded by a vowel add *-k* in inflection (eg *I magi__c__, I magi__ck__ed, magi__ck__ing*).
- Single-syllable verbs ending in a single consonant, and verbs whose final syllable is stressed and ends in a single consonant, often double the consonant in inflection (eg *ba__tt__ed, begi__nn__ing*).
- Verbs whose final syllable is unstressed and ends in a single consonant do not usually double the consonant in inflection (eg *budge__t__ed, gallo__p__ing*).

➤ See also **aspect, auxiliary verb, finite/non-finite verb, imperative, indicative, infinitive, lexical verb, linking verb, mood, phrasal verb, subjunctive, tense.**

veritable
▷ is spelt *-able*.

verso
▷ has a plural *versos*.

vertebra
▷ has a plural *vertebrae*.

vertex / vortex
▷ *vertex* means 'peak, tip' and has plurals *vertexes* and *vertices*; *vortex* means 'whirlpool' and has plurals *vortexes* and *vortices*.

victualler
▷ is spelt *-ctu-*, but pronounced *vit-lur*.

victuals
▷ is spelt *-ctu-*, is pronounced *vit-ulz* and is plural.

video
▷ has a plural **videos**.

vigilant / vigilante
▷ the first is an adjective meaning 'watchful'; the second is a noun meaning 'self-appointed enforcer of law and order' and is pronounced with four syllables.

vigorous
▷ is spelt *-orous*.

vigour
▷ is spelt *-our*.

villain / villein
▷ a **villain** is an evil-doer; a **villein** is a serf.

vingt-et-un
▷ is spelt *vingt* and pronounced va^{ng}t-e-uh^{ng}.

virtuoso
▷ has a plural **virtuosos**.

virus / bacillus / bacterium
▷ doctors know that each of these three words denotes a different sort of germ, but ordinary people use them interchangeably. **Bacillus** has a plural **bacilli**; **bacterium** has a plural **bacteria** (which must not be treated as a singular) and **virus** has a plural **viruses**.

vis-à-vis
▷ is spelt with an *à*, pronounced *vee-za-**vee*** and has a plural **vis-à-vis**.

viscid
▷ is pronounced **vis**-id.

visible
▷ is spelt *-ible*.

visitor
▷ is spelt *-or*.

visor
▷ is spelt -*or*.

viva
▷ the verb has a past tense and past participle **vivaed** and a present participle **vivaing**.

vivarium
▷ has a plural **vivaria**.

voice
▷ denotes in Grammar one of the sets of forms taken by a verb. In English there are two voices:
- ○ **active**, where the subject of the verb performs the action that the verb describes (eg *Bert kicks the ball*).
- ○ **passive**, where the subject of the verb suffers or experiences the action that the verb describes (eg *the ball is kicked by Bert*).

vol-au-vent
▷ is pronounced ***vol**-oh-voh^{ng}*.

volte-face
▷ is pronounced *volt-**fahs***.

vomit
▷ the verb has a present participle **vomiting** and a past tense and past participle **vomited**.

vortex / vertex
▷ **vortex** means 'whirlpool' and has plurals **vortexes** and **vortices**; **vertex** means 'peak, tip' and has plurals **vertexes** and **vertices**.

vowel
▷ denotes any one of the letters *a*, *e*, *i*, *o* and *u*, or any one of the semi-vowels *w* and *y* or any of the sounds that those letters, singly or in combination, represent.

voyeur
▷ is spelt *-yeur* and pronounced *vwah-**yuhr***.

vulnerable
▷ is spelt *-able*.

W

waggon / wagon
▷ the second spelling is more common.

wake / waken
▷ both mean the same; both may be used transitively and intransitively. But **wake** (which has a past tense **woke** and a past participle **woken**) tends to be used for the literal senses (eg *she woke with a pounding headache*) and **waken** for the metaphorical ones (eg *the death of his wife seemed at last to waken in him a realization of his responsibilities towards the children*).

wallop
▷ has a present participle **walloping** and a past tense and past participle **walloped**.

walrus
▷ has a plural **walruses**.

warrantor
▷ is spelt *-or*.

Warwick
▷ is pronounced **wo**-*rik*.

wastable
▷ is spelt *-table*.

waterworks
▷ may be treated as either singular or plural eg
  - ✓ *the waterworks <u>is</u> in the next street*
  - ✓ *the waterworks <u>are</u> in the next street*

waylay

waylay
▷ has a past tense and past participle **waylaid**.

weak verb
▷ denotes any one of that class of verbs that form their past tense and past participle by adding *-ed* to the present (eg *end, ended*).

wear
▷ has a past tense **wore** and a past participle **worn**.

weave
▷ the verb has two sets of inflections according to meaning
  ○ a past tense and past participle **weaved** when it means 'move to and fro, wind in and out' (eg *they watched anxiously from the balcony as the waiter weaved his way across the crowded dance floor, balancing a tray above his head*).
  ○ a past tense **wove** and a past participle **woven** for all other senses (eg *the class wove her a basket as a wedding present*).

Wednesday
▷ is spelt *-dnes-* but pronounced **wens***-day*.

weep
▷ has a past tense and past participle **wept**.

weigh, weight
▷ are spelt *-eigh*.

weird
▷ is spelt *-ei-*.

weirdo
▷ is spelt *-ei-* and has a plural **weirdos**.

well
▷ the adverb and adjective have a comparative **better** and a superlative **best**.

werewolf
▷ is pronounced **wer**-*woolf* or **weer**-*woolf* and has a plural **werewolves**.

wet
▷ the verb has past tenses and past participles **wet** and **wetted**.

wharf
▷ has plurals **wharfs** and **wharves**.

what
▷ the basic rule is

○ when **what** means 'the thing which' it is followed by a singular verb (eg *what she needs is a good hiding*).

○ when **what** means 'the things which' it is followed by a plural verb (eg *they sorted through the books and what they didn't need were sent to a jumble sale*).
Sometimes, however, the rule is varied according to the sense, so that (for example) we might say or write ✓*what he needs is a hot bath, some dry clothes and a square meal* because the three items are thought of as a single list (meaning 'the thing which') that comes immediately into the mind upon seeing the bedraggled person at the door.

what ever / whatever
▷ always use the one-word form, except in emphatic questions (eg *what ever have you got there?*).

whereabouts
▷ the noun may be treated as either singular or plural eg
    ✓   *his present whereabouts is unknown*
    ✓   *his present whereabouts are unknown*

whiskey / whisky
▷ in British English

whizz

- ○ **whisky** (plural **whiskies**) may be used of any sort of whisky and must be used of Scotch whisky.
- ○ **whiskey** (plural **whiskeys**) may be used of Irish and American whiskies.
  In American English **whiskey** is used of any whisky.

whizz, whiz
▷ the first spelling is more common.

wholly
▷ is spelt with two *l*s and no *e*.

whoop / whooping cough / whoops
▷ the first denotes a cry of joy and is pronounced *wuup*; the second is pronounced *huup-*; the third is an exclamation of surprise and is pronounced *woops*.

wide / broad
▷ in almost all cases either word may be used, but there is a tendency to use **broad** of an object and **wide** of a gap between objects or parts of an object (eg *the wide gateway had been blocked by a pile of broad tree trunks*).

wife
▷ has a plural **wives**.

wildebeest
▷ is spelt *-lde* and *-beest*, is pronounced **wil**-*du-beest* or **vil**-*du-beest* and has two plurals
  - ○ **wildebeest**, when the group is thought of as a whole (eg *saw a large herd of wildebeest charging across his path*).
  - ○ **wildebeests**, when the group is thought of as a set of individuals (eg *a few wildebeests came past, some limping badly*).

wild-goose chase
▷ has only one hyphen.

will / shall
▷ the basic rules for formal standard speech or writing are
  ○ when simply talking about the future, use **shall** with the first person and **will** with the second and third (eg *I shall be glad to see the last of him | you will be served shortly*).
  ○ when talking about the future and also expressing determination, permission, compulsion, etc, use **will** with the first person and **shall** with the second and third (eg *I will not do it! | you shall go whether you want to or not*).
  Many variations to these two rules will be found in regional or informal speech.

win
▷ the verb has a past tense and past participle **won** and a present participle **winning**.

wino
▷ has a plural **winos**.

wistaria / wisteria
▷ the second spelling is more common.

withdraw
▷ has a past tense **withdrew** and a past participle **withdrawn**.

withhold
▷ is spelt *-hh-* and has a past tense and past participle **withheld**.

wizened
▷ is pronounced **wiz**-*und*.

Wodehouse
▷ is pronounced **wood**-*hows*.

wolf
▷ has a plural **wolves**.

woman
▷ has a plural **women**.

wondrous
▷ is spelt *-drous*.

wont
▷ means 'in the habit of' (eg *am wont to take my tea at 4.30*) and may be pronounced either like *won't* or like *want*.

woodlouse
▷ has a plural **woodlice**.

woodworm
▷ has plurals **woodworm** and **woodworms**.

Woolwich
▷ is pronounced **wool**-*ij*.

Worcester
▷ is spelt *Worces-* but pronounced **woo**-*stur*.

word
▷ denotes the smallest unit of written or spoken language that can be used independently; in writing and printing words are usually separated off from each other by spaces.
➤ See also **grammatical word, lexeme, orthographic word, phonological word**.

workable
▷ is spelt *-able*.

works
▷ may be treated as either singular or plural eg
  ✓ *the works is in the next street*
  ✓ *the works are in the next street*

wrath / wroth
▷ **wrath** means 'anger' and is pronounced *roth*; **wroth** means 'angry' and is also pronounced *roth*.

wreath / wreathe
▷ the first is the noun and the second the verb.

wring
▷ has a past tense and past participle *wrung*.

write
▷ has a past tense *wrote* and a past participle *written*.

X

Xerxes
▷ has only one *s* and is pronounced ***zerk***-*seez*.

Xhosa
▷ is spelt *Xh-* and pronounced ***koh***-*su*.

-xion / -ction
▷ the *-ction* spelling is now acceptable for almost all of these words; the few that are still spelt *-xion* are listed at their alphabetical place in this book.

X-ray
▷ is spelt with a capital and a hyphen.

y

yak
- has two plurals
  - *yak*, when the group is thought of as a whole (eg *a herd of yak could be glimpsed through the blizzard*).
  - *yaks*, when the group is thought of as a set of individuals (eg *a few yaks came past, some limping badly*).

yobbo
- has a plural *yobbos*.

yoghourt / yoghurt / yogurt
- the second spelling is more common; they are all pronounced **yog**-*urt* or **yoh**-*gurt*.

yourself
- has a plural *yourselves*.

yo-yo
- has a plural *yo-yos*.

Z

zabaglione
▷ is spelt *-glione* and pronounced *za-ba-**lyoh**-ni*.

zealot
▷ is pronounced ***zel**-ut*.

zebra
▷ is pronounced ***zeb**-ru* or ***zee**-bru* and has two plurals
- *zebra*, when the group is thought of as a whole (eg *a herd of zebra could be glimpsed through the dust*).
- *zebras*, when the group is thought of as a set of individuals (eg *a few zebras came past, some limping badly*).

zero
▷ has a plural *zeros* and usually denotes the number, figure or symbol *0*; it is also used to mean 'absolutely no' but this meaning is acceptable only in business, technical and informal English (eg *zero population growth predicted by 2050 / zero fillings when you brush with this toothpaste*).

zero plural
▷ denotes a plural form of a word which is the same as its singular (eg *deer, sheep*).

Zion / Sion
▷ use the *S-* spelling for Old Testament references and the *Z-* for modern political terms, eg *In Jewry is God known: His name is great in Sion* / *Zionist bomb kills 30 on the Gaza Strip*.

zombie
  ▷ is spelt -ie.

zoology
  ▷ is pronounced zoh-**ol**-uji or zoo-**ol**-uji.